A Lecturer's Guide to Further Education

A Lecturer's Guide to Further Education

Edited by
Dennis Hayes, Toby Marshall and Alec Turner

 Open University Press

Open University Press
McGraw-Hill Education
McGraw-Hill House
Shoppenhangers Road
Maidenhead, Berkshire
England SL6 2QL

email: enquiries@openup.co.uk
world wide web: www.openup.co.uk

and Two Penn Plaza, New York, NY 1012–2289
USA

First published 2007

A catalogue record of this book is available from the British Library

ISBN 13: 9780 33522 0182 (pb)   9780 33522 0199 (hb)
ISBN 10: 0 335 220 185 (pb)   0 335 220 193 (hb)

Library of Congress Cataloging-in-Publication Data
CIP data has been applied for

Typeset by BookEns Ltd, Royston, Herts.
Printed and bound in Poland by OZGraf S.A.
www.polskabook.pl

Contents

Notes on the Contributors

Jon Bryan moved from being a lecturer in sociology to teaching trade union studies at Newcastle College. He has been an active trade unionist all his working life and was for several years the Chair of the NATFHE, and subsequently of the UCU, Further Education Committee.

Neil Davenport teaches government and politics at Hammersmith and West London College. Since becoming an FE lecturer in 2002, he has taught social science subjects in a number of inner city London colleges. Prior to lecturing he was a journalist working for the *Manchester Evening News* and still contributes regularly to a variety of political, consumer and lifestyle magazines.

Kathryn Ecclestone is Professor of Post-Compulsory Education at Oxford Brookes University. She was an associate director for further and adult education in the university's Teaching and Learning Research Programme. Between 1993 and 1997, she ran a large university-led consortium of FE colleges offering teacher education and professional development courses for post-16 practitioners. Among her recent publications is the well-received and successful *Learning Autonomy in Post-Compulsory Education* (2003).

Claire Fox is the Director of the Institute of Ideas and among her many radio and TV credits is being a regular on BBC Radio 4's *The Moral Maze*. She worked in FE colleges in Essex and Hertfordshire for several years and has written widely on educational matters.

Dennis Hayes is the Head of the Centre for Professional Learning at Canterbury Christ Church University and is one of the authors of two best selling books, *Teaching and Training in Post-Compulsory Education* (1999) and *Working in Post-Compulsory Education* (2003), both published by the Open University Press. He has worked in FE and FE Teacher training for many years, and writes a monthly 'Backchat' column for the *TES*. From May 2006 to June 2007 he was joint President of the University and College Union, the largest tertiary education union in the world, which was formed from the merger of NATFHE and the AUT.

Patrick Hayes is Head of Research and Development at TSL Education. As a freelance journalist and researcher for the *TES* he reported on many innovative programme developments targeted at young people.

Toby Marshall is Curriculum Manager for Media, Film, Law and Psychology at Havering College of Further and Higher Education. He has extensive experience of using ICT as a teacher of communications, film and media.

Ian Nash has been the Editor of the FE Focus supplement in the *TES* since he was instrumental in its creation in 1995. In 1999 he was the joint author of a major report for the OECD, *Overcoming Exclusion through Adult Learning*. He has been closely involved with initiatives to drive forward serious thinking about FE, including the formation of the Concord Group, an ad hoc grouping of key players in the sector.

Alec Turner has taught a broad range of subjects since he began to teach in FE in 1991. He is currently a lecturer in health and social care and Key Skills co-ordinator at City and Islington College.

Patrick Turner worked in Wandsworth as a senior drug education worker and a co-ordinator of a young people's 'virtual' drugs team. Part of his work involved him in the training of Connexions advisors. He is now a lecturer at City and Islington College.

Joanna Williams taught English and was a tutor on the Certificate in Education programmes at Canterbury College and Thanet College. She is currently researching the impact of the politics of social inclusion on FE. In addition to her academic work she has written many articles on education for the *TES* and other publications.

Preface

This book came about because of our consciousness of the lack of debate about further education (FE) at a time when there is more fundamental change happening than at any previous time in the history of the sector. As we explain in our Introduction, the driver for that change is government intervention and the central theme of this book is to encourage discussion of how the consequences of their interventions are inevitably perverse. The fact that there are so many policy documents and consultations that require responses may give the appearance of debate, but it is one-sided and controlled. Outside of occasional letters and articles in the educational press, there is little serious and open discussion.

Our experience in FE colleges and on their teacher training courses was that 'debate' and discussion for lecturers meant little more than either talking about and becoming familiar and supportive of new initiatives, or of having their cynicism encouraged as a replacement for criticism. While most lecturers were keen to understand the context in which they were working, the pressure to get through compulsory training courses or just to 'survive' seemingly constant change, took over. A functional view of a lecturer's role is encouraged throughout the sector and by government. Being functional may seem a way of maintaining control of workloads but it is essentially an intellectually passive approach to working life. Likewise, being cynical may seem subversive but it is ultimately a passive approach as well. Our goal is to encourage active engagement with ideas that are dominating policy-making by encouraging lecturers to consider their perverse consequences for FE and to develop alternatives to them.

Since the introduction of mandatory FE teacher training, there is a need for a book that sets out clear challenges to the current functional and compliant approach to professionalizing FE teaching. Our approach invites the intelligent, engaged lecturer to join in a debate with other lecturers. It is our view that debate is necessary before policies are produced and before academic research begins. Only in a climate in which there is debate about a vision for FE will we begin to see adequate long-term policy-making and the independent research that will ensure its continuing success. We hope that this book will kick-start that debate.

About this book

The chapters in this book can be read independently. They deal with all aspects of working in FE. In a sense they cover a very basic range of topics from starting to teach in FE, management and industrial relations, supporting students, qualifications, ICT, key skills, the transition to work, professional training, to a final 'head to head' discussion of the future of FE. But they are distinctive. Each puts forward a perspective that we hope is both challenging and different. The contributors were, at the time of writing, mostly lecturers in FE or FE teacher training, and were chosen because they had something original or controversial to say. The book is a step toward encouraging the 'lecturer voice' which is often transmitted only through academic studies and the consultations of policy-makers and unions. We do not expect everyone, or anyone, to agree with their arguments but we hope they will provoke debate and criticism. As a taster we give here an outline of what we see as an original or challenging idea from each chapter.

The Introduction was written after the individual chapters were completed and identifies what can be read in them about the state of further education at the present time. What the various contributors identify in their different ways is the 'perverse' consequences of policy-making by government and its quangos. By 'perverse' we mean that the increased interventions often have the opposite result from that intended and that these perverse consequences are responded to by more and often hasty policy-making that produces further perverse consequences. The spiral of perverse consequences is a feature of the frantic policy-making that characterizes New Labour's 'third way' politics. The outcome of which, we argue, is an increasingly therapeutic FE culture that has a diminished view of the potential of young people.

Joanna Williams, who moved from secondary school teaching to FE, starts the chapters with a critical examination of the role of FE from the standpoint of a new lecturer. She looks at the history of the sector and concludes that the emphasis on social inclusion that comes out of government policy is encouraging student attendance not for its stated aims, such as developing skills or the values that a good citizen should have, but as being about *participation for its own sake*. She sees this emphasis merging with the children's 'well-being' objectives that come out of the *Every Child Matters* (ECM) objectives in compulsory education to foster a practice based on 'safe participation'. For this – clearly therapeutic practice – a new sort of lecturer is needed, one who is more concerned with student safety and participation than subject knowledge and skills. In this new professional practice she argues, both lecturers and students are infantilized.

In Chapter 2, Jon Bryan and Dennis Hayes introduce the concept of 'McDonaldization', and explore its application to FE. Although they raise the spectre of the 'McCollege', their analysis is different from what the title might lead a reader to expect. They argue that McDonaldization, like the 'commodification' of education, is not necessarily a bad thing but that the McCollege fails because it cannot even live up to the challenge set by McDonald's restaurants. Colleges are not McDonaldized but bureaucratized institutions. Their ability to deliver even commodified education is frustrated. One of the criticisms of the 'McDonalization' thesis that they deal with is that it is *unstoppable*. Against this inevitability argument, both being active trade unionists, they identify the resistance that there has been, particularly to the deskilling of the work of the lecturer and the creation of the McLecturer.

Chapter 3 is a polemical look at student 'motivation' by Patrick Hayes, drawing on his experience as a researcher for the *Times Educational Supplement*, and a period as an FE student. He compares what is actually happening within FE with the theory on offer in teacher training textbooks. He identifies a serious problem in saying that attempts in theory and practice to motivate students are at the heart of the problem of students lacking motivation. Enjoying an apparent paradox, he argues that if lecturers want to motivate students the first step is to stop trying to 'motivate' them.

Hype about ICT is analysed next in Chapter 4, not by a Luddite or technophobe, but by a head of media and communications, Toby Marshall. Reflecting in his terminology the animal metaphors in which some of the debate about ICT is conducted, he argues against both bullish hype and mulish rejection of the potential of ICT. Examining the literature from B.F. Skinner's early work in *Teaching Machines* in 1958 to the present day, his central argument is that what determines the success or otherwise of ICT is not the technology but the pedagogical framework in which the technology is applied.

Alec Turner is in many ways a traditional FE lecturer, coming to work in FE from industry. In Chapter 5 he uses his own experience as a student and lecturer to illuminate an important argument. He states that he finds the concept of 'key skills' confused and difficult, and that concentration on such 'skills' is removing real knowledge and skills from the curriculum. Developing 'key skills' is, he says, no more than a bureaucratic exercise devoid of subject content.

The transmission of knowledge and skills in FE may be declining but the achievement and award of qualifications continues to rise. The idea of 'credentialism' gives Neil Davenport, a politics lecturer and journalist, a hook with which to explore the secular increase in qualifications on offer in FE. Despite the constant iteration of the backwardness of British youth and workers in relation to the achievement of a variety of qualifications, people today have more qualifications than ever before. Something else is going on behind the drive for more credentials. In his opinion it is a cover for the emptying the content of courses. This leads him to a rejection of FE funding being tied to working for often meaningless credentials. What is needed he concludes, is a defence of education for its own sake, an aim that has previously been an essential part of not only FE, but of all forms of education.

In a sense any book about FE is about the transition from school to adult life, something which is now an extended process. Patrick Turner, a youth worker and a trainer of youth workers, provides in Chapter 7, what in many ways is a summary of the themes of this book. He draws upon a broad range of philosophical perspectives to explore what is different in the transition to adulthood today. He analyses the way in which this transition has been significantly changed by a managerial government intruding into and controlling private life. Government now considers the teenage years of the underprivileged so fraught with risk that 'youth' must be monitored at every turn if they are to take their allotted place in the social order, so maintaining the status quo.

He draws attention to the fact that the methods adopted by the state to control young people are different from those of the past. The state increasingly uses therapeutic interventions rather than letting young people follow the risky path to adulthood that he and other young people of an earlier generation managed, without the state holding their hand and, as a consequence, holding them back.

Teacher training provides Dennis Hayes, in Chapter 8, with an opportunity to rehearse some arguments from his previous papers on the dangerous therapeutic trends in FE teaching. His initial focus is both the lack of critical thinking and the damage this does when replaced by essentially therapeutic notions, although the term 'critical' still remains. He then looks at the ideologies of teacher training drawn from key textbooks in the field and suggests that instead of promoting 'reflective practice' there should be developed what he calls *descriptive practice*. Descriptive practice is the art of describing in detail what happens in the classroom, and in meetings and tutorials with students. There is no pretentious philosophy behind descriptive practice but it does demand careful observation, listening and the ability to write down what is seen and heard. In a witty aside, he then takes trendy teaching methods to task as being the ways not to teach. So what is good FE teaching? He gives an answer that looks forward to the changes in teacher training from 2007 and provides a straightforward reduction of all the professional 'standards' and 'competencies' for FE lecturers and FE teacher educators to one simple criterion.

Our experience of working in FE, and in FE teacher training, has convinced us that there is a great need for the sort of debate exemplified in the final chapter of this book, Chapter 9, where Ian Nash, Kathryn Ecclestone and Claire Fox, discuss their visions for FE. In an age when new and existing lecturers are encouraged to have narrowly instrumental views of their work, the perspectives they offer raise profound problems about the nature and future of FE.

Key readings

Each chapter provides a short list of key readings. We have asked the authors to provide not just the obvious key readings, such as policy documents, legislation and well-known textbooks, but books that may offer a critical perspective. They do not attempt to be exhaustive but answer the question, 'What do you have to read to be able to talk about this issue intelligently?'

Using the chronologies

Each chapter also contains a short chronology which varies in length and content, according to the author's interest. They are varied and provisional in that they can be adapted and updated. As they are very short they can be contextualized and even supplemented with the longer and fuller version in Armitage et al. (2007) where readers will find a detailed explanation of the uses of a chronology. To summarize that explanation, their purpose is three-fold: first, to give at a glance the key dates that the authors of the chapters think are crucial to understanding the topic; second, they are intended to provide a more distanced and historical perspective on the issues discussed; third, and most importantly, they should allow the reader to see many aspects of what is different now in FE. In our view the differences, between what is happening now and what happened in the past, are always more important that the similarities, and we should avoid the easy and habitual approach of always looking for the latter.

List of abbreviations

As many of these abbreviations refer to historical initiatives or defunct organizations, the dates when these were established are given. For a fuller account of these, see the Chronology of Post-Compulsory Education in Armitage *et al*. 3rd Edition 2007.

ABC	*A Basis for Choice* (FEU publication 1979)
ACM	Association of College Managers
ALI	Adult Learning Inspectorate
AoC	Association of Colleges (1996; formerly the CEF)
APIR	Assessment planning implementation and review
AQA	Assessment and Qualifications Alliance
ASBO	Anti-social behaviour order
ATCDE	Association of Teachers in Colleges and Department of Education (1943)
ATL	Association of Teachers and Lecturers
ATTI	Association of Teachers in Technical Institutions (1904)
AUT	Association of University Teachers (1919)
BECTA	British Educational Communications and Technology Agency
BERA	British Educational Research Association
BIP	Behaviour improvement programmes
BTEC	Business and Technology Education Council (1991; formerly (1983) Business and Technician Education Council)
CCEA	Council for the Curriculum, Examinations and Assessment (Northern Ireland)
CEF	Colleges' Employers' Forum (1992)
CEL	Centre for Excellence in Leadership
Cert. Ed	Certificate in Education
CETT	Centre for Excellence in Teacher Training
C&G	City & Guilds
CKSA	Common knowledge, skills and attributes
CNAA	Council for National Academic Awards (1964)
CoVEs	Centres of Vocational Excellence
CP	Community Programme
CPD	Continuing Professional Development

CPVE   Certificate of Pre-Vocational Education (1985)
CSE   Certificate of Secondary Education (1964)
DES   Department of Education and Science (1964)
DfE   Department for Education (1992)
DfEE   Department for Education and Employment (1995)
DfES   Department for Education and Skills (2001)
DoH   Department of Health
ECM   *Every Child Matters*
EDEXCEL   Formed from BTEC and London Examinations Board (1996)
EI   Emotional intelligence
EIQ   Emotional Intelligence Quotient
ELS   Education Lecturing Services
EMA   Education Maintenance Allowance
EQ   Emotional quotient
ERA   Education Reform Act (1988)
ESOL   English for Speakers of Other Languages
ESSA   English School Students' Association
E2E   Entry to Employment
FE   Further education
FEC   Further Education College
FEDA   Further Education Development Agency (1995)
FEFC   Further Education Funding Council (1993)
FENTO   Further Education National Training Organization (1998)
FEU   Further education unit (1977)
FHE   Further and Higher Education
GCE   General Certificate in Education (1951)
GCSE   General Certificate of Secondary Education (1988)
GERBILL   Great Education Reform Bill (1987)
GNVQ   General National Vocational Qualification
GTC (E)   General Teaching Council (England)
HE   Higher education
HEA   Higher Education Academy (formerly the IfLT HE)
HEI   Higher education institution
HMI   Her Majesty's Inspectorate
HO   Home Office
IBM   International Business Machines
ICT   Information and communication technology
IEP   Individual education plan
IfL   Institute for Learning (formerly IfL PCET and, before that, IfL FE)
IFP   Increased Flexibility Programme (for 14–16-year-olds)
ILA   Individual learning account
ILP   Individual learning plan
ILT HE   Institute for Learning and Teaching in Higher Education (now
          absorbed in the HEA)

INSET	In-Service Education and Training
IQ	Intelligence quotient
IT	Information Technology
ITALS	Initial Teaching Award Learning and Skills
ITE	Initial Teacher Education
ITT	Initial Teacher Training
IWB	Interactive whiteboard
LAs	Learner Accounts
LEA	Local education authority
LLSC	Local Learning and Skills Council
LLUK	Lifelong Learning UK
LSC	Learning and Skills Council (replaced the FEFC in 2001)
LSDA	Learning and Skills Development Agency (formerly the FEDA)
LSN	Learning and Skills Network
MA	Modern Apprenticeship (1993)
MSC	Manpower Services Commission (1974)
NAO	National Audit Office
NATFHE	National Association of Teachers in Further and Higher Education (1976)
NC	National curriculum
NCVQ	National Council for Vocational Qualifications (1986)
NDPB	Non-Departmental Public Body
NEET	Not in employment, education or training
NETT	National Education and Training Targets
NFER	National Foundation for Educational Research
NIACE	National Institute of Adult Continuing Education
NQF	National Qualifications Framework
NTI	New Training Initiative (1981)
NTO	National Training Organization
NUS	National Union of Students
NVQ	National Vocational Qualification
OECD	Organization for Economic Co-operation and Development
OfSECSS	Office for Standards in Education, Children's Services and Skills
OfSTED	Office for Standards in Education (1992)
PA	Personal Advisor (Connexions)
PCE	Post-compulsory education
PCET	Post-compulsory education and training
PELTS	Personal, employability, learning and thinking skills
PGCE	Post-Graduate Certificate in Education (or Professional Graduate Certificate in Education)
PISA	Programme for International Student Assessment

QCA	Qualifications and Curriculum Authority (formed in 1997 from SCAA and NCVQ)
QIA	Quality Improvement Agency
QTLSS	Qualified Teacher Learning and Skills
QUANGO	Quasi-Autonomous Non-Government (al) Organization
QUEST	Quality of Experience in Schooling Trans-Nationally
SCAA	School Curriculum and Assessment Authority (1993)
SCETT	Standing Committee for the Education and Training of Teachers
SEU	Social Exclusion Unit
SIR	Staff Individualized Record
SSC	Sector skills council
SSDA	Sector Skills Development Agency
STAR	(Not an abbreviation) DfES/QIA awards scheme for FE staff
SVQ	Scottish Vocational Qualifications
SVUK	Standards Verification UK
TDA	Training and Development Agency for Schools (2005)
TDLB	Training and Development Lead Body
TEC	Training and Enterprise Council (1991)
TES	*Times Educational Supplement*
TTA	Teacher Training Agency (1994)
TUC	Trades Union Congress
T2G	Train to Gain
UCET	Universities Council for the Education of Teachers
UCU	University and College Union (formed from the merger of the AUT and NATFHE in 2006)
VLE	Virtual learning environment
WBL	Work-based learning
WEA	Workers' Educational Association
WEEP	Work Experience on Employers Premises (YOP)
WISE	Women into Science and Engineering
YT	Youth Training (1989)
YTS	Youth Training Scheme (1983)
YOP	Youth Opportunities Programme (1978)

Introduction: the perverse consequences of further education policy

Dennis Hayes, Toby Marshall and Alec Turner

Further education colleges were once heterogeneous community-based institutions providing skills training, adult education and 'remedial' education. Constant government interference over the last three decades has transformed them from the traditional 'tech', first into youth containment camps and then, as a result of more and more interventions focused on individuals and their personalities, into therapy centres. In our view this is the trajectory of contemporary further education (FE). Of course, this is an argument about a general trajectory and counter-examples of good plumbing, hairdressing and philosophy courses can still be found. Where they do exist they exist within a framework that we would, nevertheless, describe as 'therapeutic'. By 'therapeutic' we mean that in all, not just specialist, courses increasingly focus on the private and internal emotional lives of students. This process of change, which we will explain, was not a deliberate consequence of any policy. What it reflects is a changing view we have of young people and one that is difficult to articulate in a philosophical way.

The authors of the *Nuffield Review of 14–19 Education* recognize that something has changed. They argue that government has neglected discussion of values, and that more needs to be said about educational aims because 'They reflect the kind of life that is thought to be worth living, the personal qualities worth developing and the sort of society worth creating' (Hayward *et al.* 2005: 24–5). The question they raise as being most important is 'What counts as an educated person (19-year-old) in this day and age?' Their remarks are typical of criticism made by many teachers and lecturers, that government policy is instrumental and managerial and does not deal with over-arching values. It is our contention that this cannot be easily answered because the view that comes out of most education policy is no longer a positive vision of a young person but a negative one. Young people are presented as vulnerable and as potential victims of themselves or others and, as a result, we are offered a diminished concept of their potential as human beings (Hayes 2006e; Ecclestone and Hayes 2007). It is not merely an omission from policy but is something altogether more problematic. A negative and diminished vision of young people is, by its very nature, difficult to express in policy documents except in terms of 'caring', 'protection' and 'safety'.

The explanation for this diminished concept of a young person lies in the increased intervention in education. Intervention by government and its quangos – what we call the 'quangocracy' – has become so commonplace that we do not recognize that the very process of constant intervention is not merely disturbing but produces substantive consequences. This is not merely because the recent policies are constantly changing and contradictory or that they challenge established values (Newman 2001; Coffield *et al.* 2005). We will argue that what is distinctive about recent government interventions in FE, and elsewhere, is that their consequences are always *perverse*. By 'perverse' we mean that in the attempt to meet their stated aims, they produce the opposite effect to that intended. To take the example of the broad description of change given in the opening paragraph, the overall aim of policy was to ensure that FE colleges met the needs of the economy by ensuring that the work force of the future had the appropriate skills. Through a series of often poorly thought out, under-developed and chaotic initiatives looking at 'skill gaps', they have come to focus more on the personal weaknesses and vulnerabilities of students to the extent that the latter are less likely to develop the resilience that is needed to survive in the workplace.

Our analysis of this process of intervention may seem to be a version of the criticism that government is trying to 'micromanage' further education. We are not primarily concerned with the form government intervention takes, whether it involves micromanagement or, what we consider to be more important, the over-regulation of FE. What we and our contributors focus on is not the form but the content of these continual interventions. Critics of 'micromanagement' are often at ease with the philosophy and outcomes of interventions but reject the method and, not least, the meanness of trying to implement policies within a climate of the systematic under-funding of FE. We want to focus on the *content* of innovations more than the forms they take.

The most significant change that we want to focus on is how the image of the student has been transformed into the more vulnerable young person that fills government policy documents and textbooks, if not the FE classroom. We illustrate this transformation starkly before touching on how management, vocational training and the professionalism of lecturers have all suffered from the perverse consequences of government interventions.

From fear of youth rebellion to fear of youth self-harm

We argue that the last 30 years of developments in FE have taken place alongside, and may well have contributed to, a complete reversal of the idea we have of a young person. This may not seem so troubling if considered in an abstract way, because the way in which young people are viewed has always been paradoxical: they are seen as threatening or threatened, and often as both. Writing in the aftermath of the introduction of the youth training schemes in the 1980s, sociologist Paul Willis neatly expressed the social category of 'youth' in terms of this paradox:

> . . .Youth', as it has been socially constructed, can conjure up a set of menacing and largely masculine images which in various moral panics have defined young people as a threat . . . On the other hand, youth has itself been seen as threatened and at risk. It is a fragile, vulnerable stage of physical and personal development through which we must pass to independence and maturity.
>
> (Willis 1987: 5)

While the paradox is always present, it is the social context that determines what emphasis is given to the threatening or threatened aspects of 'youth'. In the context of mass unemployment in the 1980s, what dominated the mind of government was the threatening possibility of 'youth' responding to the prospect of long-term unemployment by challenging the social order. The images of rioting in Brixton, Handsworth and Belfast, and of unemployed youth marching for jobs were the social background against which FE training policies were developed. Fear of social disorder was real.

To illustrate the paradoxical nature of 'youth' and the way in which the perverse consequences of government intervention arise, we have drawn up two case studies. The first is of a student, Mark, who was seen as a 'new' entrant to FE in the early 1980s and, the second of a student, Susie, who we believe is the 'new' entrant to FE of the 2000s. We chose examples of students two decades apart, both to make what we are arguing more concrete but also to make the historical differences clear for those, and that is most of us, for whom the current student represents the eternal student. We are drawing attention to the *differences* between our case studies rather than to the similarities.

Mark: a case study of troublesome youth (1980s)
Mark is 17. After spending a year on benefit doing odd jobs on the side, he has been forced to join a Youth Opportunities Programme. He does so only after receiving several threatening letters and facing the prospect of having his benefit withdrawn. His brother is an apprentice car worker and a member of the Young Socialists who thinks the YOP is pointless and that the work experience Mark is getting is just slave labour. His father has worked in the paint shop of a car plant for 20 years and is a shop steward and Labour councillor. His mother does clerical work for a local insurance broker in the mornings and is doing an intermediate French class at her local adult education centre. Mark and the other trainees are looked down upon by the lecturers and students on more traditional courses. Several of his fellow trainees have reading and writing problems. He is taught by indifferent lecturers redeployed from the college's general education department, which is closing. One of the lecturers is a political activist and encourages Mark to join an Anti-Fascist Action group, so he spends most of his time working for them, speaking, leafleting and sometimes defending families threatened by local racist thugs. After a few months of poor attendance, a job comes up at the local car plant. He leaves straight away, wanting never to go on a college vocational course again. He has had enough of 'education' although he might think about an A level politics evening class run by the politically active lecturer who influenced him.

The context in which Mark endured a forced and unwanted period of training is set in a climate where there existed active traditions of involvement in politics and trade unions, the community and a strong sense of family and continuity of interests. Education is seen as something which is about extending personal knowledge and horizons. Entry to education is initiated by individuals and is voluntary.

The contemporary social context is more difficult to describe although the terms 'culture of fear' or 'culture of risk' express the mood of the times the context is best described by the term 'lifelong learning'. Instead of rebellious youth there is a vision of 'Chavs' who are the victims of binge drinking, drug taking, unwanted early pregnancies and who can't control their feelings of aggression unless threatened with anti-social behaviour orders (ASBOs). All these activities are self-destructive and their cause is usually identified as low self-esteem that requires intervention from outside agencies.

Susie: a case study of troubled youth (2000s)
Susie is 17. She has dropped out of education, having had a year off school after being bullied because she was over-weight. She occupied herself helping her mother who is suffering from depression. Her mother was on medication after finding it impossible to cope with her twin babies after their father left. Eventually her doctor recommended that Susie's mother join a mums' support group at a local community centre. She enjoyed this and everything went well. She made friends and attended a parenting class at the local college. Feeling comfortable at the college, she looked for a work-related course. After talking to a student advisor she applied for, and was accepted on, an IT at Work Introductory Diploma. Susie, like her mother, also has a history of depression related to low self-esteem because of her appearance and social isolation. Her elder sister was close to finishing her training as a beauty therapist and encouraged Susie to talk to her Connexions' Personal Advisor (PA) about her future. Her PA suggested a Skills for Life class. The college provided a crèche and this meant that mum and daughter could both attend classes during the day. Susie stuck at her course, never missing a session, and also took advantage of the student counselling service. Next year she hopes to do a more demanding Skills for Working Life course. All of the family members feel supported at college and hope to continue doing courses as long as they enjoy them. They have just heard that Susie's sister has been accepted to do a foundation degree. She will be the first member of the family to go into higher education.

Susie's period of change and achievement focused on her emotional and social development facilitated by a series of professional advisors and semi-professional counsellors. Her entire family is supported by caring, educational and training institutions.

They typify many beneficiaries of the era of lifelong learning who escape 'social exclusion' through a framework of education and training qualifications.

How have we moved from seeing Mark as the 'new' FE student to seeing Susie as the 'new' FE student? At one level the issue is about a conceptual shift from a concern with *education and knowledge* sought by an autonomous learner, to a concern with the *process of learning* covering all aspects of life. Mark saw education as a stage you passed through before going on to a job, returning voluntarily to enhance your knowledge or skills. For Susie, learning goes on throughout life and is structured by others. Although she feels empowered, she is a dependent rather than an independent learner. She relies on courses and agencies to support her and the likelihood is that this will be a never-ending process.

This dependence is something that once only the most vulnerable young people would need. Perhaps Susie may seem like such a person. Whether this is true or not, she is the model for all young people. Even the most able students now accept that they are potentially vulnerable and that they need help from PAs and courses in stress management and even in happiness.

Susie illustrates for us the perverse consequence of the many government interventions over the last 30 years. The attempt to produce less dependent young people, to keep them off the dole queue and the protest or picket line, has led to young people being more dependent on provision by the government and its learning agencies. The process began with *A Basis for Choice* (ABC), published by the Further Education Unit (FEU) in 1979, which emphasized 'transferable' skills and a young person's 'learning experiences'. Since ABC there have been ever more interventions that change the focus of the curriculum from knowledge to process and from acquiring content to acquiring personal skills.

These interventions have made autonomy in young people's personal and educational lives impossible. Although there is now no need to deal with the social consequences of mass unemployment, we have a situation where everyone has to have more and more aspects of their lives assessed and certified. Much of it seems to lack any purpose as most of this newly certified 'learning' once referred to the things young people just picked up without any teaching. One purpose may be control, but there is no evidence of the need for this. What the structuring of everyday learning around qualifications and courses does achieve is the transformation of young people into dependent lifelong 'learners'.

Young people do not have to be seen as vulnerable or as incapable of normal social life without qualifications in most aspects of everyday experience. The most important thing is for FE lecturers, first, to see young people as being educable and, second, to educate by, opening up for their students in Matthew Arnold's words, 'the best that is known and thought in the world' (Arnold [1864] 2003: 50).

Training and skills may come to mind here. Are we ignoring training for work in mentioning Arnold's vision of education? The answer is that before we can return to the traditional debate between education and training, we have to move beyond the impoverished vision of young people as hapless and hopeless individuals in need of improving their confidence and self-esteem. This involves the not inconsiderable philosophical task of regaining our vision of education. Nothing less will do (see Hayes 2006e).

The philosophical task of regaining a positive vision of an educated young person or adult is made easier because there is a general feature shared by all government interventions. Their perverse consequences make them *fragile*. This is why there are so many changes of policy and direction in FE. To explain this fragility we will examine the perverse consequences of government intervention in FE in relation to Further Education College (FEC) management, its vocational or 'skills' orientation, and in relation to the new professionalization agenda.

The perverse consequences of managerialism

In 1967 Professor Teddy Chester and his research team at the University of Manchester, were asked by the Department of Education and Science (DES) to conduct a 'study of the administration of technical colleges' (Charlton *et al.* 1971: vi). Nearly 40 years later the government approached Sir Andrew Foster, Deputy Chair of the Royal Bank of Canada, to review further education. Comparing these two studies should enable us to clarify the key changes in the sector.

Cohort and size

Professor Chester's team records that between 1956 and 1966 further education underwent a period of rapid expansion, with full time enrolments increasing from 76,000 to 173,300. By this point the total number of students had reached nearly two million and there were 675 colleges in England and Wales, not including the numerous evening class institutes. The annual expenditure of the sector was £180 million (Charlton *et al.* 1971: 11–15).

Currently, close to 3.5 million learners are enrolled, even though the number of colleges has declined. In England there are now roughly 250 general FECs, more than 100 sixth-form colleges, and 38 colleges with a specialist focus, such as horticulture. Further education is the single biggest provider of education for 16–18-year-olds, and its student body includes a greater than average proportion of females, the deprived and members of ethnic minorities (DfES 2005d: 81–3).

The average student roll in a general FE college is 12,000. Mostly, these students are part-time adult learners on short courses, although 16–18-year-olds on longer vocational courses receive approximately 50 per cent of the available teaching hours (DfES 2005d: 83). The vast majority of courses are work-related, with ICT (18%) and health, social care and public services (17%) being the largest areas of learning (Mounts and Bursnall 2004: 42).

Governance

The quantitative changes in FE have been matched by qualitative shifts in its system of governance. In the mid-60s college principals were accountable to local education authorities (LEA), which in turn, were accountable to local councillors and ultimately to the electorate. For this reason, older residents in the vicinity of your FE workplace may sometimes be heard talking proprietarily of 'our college'.

Technical Colleges also came under the purview of the regional advisory councils (RAC). These bodies included representatives from a range of constituencies, including employers' organizations, teacher training institutions, universities and trade unions. The purpose of the RACs was to ensure that provision matched regional needs (Charlton *et al.* 1971: 56–73).

Governance changed with the Further and Higher Education Act of 1992. The motivation for this is explained in the autobiography of the former Conservative education secretary, Kenneth Baker. 'Further education colleges', Baker argues, 'were being held back by their local authority *controllers'*.(Baker 1993: 244, emphasis added). In an attempt to liberate them, the Conservative administration resolved to take colleges out of local authority control and to establish them as self-governing charitable institutions. This meant that, from 1 April 1993, the newly 'incorporated' colleges were free to establish their own corporate objectives, to contract with government to deliver training via the Further Education Funding Council (FEFC), and to manage their staff and services. One immediate consequence of the demands of these changes and funding freezes, was to catalyse institutional concentration through a series of mergers.

Quango capture: shell-shocked managers

The independence conferred by incorporation has proved more nominal than substantive. It's true that further education colleges have much of the epiphenomena of the private sector, such as derivative branded signage and biros. But colleges for the most part continue to be dependent on the state for funding. While larger institutions now command budgets of up £65 million, 78 per cent of the sector's income is sourced from the Learning and Skills Council (LSC) (DfES 2005d: 81–2). The immediate cost of state funding is in regulation. So far from liberating colleges, incorporation has substituted Baker's local council controllers for an army of unelected national state controllers, less of a rolling back of the state than its extension, diversification and buttressing.

In their submission to the Foster Review, Professor Steven Fox and his colleagues distinguish between internal and external challenges confronted by senior management teams, and in doing so they alert us to the very real consequences of the regulatory burden that is being imposed on the sector. In terms of external challenges that confront managers, they note the primary importance of the 'audit culture and regimes . . . [that] drive what college leadership does and absorb scarce management time' (Fox 2005: 2). Tellingly, they point out that this diverts attention from arguably more important and meaningful external relationships that could be developed with the business community.

To put this bluntly, further education is experiencing what could be termed 'quango capture'. The intrusion of government agencies, including Ofsted, the Learning and Skills Council, and the newly formed Quality Improvement Agency (QIA), to name but a few, contribute little to the quality of these services and does much harm. Most particularly, it restricts managers' autonomy, and by extension their effectiveness, by ensuring that they are constantly trying to guess what the regulator deems to be 'best practice'. In doing so, vital energies are diverted from more important external tasks, such as those noted above, as well as the critical task of addressing how the quality of lecturing might be improved. For senior management teams there often seems to be no alternative, as the principals of institutions that are judged as non-compliant by Ofsted soon find that they lose their positions.

Quango capture gives rise to a state of executive insecurity. Anybody who has played the game of 'guess what the inspectorate is thinking', or 'hunt the funding stream', understands that this is a life dominated by quixotic, fast moving, externally imposed and, often, poorly rationalized decisions. Consequently, senior and middle managers, who try to remain upright on the shifting sands of a policy desert, can often exhibit a brittle and sometimes aloof approach to their staff. However, the one issue on which they are consistent is the need to produce ever greater volumes of paperwork, including lesson plans, schemes of work, course performance reports, in order to ensure that they have an extensive dossier with which to demonstrate evidence compliance. Managers within FE would act with greater confidence and compassion towards their staff if they knew they had the weight of numbers behind them: of their community, their staff and their learners.

Aside from its insecurity, the management of many FE colleges is notable for the dry argot through which it communicates. As McGrath (2004: 193) has noted, they speak using the language of generic management, with their controlling concepts being economy, efficiency and effectiveness. In adopting this language, senior management teams mirror the political and regulatory elite, but undermine their own position. The lexicon of audit, control and measurement generates as many problems as it resolves. While it may give the appearance of hard-nosed accountability, it fails to inspire commitment in staff, because it lacks a substantive moral core. It's not, in fact, the language of education and training, as it could be used to describe the manufacturing of tins of baked beans. For this reason it cannot be projected with much authority and credibility, which compounds their sense of isolation.

Policy churn, ambiguity of purpose, regulatory ambush and capture: all this ensures that in the post-incorporation era there are few of the buccaneering and entrepreneurial managers that incorporation promised. A perverse consequence indeed!

This new and diminished management, with little real character, still has to function and its operation has further perverse consequences for lecturers and students.

Reluctant lecturers: 'only 3457 days until retirement . . .'

The erosion of management character within FE has had multiple effects on the working lives of the practitioners, most immediately through the creation of a control culture and the associated erosion of their professional autonomy. Gone are the days when, in the words of one respondent to the Chester survey, colleges were run on a '90 per cent trust and 10 per cent check basis'. Characteristically, lecturers respond to this in one of two ways. The best get on with their jobs and find meaning in the isolation of their classrooms, although privatized engagement is hard to sustain over time. Many more are openly, or privately, cynical: at lunch times they plan their exit strategy or work out how many days remain until retirement.

A survey produced in 2000 by the Learning and Skills Development Agency (LSDA) received questionnaire responses from 9515 individuals working in the sector. They were asked to rate a variety of statements in relation to their experiences. The findings make for rather depressing reading. According to the authors: 'In our experience, it is uncommon for average ratings to be as negative within a single organization and very rare for them to be so negative across a whole sector' (Davies and Owen 2001: 7). In particular, they argued, two factors seemed to be linked with the perceptions of satisfaction where they were rarely found. First, the feeling that the 'college cared about them' and their contribution was valued and, second, the extent to which they were communicated with and involved in the decision-making process. Perhaps one consequence of regulatory capture is that staff contributions to the decision-making process are increasingly considered incidental by college management teams. The sourness produced by this marginalization is a familiar part of the 'demoralization' of FE. To illustrate this demoralization, here are three practitioners speaking for themselves in an edited selection from the *TES*'s online FE Staffroom:

> I am currently employed as a Lecturer in Computing and Multimedia at my local FE college (6 years standing) and am considering moving out of FE altogether. This is due to a number of factors such as lack of recognition/appreciation, poor management etc rather than a dislike of teaching or working with students.

> . . . In many environments the useless are promoted because they cannot do the job they are employed for. This seems to be the case in FE also, and is based on the lack of will to actually boot people out who are grossly incompetent. I will not describe the management wonders of my College because it would identify it, but I wonder how many Colleges also have NO academics in senior positions who then control curricula and teaching. Seems bizarre to me.

> Tell me . . . of all the managers you came across in college how many were professional?
> I should imagine not many, judging from my experience. The reason being that there is a combined culture of nepotism and sheer indolence in many areas. I can think of some startling examples of people given posts at heads of department and above, who were only there as a political favour or were in a sexual relationship with the principal. Sound familiar?

Management and leadership is important, but a perverse consequence of the new management being compliant in the face of over-regulation is that in many colleges managers at a variety of levels adopt an autocratic style and seem to be remote from both workforce and students. However, this distancing from day-to-day activity and engagement with students does not preclude a concern for ensuring that FECs are 'student-centred' and empower their students.

'You will have a voice': the compulsory empowerment of students

Surveys of students' perceptions of FE need, of course, to be treated with caution. Too often respondents use research of this type as a means of attacking lecturers, whose behaviour senior managers often see as the cause rather than the solution to their problems. Equally, if we accept a fundamental asymmetry between student and lecturer in terms of knowledge and experience, then it follows that students' perceptions of quality should, at the very least, be interpreted with some critical distance.

Sadly, the ideology of the pedagogic quangocracy often elevates students to the status of co-pedagogues. A recent report produced by the LSDA provides evidence of this approach and you may have experienced variants in your institution. After discussing the importance of students' contribution to the pedagogic decision-making, it concludes, with a noticeable lack of irony, that the students should be 'empowered', even if they choose not to be:

> Active and constructive involvement by students in the design and delivery of their learning does not usually happen if arrangements are *merely permissive and voluntary*. It requires specific encouragement via such steps as support for the training of student representatives.
>
> (Davies 2006: 10, emphasis added).

However, there are some interesting findings that can also be drawn from research of this type. The Davies and Owen staff survey also mapped its findings against the results of a parallel student survey. They found a correlation, as one might expect, between staff and learner dissatisfaction. They note that the results: ' . . . indicated that there was a positive relationship between the relative strength of agreement of staff [to positive statements on their working lives] and the likelihood that students at the same college would encourage others to attend' (Davies and Owen 2001: 32).

Equally, the largest scale survey of learner perceptions, the LSC's *National Learner Satisfaction Survey* indicates that while many learners have indeed picked up anti-lecturer attitudes that surveys of this type often promote, the biggest single factor that contributes to their satisfaction in relation to their studies is not the degree to which they have become co-pedagogues, rather it's the more traditional expectation that the teacher has sound subject-knowledge (LSC 2004: 8). This 'voice' is, we would argue, the most important but we can be sure it will not be heard.

In summary, management's abandonment of the role of strategic academic direction, whether or not they are academics, and their complete capitulation to external regulation has several perverse consequences. It undermines both the nature of FE and makes it a market without a clear commodity on sale. They are no longer supported or trusted by lecturers who see them as having no interest in education and as weak, vacillating and powerless in the face of the FE quangocracy. This capitulation has so undermined their character that the most perverse consequence is that they fail to manage in ways that are straightforward and have to rely on ambiguous pressure from students, whether directly through evaluations and feedback or through surveys. This has further perverse consequences, as we shall see.

It may be objected that managers have not given up on 'education' but have rightly begun to focus on the vocational elements of FE, which were always its real focus. Far from abandoning 'education' they are ensuring the development of the nation's skill base and play a vital economic role. In the next section we will show that this, the best line of defence that managers the quangocracy and government can come up with, has even more perverse consequences.

The perverse consequences of being 'skill crazy'

The language and discourse surrounding and enveloping the FE sector has changed beyond recognition in the last 25 years. For teenagers FE was once a choice with pretty clear and definable outcomes. For the boy or girl emerging from a comprehensive school with little academic inclination, the FEC was a place of learning one day per week during their period of apprenticeship. Away from the hurly-burly of the building site, garage workshop or hairdressing salon, the youngster would learn theoretical aspects of their chosen trade as well as having a period of general studies in recognition of the fact that life involved rather more than simply work. For those with a proven track record of successful academic study, full time vocational courses were available, for instance in business studies, where students attended college five days per week, with a timetable not dissimilar in structure and length to the type they would have been familiar with at school. Successful completion of the course fairly well guaranteed reasonable employment or a place at a polytechnic on a higher level course coupled with substantial periods of work experience. The local college would also have a general education section where students could enrol for academic study to A level with future progression to university in mind. Then, of course, the college fulfilled wider community needs, providing special interest, part-time courses for adults who simply wished to enrich their personal lives through engaging in learning and practical activities that were quite new to them.

To suggest that these were halcyon days would constitute an over-statement. That the demarcations existing within those colleges met everyone's needs was simply not true. Nevertheless, attendance at an FEC represented a choice made by the individual who was expected to be robust in making that decision and in accepting full responsibility for the consequences: good, bad or indifferent. While outcomes could not be guaranteed, the vast majority of students would acquire valuable knowledge, facilitated by lecturers sharing their knowledge, expertise and wisdom. Relationships within this setting were based on trust. Students trusted their lecturers' expertise, lecturers trusted their charges to use their newly acquired knowledge for their own and, hopefully, the wider community's benefit, and all placed some trust in the body charged with the administration and management of the FE college: the local education authority (LEA), comprising democratically elected councillors imbued with a public service ethos and intimate knowledge of the community they served.

Having considered the description above, the practitioner fresh to the world of FE might be forgiven for asking, 'So, what has changed?' After all colleges are still full of teenagers engaged in vocational and general education study, and with adults putting in an occasional appearance, even if the day-release students have all but disappeared.

In response to this question, the first point to make is that the element of choice has all but disappeared. Although compulsory education is completed at the age of 16, there are virtually no employment opportunities or apprenticeships on offer to people of this age, regardless of the individual's inclinations, attributes or abilities. To all intents and purposes, entry into the labour market without a sheaf of certificates is a non-starter. It is very easy to believe this is the way things have always been, but it is in fact a fairly recent phenomenon. In reality, entry to post-compulsory education and training (PCET) is no longer a choice, and the very idea that compulsory education finishes at age 16 is increasingly outdated. It is, perhaps, equally easy to assume that the nature of the labour market has changed beyond recognition as a result of globalization, the service sector overhauling the manufacturing sector in terms of contribution to GDP and the increased use of advanced technology with a corresponding need for qualifications and certification. However, this is far from being the case. If anything, the service sector generates a greater number of unskilled, routine jobs than the manufacturing sector and many people with PCs on their desks simply use them as glorified typewriters.

In truth, despite the seemingly endless supply of and demand for qualifications, the economy is no more in need of them now than it ever was. The qualification-hungry economy is a myth created by those who control the economy and the institutions of power. More than anything else, this situation is symptomatic of a government that is struggling to fill a void created by sporadic, low-level economic growth and their lack of a vision for the future with which to engage citizens.

As with many developments in modern history, the outcomes we are witnessing today of events that occurred 25 years ago may be quite unintentional but, nevertheless, can soon be whipped into the service of the state and those with an interest in maintaining the status quo. The events in question started in the late 1970s with the shocks to the UK economy of a quadrupling of oil prices and the rapid development and industrialization of the Asian 'tiger' economies on the Pacific rim, utilizing new technology and cheap labour. The primary victims of this economic downturn in the UK were working class teenagers with the disappearance of new job opportunities for school leavers as companies contracted. The initial response of the Conservative government was simply to cut the benefits system in the face of rising unemployment. However, further means were required to contain mass youth disaffection. The government hatched a variety of make-work schemes with little or no prospects and the FE sector was corralled into the process, delivering life skills, study skills and any number of other skills which were grouped together as 'skills for life' or 'employability skills'. Given the lack of job opportunities, 'employability skills' were simply a metaphor for youth containment. Their degree of success in terms of containment is somewhat debatable given the profusion of urban riots erupting in the 1980s and the glee with which youth attached itself to anything resembling opposition to a widely hated government, including the coal miners' strike of 1984/5 and the poll tax riot of 1990.

The imperative for governments to contain and control youth in the absence of real opportunities was writ large and from these rather crude beginnings, we have now moved into an all-embracing and expanding skills agenda. With each inquiry, report and subsequent government initiative related to FE, the skills agenda is further concretized and, of course, the White Paper issued in March 2006, the *Further Education: Raising Skills, Improving Life Chances*, is no exception in taking this agenda to new heights. If we are to understand the real motivation behind 'skills' in FE, then we must, first of all, reveal the contradictory and, even, nonsensical educational/training-speak emanating from government in this document. Four extracts will serve us well:

> The FE system must be the powerhouse for delivering skills at all levels that are needed to sustain an advanced, competitive economy . . .

> Since 1997, participation in post-16 training has expanded, with total learner numbers rising from around 4 million in 1997/8 to around 6 million in 2004/5.

> The proportion of our young people staying on in education and training remains scandalously low: the UK ranks 24th out of 29 developed nations. We lag well behind France and Germany . . .

The initial report in autumn 2005 by Lord Leitch on the skills needs of the economy in 2020 presents a daunting picture of the rate at which other nations such as China and India are improving their skills base . . .

(DfES 2006a: 3–4)

First, FE cannot deliver skills at all levels. FECs are, essentially, places of learning and removed from the workplace. As such, any skills development is decontextualized and fairly meaningless. Skills development is best situated in the workplace. However, within the UK, employers have long shown a marked reluctance to invest in training, research and development or cutting-edge technology, all of which would facilitate real skills development. With regard to participation rates, France and Germany's economies are even more stagnant than the UK's, with Germany experiencing chronically high levels of unemployment. Meanwhile, China seems to understand the demands of a fast-growing economy rather well, delivering high-quality general education to virtually all those participating up to the age of 18. The lesson learned is that skills are best developed within the workforce on the back of the acquisition of knowledge, rather than replacing knowledge with superfluous and meaningless notions of skills.

The reality of the skills agenda is, in fact, markedly different to anything the government might claim on its behalf. Since the shocks of the 1980s and the panics suffered by the elites in this country, FE has taken on a new role: a residuum for the large number of young people that a stagnant economy can no longer accommodate. A recognition of this fact allows us to better understand the politicization of FE. Far from being a sector whose core purpose is to deliver education, it has now become the place where teenagers' thoughts are policed. Rather than being a sector in which young people can learn a trade or job-specific skills, it is now the place where youngsters' behaviour will be managed in line with the crude principles laid down by politicians, their friends in quangos and the captains of industry. More so now than at any point in history, the FE sector will orchestrate the construction of an uncritical, malleable and subservient workforce designed to meet the needs of the economy and for the benefit of those who run it rather than offering anything by way of satisfying the natural thirst for knowledge or quest for personal fulfilment. The gradual emptying-out of knowledge from vocational curricula becomes the opening of the floodgates as a consequence of the White Paper. Following on from Tomlinson's 2004 report on the 14–19 curriculum, the government has adopted his proposals for specialized diplomas in work-related sectors, to be launched in 2008. The step-change in the skills agenda is quite breathtaking. For several years, policy-makers have witnessed the abject failure of the wider or 'soft' key skills (Improving Own Learning and Performance, Working with Others and Problem-Solving), largely because there was no element of compulsion, and students and lecturers alike rejected them as being a tedious distraction from real learning and meaningful education. Re-branded for the new diplomas, these skills will dominate the curriculum. The DfES has transformed Tomlinson's common knowledge, skills and attributes (CKSA) into personal, empoyability, learning and thinking skills (PELTS). While generic learning will comprise 26 per cent of a level 2 diploma curriculum and include functional skills in English, mathematics and ICT, as well as a project demonstrating PELTS, PELTS will be assessed in the remainder of the curriculum consisting of principal and additional learning. The six groups of PELTS recast the young people in our classrooms as team workers, self-managers, independent enquirers, reflective learners, critical thinkers and effective participators (taking the first letters as acronym and, then, as anagram, we could rename our students Clempwitters). Each PELTS group is accompanied by a focus statement and six statements of outcome. A reading of this exhausting list raises several questions in relation to the government's mindset not least of which is if student and lecturer alike are to manage and observe all of these focus statements and outcomes, where is the time for real teaching and learning? This minor inconvenience is clearly of little import to our masters who have rather more pressing details of social engineering to drive through, and goes some way to explain the increasing contempt in which they hold meaningful education for the lower orders in society. Equally well-illustrated is both the distrust and lack of confidence in FE lecturers held by those same people. For instance, the independent enquirer must support conclusions using reasoned arguments and evidence while the creative thinker must ask questions to extend their thinking. It would appear that the award of a good grade will no longer be indicative of a student working well and the lecturer recognizing this, but that student and lecturer need reminding of what underpins good teaching and learning. Given the current skills-based nature of teacher training curricula, littered as they are with competencies rather than challenging learning, perhaps this is not altogether surprising.

The major issue, though, is the moulding of behaviour and outlook that students will necessarily have to undergo in order to meet the demands of these outcomes. The overall aim is highly instrumental and designed to inculcate a value system in young people who are plainly not ready to receive it at such an early stage in their lives, when they have insufficient experience or knowledge of the world to make such judgements about the good or moral life. On the one hand, students will learn the injunctions of valuing diversity, learning emotional literacy and how vulnerable they are. They will 'recognize that others have different beliefs and attitudes', that they must 'consider the influence of circumstances, beliefs and feelings on decisions and events', that they will 'evaluate their strengths and limitations' and that they must 'discuss areas of concern'. Having learned to value others' beliefs which nevertheless, they might find faintly ridiculous, got in touch with their emotions and doubts and realized that reaching for the stars is to be ridiculed, they will then be in a position to 'act as an advocate for views and beliefs that may differ from their own'. The merging of the worlds of therapeutic counselling and education becomes quite seamless. Once the values are in place, a further string of outcomes will determine behaviour. Students will 'play a full part in the life of their college or wider community'; 'take responsibility showing confidence in themselves'; 'adapt behaviour to suit different roles'; and 'identify improvements that would benefit others'. While any or all of these statements might make sense at times in certain situations in the workplace they are, by and large, entirely contrived, artificial and meaningless in the classroom and within the context of learning. It would appear that the days of the independent teenager, striving to assert him- or herself and, incidentally, making plenty of mistakes along the way, are numbered. Behaviour and emotions will be codified, regimented, measured, monitored and recorded on a daily basis. Within this regimented world of FE, what are we to understand by 'anticipating, taking and managing risks'? College classrooms are not, after all, renowned as risky places to be. Perhaps this is a reference to catching the right bus to college or asking the wrong question in an attempt to extend their thinking? In this fragile, brave, new world, any and every action or word takes on the appearance of risk.

The real irony, the perverse consequence of this skills agenda, is that the last thing developed is a skilled, competent, confident workforce-in-waiting. With every single element of a student's basic functioning subject to an assessment decision, real life is suspended. Far from encouraging independence, this remorseless assessment of attitude and behaviour creates a new dependency. Anyone unfortunate enough to be rigorously forced through this process will become an ideal candidate for the world of lifelong learning. The inhabitants of this world, having been exhorted to accept and understand everyone else's values, opinions and beliefs will know no certainties or moral absolutes, and lose all sight of direction and purpose. The only respite will be a further round of behaviour modification, courtesy of the skills agenda. The aggressive, thriving, dynamic workforce is simply a pipedream. The workers of the future will be forever looking over their shoulders asking someone else whether or not they have got it right and whether another box can be ticked.

The perverse consequences of professionalization

The idea of being a 'professional' FE lecturer no longer seems strange. In the days of the old 'tech' it did. Then a lecturer was just an expert or specialist with knowledge and skills. The idea of being a 'professional' lecturer was not really discussed and the earliest textbooks, such as L.B Curzon's (1976) *Teaching in Further Education* did not discuss the subject, it is also omitted in the latest edition. Later textbooks continued to devote little space to the topic except in the discussion of 'professional' or managerial and administrative tasks, lecturers had to undertake (Reece and Walker 1992) or in terms of 'professional development' (Huddlestone and Unwin 1997). Occasionally there is a short philosophical discussion of what 'professionalism' means (Armitage *et al.* 2007) but little else. Recent textbooks show a change, typically in response to the introduction of Key area H of the then Further Education National Training Organisation (FENTO) standards 'Meeting Professional Requirements', with the sub-headings 'Work within a professional value base' and 'Conform to agreed codes of professional practice', which has led to more sociological discussions around 'values' and social policy within the framework FENTO set out to which compliance was required (Fawbert 2003: 314–35).

This change accelerated between 2004 and 2007 when the Teacher Training Agency (TTA), and its reincarnation as the broader and more opaque Training and Development Agency (TDA) for schools, began a discussion of a 'new' professionalism in education that involved setting generic standards for the wider school workforce. Standards were being set for everyone and it was only to be expected that FE would follow after the attention it had been given in 2005/6 through a series of reports (Tomlinson, Foster and Leitch), and a White Paper, but more significantly after the damning OfSTED survey inspection of ITT in FE, which declared that: 'The current system of FE teacher training does not provide a satisfactory foundation for professional development for FE teachers at the start of their careers' (OfSTED 2003: 2) and the almost immediate response by the DfES. The latter pointed out the 'common elements between teacher education in schools and in the learning and skills sector (DfES 2003e: 13).

Arguably, this was an extension of previous trends in training for compulsory schooling, but it is sudden and accelerated in FE. What took over a decade to achieve in teacher education is being imposed in two to three years in FE. This 'new' professionalism has one major perverse consequence. It undermines professionalism. Whether slowly as in compulsory education, or quickly, as in FE, if the government is telling you that you must be professional in certain ways, this undermines professionalism. Being 'professional' is not about doing what the government or its regulatory quangos say. Professionalism is necessarily autonomous and is based on personal knowledge and skills alone. Once a list of criteria are introduced the autonomy is lost, students increasingly get the 'service' or treatment the government wish them to have and professionalism is lost. As FE is playing 'catch up' and highlighting influential ideas taken from compulsory education's 'new professionalism' it may make explicit the undermining of professionalism that is masked in the compulsory sector. We argue that a professional has knowledge and skills. A professional's 'morals' are his or her own business. They are subject to moral criticism but not to professional control. There is a philosophical issue here, namely, 'Can a good lecturer be a bad person?' The answer was once obviously 'Yes', but now it is not so clear. When the answer was, 'Yes', the ethical values a lecturer had as a lecturer were values such as honesty, consistency, avoidance of contradiction, respect for evidence and truthfulness. All of these are what we might call 'epistemological' values. These are the values that are necessary if we are concerned with knowledge and truth, and if we wish to pass on to students not only knowledge and skills, but a respect for what constitutes knowledge. These are the values peculiar to teaching; other values, however noble, are irrelevant to the profession. In FECs too, 'mission statements' or 'professional' codes will incorporate all sorts of external and irrelevant values.

The answer is not so clear now because we are told that, among other things, a professional is someone who cares about the environment. Whatever people's views are about the environment it seems to us an irrelevant matter in deciding whether a lecturer is professional to look at whether or not they recycle their wine bottles or fly to their holiday destination with a guilty conscience. However, in the IFL discussion of its green and professional code, such a response gets short shrift and 'knowledge' does not get a look in (IfL 2006a, b).

The IfL provides a good example on its website of what we might reflect on as the characteristics of good professional ethics in *Towards a Code of Ethics* (IfL 2006c). Based on the assumption that we live in a rapidly changing world where there is no fixed body of knowledge, no body of facts to impart we have to recognize a unique 'level of uncertainty' in which 'learning to learn' is the most important thing for students. All this is familiar hype of the sort that management gurus come out with but it does away with, among other things, two thousand years of scientific knowledge. Yet lecturers are said to be able to accept this and still have some sort of expertise based on our acquired understanding. What 'understanding' could lecturers have that isn't based on a body of knowledge? Once we abandon knowledge what sort of professionals would we be? The essential 'ethics' they take from a discussion of Mike Bottery's early work on professionalism, gives it away:

Underpinning their professional practice, will be five essential ethics:

1 **An ethic of truth disclosure:** which must override personal advantage
2 **An ethic of subjectivity:** for each individual must recognize the limits of his or her perceptions, the individuality of his or her values
3 **An ethic of reflective integrity:** as each professional recognizes the limits of personal perception, of the need to incorporate many understandings of a situation
4 **An ethic of humility:** as each professional recognizes that such subjectivity means that personal fallibility is not a failing but a condition of being human
5 **An ethic of humanistic education:** of the duty of the professional to help the student help themselves.

(IfL 2006c)

Apart from the first, rather banal, point which implies that we might lie rather than tell the truth, all these are thinly disguised attacks on objective knowledge. The second 'ethic' implies that all knowledge is subjective. The third asserts a variant of relativist thinking, positing a post-modern plurality of equally valid viewpoints. The fourth suggests we celebrate the fallibility of our knowledge, and the last merely recognizes that, as we can't assert anything, we must put the student in the driving seat. Whatever the intentions, these are ethics for the know-nothing lecturer. If all knowledge is changing, subjective and fallible the students really will need more and more support and help because they really are learning on their own. These 'ethics' presents a dispiriting and isolating idea of further education dressed up as something humanistic. It also takes away all of the authority and autonomy of the lecturer and therefore anything that could be called professionalism.

A crisis of professional identity

Once this popular but nonsensical track of abandoning knowledge has been adopted, another perverse consequence results: the concern with the professional 'identities' of lecturers (Avis *et al.* 2002; Gleeson *et al.* 2004). The same is true of teacher education where the formation of professional identities has become a major research topic and teachers' identities are often unstable, occasional, fragmented and uncertain (Day *et al.* 2006). Despite the growth in literature the situation is easily explicable without drifting into post-modern celebrations of lecturers' multiple identities. Once you abandon knowledge there can be no professionalism. No wonder there is a crisis.

The neglect of professionalism and its academic study in FE has staved off the slide into the post-modern morass. It will not last. At the moment there is only a certain amount of schizophrenia. The IfL, for example, has been promoting a 'dual model of professionalism' which it hopes will place the sector in 'the vanguard of professional development'.

A key feature of the Institute's model for professional development is the recognition that teachers in the post-compulsory sector have clearly defined dual professional identities, based on subject specialism and teaching/supporting learning. The model encourages teachers to value both aspects of their professionalism and to draw on various feedback conduits to improve their practice through CPD (IfL 2006d: 3).

Although the professionalization of the sector is accelerated, the simple assertion of a dual role does not create a dual role. The introduction of the professional ethics that lies behind the teaching and supporting of learning is used to undermine professionalism based on subject specialism. Something else is going on and to understand it necessitates an understanding of the politics behind the drive for contemporary professionalism.

The politics of professionalism

In a speech to the Social Market Foundation in 2001, Estelle Morris, then Secretary of State for Education and Skills, defined the contemporary problem of professionalism from the viewpoint of New Labour:

> Gone are the days when doctors and teachers could say, with a straight face, 'trust me, I'm a professional'. So we need to be clear about what does constitute professionalism for the modern world. And what will provide the basis for a fruitful and new era of trust between Government and the teaching profession. This is an arena ripe for debate and we welcome views from all round the education system and from others, including parents and business people.
>
> (Morris 2001: 19)

Morris makes the process of the political construction of a crisis of professional identity explicit in this quotation from the aptly entitled *Professionalism and Trust*. First, there is the scathing rejection of the teacher as an autonomous expert. Second, there is an abstract semantic search for the meaning of trust – something that must follow once the autonomy that is the essence of trust has been rejected. Finally, we get an elevation of 'others' to the role of experts in a search for meaning. Out of such a process can only come confusion and a loss of meaning, but one thing Morris is

categorical about is what is not on in the development of this new professionalism:

> It is important to trust our professionals to get on with the job.
> That does not mean leaving professionals to go their own way,
> without scrutiny – we will always need the constant focus on
> effective teaching and learning, and the accountability measures
> described above. But what it does mean is that we shall
> increasingly want to see professionals at the core, to join us in
> shaping the patterns for the schools of the future.
>
> (Morris 2001: 26)

This is not an open approach to debate about professionalism but an
expression of an anxious authoritarianism.

Why raise the issue of creating a 'modern' professionalism at all when
you have no confidence in professionals? The obvious reason is New
Labour's simple desire to get people on side but on their terms. In Anthony
Seldon's monumental *The Blair Effect*, he concludes that 'The Net Blair
Effect' is a matter of style. New Labour has 'become more national and
classless and less of a sectional and class-based party, and it reached out as
never before to embrace the establishment, including the City, business, the
professions, the media and the Church of England, and even independent
schools' (Seldon 2001: 594). Trying to get professionals on side is one of the
major motivations behind New Labour policy and the growth of 'managers'
in colleges and the expansion of the quangocracy that governs FE is an
expression of the success of New Labour in getting professionals on side.

Although the growth of a new professional class has happened, it is far
from clear what it is that keeps the new professionals on side when their
professionalism is yet to be defined and is subject to constant change. Alan
Smithers has tried to understand the constant shifts in New Labour's
educational thinking. New Labour, he suggests: 'desperately wanted to be
seen to be doing good things' to the extent that 'Everyday without a new
education headline was regarded as a day wasted . . .' And he asks:

> What are we to make of all this activity? Has the Blair government
> really had 'a big picture', with the many initiatives necessitated by
> numerous faults in the system? Or has it tended to dissipate its
> political capital by failing to focus sufficiently on the main issues,
> rushing off in all directions?
>
> (Smithers 2001: 425)

Smithers inclines to the second suggestion and blames the private
educated 'ideas-people' that surround Blair as being responsible for a

situation in which 'Idea after idea seems to have come tumbling out, often encapsulated in a catchy two- or three-word phrase, without a full appreciation of the education system's capacity to absorb them or their relevance to ordinary pupils' (2001: 425). Smithers' response is the same as many others, for example, Hodgson and Spours in their study of New Labour's education policy argue that 'New Labour does not appear to know what kind of direction it wants the education and training system to follow' (1999: 145).

A cynical view might be that any policy will be tried if it looks like reaching an audience that might support the government and even vote for it. But all these responses simply miss what is emerging from policy churn.

Professionalism's 'Three Ways'

The best way of understanding what is developing out of the policy churn is to look at it through the politics of the 'third way' and to ask the simple question, 'If this is the period of "third way" politics, what were the "second" and "first" ways?' (For a fuller discussion, see Blair 1998; Giddens 1998a; Hayes and Hudson 2002; Armitage *et al.* 2007).

The 'first way', as a historical period, ran from the time of post-war reconstruction until the middle of the 1970s. Throughout this time we find an idea of professionalism that was based on a lecturer's or teacher's independence and autonomy in all areas of their work, based on their (subject) knowledge. Their teaching methodology, their relation to students and their judgements, as far as assessment and examination were concerned, were all their responsibility. It is important to understand that the consensus about professional autonomy was an accidental feature of a historical period. It was not worked out from an epistemological or philosophical position. This explains in part why those thinkers we associate with this period – perhaps Paul Hirst and his defence of a liberal education founded on the 'forms of knowledge' is the exemplar of this – have moved with the times and changed or abandoned their views. What made this period unique was the post-war boom, touched on already in our discussion of skills, which allowed the expansion of education and the luxury of Socratic and disinterested inquiry for a short period even if it never amounted to a 'golden age' (Hayes 2002).

The post-war economic boom was over by 1972 and was marked by the various oil crises and the rise in unemployment. The key date for FE is 18 October 1976 when Callaghan's Ruskin College speech launched his 'great debate' about education that culminated in giving business a greater say in what went on in education and put an end to consensus. In a sense the 1980s and the 'second way' of Thatcherism began then. The Thatcherite 'second way' set out to destroy what she called 'socialism', that is, trade unions and the communities of the period of welfare consensus. However, Thatcherism left nothing in their place, only the illusory 'market mechanisms' imposed on all public sector institutions, including colleges. The legacy of the 'second way' is a morass of managerialist and bureaucratic practices.

And so to the 'third way', in which no return to the welfare consensus seems possible, and the market mechanisms are equally unacceptable. Often represented as a positive period in which creativity can be unleashed and we can experiment with new ideas, the reality is the opposite. The new freedom is not a happy thing but leads to uncertainty and constant change. We have already seen how the new epistemology and ethics of FE professionalism is based on 'uncertainty' as a 'positive' value.

Policy-making becomes arbitrary because policies are not aimed at any stable or traditional communities. They cannot be because, after the destructive period of the 'second way', traditional communities no longer exist. In these circumstances what characterizes the third way is the artificiality and *fragility* of all policies and practices.

This political climate of the 'third way' is fundamentally about the uncertainties of a political elite anxious about ordinary people. Lacking traditional organizations that represent, and also discipline people, the political elite can only, in an entirely spontaneous way, encourage low horizons and low expectations. To gain reassurance for themselves about their role they promote ideas and policies of self-limitation and self-regulation.

Towards a therapeutic professionalism

Estelle Morris, in the discussion referred to earlier, expresses the politics of the third way very clearly (Morris 2001). She seeks a sort of trust and yet scathingly rejects the first way approach of giving people the autonomy that could make them truly professional. But neither can she leave the development of a new form of professionalism to the market. Fearful of both autonomy and the market she wants to regulate what teachers do, which merely illustrates the fragility of the whole New Labour project. They want to trust professionals and people in general, but only to work with the government and the quangocracy. The problem is, however, that they just don't know what they want. 'Big' ideas come and go. The uncertainty and constant change that are a consequence of this, in turn exacerbate this deep-seated lack of trust in people. For, even if some people such as FE managers and lecturers come on board, the ways in which they do so are arbitrary and the consequences, as we have seen, are perverse.

However, the solution for government and the quangocracy is slowly emerging. We describe this solution as the inculcation of a therapeutic approach to FE. However, the consequences of this for students and lecturers are worse than being subject to the vacillations of the 'third way'.

Towards the therapeutic college

The basis of this new professionalism, that is gaining ground in FE, is neither conservative nor radical and transformative. Rather, it has at its core a largely therapeutic ethos.

We are moving towards the creation of what we call the 'therapeutic college' that will close the gap between the 'therapeutic school' (Nolan 1998) and what one of us has labelled the 'therapeutic university' (Hayes 2002, 2003; Hayes and Wynyard 2002a, b). The therapeutic ethos has developed late in FE because of its neglect by government and the strong links the sector traditionally had with the world of work. This economic nexus gave it some distance from more developed trends in schools. That distance will always be there, however, as we stated at the outset, the tendency is for the therapeutic initiatives to dominate the cultural climate of FE.

In the areas of management, skills and professionalism management, the issues we have addressed may not seem to lead to a conclusion that the trajectory of the perverse consequences is therapeutic. This is because the therapeutic culture arises spontaneously in the vacuum produced by constant, almost meaningless change. Out of the policy churn comes not a post-modern celebration of churning, but therapeutic methods of coping or enabling us to cope.

In the area of management the authoritarian is giving was to the caring, although the process is slow. Management-speak is not just from business but from the therapy couch. Terms like 'inclusion', 'empowerment' (or 'empowering'), 'communicating', 'sharing', 'facilitating', 'ownership', 'responsive', 'listening', 'respect', 'valuing', 'open', 'safe', 'secure' and 'non-confrontational' are broadly 'therapeutic' terms used by college managers. Added to the list are the 'playful' away-days and staff development activities, such as the training they provide on 'coping' with various issues from 'stress' and 'bullying' to 'working with others'. Even management consultations about issues, such as the constant restructuring that goes on in FE, are designed as therapeutic opportunities for staff to air their views. And when you leave, you can have a 'therapeutic' exit interview to clear the air about any issues.

Skill craziness has also taken a therapeutic turn. This is made easier because the definition of a 'skill' is so flexible that it now covers almost anything. Even critical thinking is considered a 'skill'. Yet out of this semantic vacuum has come a new focus for skills training on what are sometimes called 'soft', 'aesthetic' or 'emotional' skills. When this is not about superficial matters, such as the etiquette that modern work requires, it can take the explicit form of developing emotional intelligence (EI) or merely of emphasizing the importance of feelings. A case could be made against the previous argument about the perverse consequences of skill craziness being that the new skills agenda takes us away from real workplace skills, this case being that these emotional skills are exactly what are needed in today's employment market. The employment market in the UK is largely in the service sector where 'inter-personal' skills typified by the ever-smiling –'Have a nice day!' – customer-oriented approach is important. Although there is some truth in this, the perverse consequence is deeply damaging to young people. Behind the superficial smiles and talk, the general emphasis on the emotional constantly diminishes young people by getting them simply more involved in exploring their feelings than their minds. The shift from concern with the intelligence quotient (IQ) to a concern with the emotional quotient (EQ) is not just another development or a sudden awareness of the need to balance aspects of the whole personality, but an abandonment of a concern with what makes people essentially human: their rationality. Beneath this fashionable concern with emotions is really an old fashioned attitude towards most young people in FE. This being that they are not up to education, 'not academic' is how it is usually put, and they need help with their emotional inner lives. Just consider the growth in counselling and support services in any FE college if there is any residual doubt about this.

It is through teacher training that the 'therapeutic college' is being constructed. Once only eccentric teacher trainers had a flirtation with the 'hug your students' psychology of Carl Rogers, and now, without ever mentioning his work, therapy is everywhere. Circle time, facilitation, sharing, confessional reflective logs form the basis of training and the result is passed on in every class in every college. However behavioural the 'standards' that frame the teacher training programmes, their delivery is often humanistic. This paradox is discussed in Chapters 2 and 8 of this book.

The charge, 'It's not teaching, it's therapy', may be said to be premature but the general tendency is towards the therapeutic college. Even if the therapeutic college was extremely well-funded it should be opposed. If we see nothing better for students than increasing the therapeutic treatment they need, then we are giving up on any future for them or for anything like further *education*. We believe that what is coming out of the policy churn is precisely this diminished sense of the potential of young people. Keeping them on the therapy couch will keep them happy and docile. They won't hurt others or themselves. No wonder 'happiness' is the new science that is already invading the school curriculum (Goodchild 2006; Layard 2006).

The plurality of perverse consequences

In trying to improve college management with a meaningless market-oriented approach, the government bureaucratizes college life and shifts resources and effort away from effective delivery of education and training. When policy-makers seek to improve skills they adopt a negative perspective and look at what they see as the deficiencies of young people. The shift is from a focus on skills to a focus on personality, on character development. In trying to professionalize lecturers they make them subject to external standards or a schizophrenic dualism that undermines professionalism.

The politics of the third way is the politics of perverse consequences. In its most general form it expresses a shift from 'knowledge' to 'process' that is expressed in all areas of education. The replacement of coming to know and understand by 'learning' is one expression of this and has the consequence that we now focus on learning to learn, and knowing becomes an ever more distant possibility.

We have argued that what has spontaneously arisen from this is a broadly therapeutic approach to FE. If you replace knowledge by a focus on the learner, their character and the learning process, and the only thing you can offer is a therapeutic environment, then the ultimate perverse consequence is that FE should become 'learner-led'. This was one of the themes of the Foster Report and has been taken up by the DfES, the QIA, OfSTED and, most importantly, by the NUS in its 'Loud and Clear' campaign of 2006 to develop the student voice in FE (NUS 2006).

The student voice in a wave of school student strikes and demonstrations against YOP/YTS 'slave labour' schemes in 1985 (Taaffe 1995) stood firmly against state action. Now the situation is entirely different and NUS radicalism – in this area – is reduced to making demands on college principals and managements that it be given the voice that the policy papers and government ministers want. The NUS has backing from the state and the quangocracy to take a leading role in further (and higher) education. Their criticisms are merely of the patchy take up of what the quangocracy wants. The NUS and the state want the student voice to be heard at all levels. Who but a few reactionary and autocratic principals, managers and lecturers could deny students their say? If you're having therapy, you need to have your 'voice' heard.

Conclusion

In January 2007 it was announced by Alan Johnston, Secretary of State for Education and Skills, that plans would be brought forward to raise the school leaving age to 18 by 2013. Many people supported this move as being a step forward in the education of young people. However, the majority, some 75 per cent of young people, stay on anyway. Forcing all to stay at school would only be as a step forward if they were offered a good liberal education or proper training. The churn and change in qualifications, and the switch to 'personalized learning' rather than the teaching of subjects, means that more and more introspective and therapeutic courses will be offered to keep those forced to stay at school happy. Absurd as it may seem, specialist diplomas in the 'new science of happiness' may not be far away.

One consequence of raising the school leaving age, may be policy changes that will see all 14–19 education effectively back in the school system with adult skills training being done by businesses and private providers. Who knows? An immediate and damaging loss to FE would be the distinctly voluntary nature of the education and training on offer. Students previously chose to go to FE colleges and this contributed to the 'adult' atmosphere that so many people valued. We, and many of the contributors to this book, would take the raising of the school leaving age to be a further sign that the government and the quangocracy see young people as little children. Just by keeping them 'at school' the government are ensuring what can be called the infantilization of young adults. We would rather they were all allowed to grow up. Freely choosing an FE course, or not to be at school, is part of that growth.

Chronology of Change in FE

1974   The MSC is established after much lobbying by the TUC. The MSC is the original further education quango. It was subsequently replaced by the FEFC (1993) and then the LSC (2001).

1979   *A Basis for Choice* published by the FEU, which looks at what is needed to prepare young people for work, such as their 'core skills', and starts the shift from imparting 'knowledge' to developing character.

1985   School student strikes against 'slave labour' schemes.

1993   Incorporation of FE colleges on 1st April. Formation of the FEFC.

cont.

1993	The *Charter for Further Education* published by the DfE. All colleges are required to produce their own versions.
1994	TTA is established with a remit that almost entirely excludes further education.
1998	*The Learning Age – A Renaissance for a New Britain*. This green paper sets the tone for the next decade with its first statement, 'Learning is the key to prosperity'.
2003	OfSTED's Survey of Initial Teacher Education finds it does not provide a 'satisfactory foundation for professional development'.
2005/6	The regulatory professional quangos (the 'quangocracy') are reformed and begin to have powerful influence – LLUK (FENTO), QIA (LSDA) and in particular the IfL that from September 2007 will oversee entry to FE teaching and monitor CPD.
2006	Learner voice. The NUS FE 'loud and clear' campaign for a 'learner-led' FE is the focus of its activity. ESSA is launched, and OfSTED decides to give more emphasis to the pupil voice. The new buzz concept 'personalized learning' is increasingly about learner voice (see the Futurelab handbook by Rudd *et al.* 2006)
2007	Plans are put forward by the DfES to raise the school leaving age to 18 in 2013. The last time it was raised was in 1972 when the leaving age became 16.

Key readings

This introductory list of key readings goes beyond those cited in the text in order to encourage some independent thinking. A good web-based resource for those interested in adult education, youth transitions and philosophy of adult education is the *Encyclopaedia of Informal Education*. This developing resource can be found on the Infed website run by Mark K. Smith and colleagues since 1995: http://www.infed.org/encyclopaedia.htm

Standard Works

Armitage, A., Bryant, R., Dunnill, R., Hayes, D., Hudson, A., Kent, J., Lawes, S. and Renwick, M. (2007) *Teaching and Training in Post-Compulsory Education*, 3rd edn. Maidenhead: Open University Press. (Contains a full chronology of post-compulsory education with an essay on how to use it.) Lea, J., Hayes, D., Armitage, A., Lomas, L. and Markless, S. (2003) *Working in Post-Compulsory Education*. Maidenhead: Open University Press. (A companion volume that offers lively essays from widely differing viewpoints with a linking commentary.)

There is an overview of other books and textbooks in Chapter 8 of this book.

Critical perspectives

For new and experimental ideas the work of think tanks provides interesting material.

The work of DEMOS is a good starting point as they have a strong influence on policy-making. Most of their publications are downloadable at no cost: http://www.demos.co.uk/

There are also two best-selling books that provide contrasting ideas about the direction of education. They are not specifically about FE, but are a stimulating read from the 'left' and 'right' of educational thought.

Bentley, T. (1998) *Learning Beyond the Classroom: Education for a Changing World*. London/New York: Routledge/Demos.
Phillips, M. (1996) *All Must Have Prizes*. London: Little, Brown and Company.

Historical comparisons

It is always useful to look at books published by earlier generations to get an indication of how different educational thinking was. The Oxfam shop is a useful resource! Readers might like to compare books, such as the two below, with contemporary publications:
Benn, C. and Fairley, J. (eds) (1986) *Challenging the MSC on Jobs, Education and Training*. London: Pluto Press. (A mock red stamp on the cover of this book reads ENQUIRY INTO A NATIONAL DISASTER.)
Finn, D. (1987) *Training Without Jobs: New Deals and Broken Promises*. London: MacMillan.

Movers and shakers

Getting to know the key players and what they are thinking and writing is essential. A useful start is with the *TES*'s 'Guide to Who's Who in FE', available at: www.tes.co.uk/fefocus/who's_who_in_fe/

Increasingly influential is the voice of the student and there are useful resources on the NUS websites, including a guide to FE jargon. Since Ellie Russell was Vice-President (FE) in 2005 there is an officer's 'blog,' available at: http://www.officeronline.co.uk/fe/

Of particular interest will be updates of the 'learners voice' campaign document:
NUS (2006) *Loud and Clear: Developing the Student Voice in FE Colleges.* Available at: http://resource.nusonline.co.uk/media/resource/loudandclear guide%20UPDATE2.pdf

A general introduction to 'learner voice' and the relevant research is given in: Rudd, T., Colligan, F. and Naik, R. (2006) *Learner Voice: A Handbook from Futurelab.* Available at: www.futurelab.org.uk/research/handbooks/04_01.htm

1 A beginner's guide to lecturing
Joanna Williams

This chapter explores the role of the lecturer in post-compulsory education through a focus upon working in a further education (FE) college and some of the ways in which this differs from teaching in a school. Work in either sector can offer practitioners a unique set of challenges: from managing unruly 13-year-olds to retaining adult learners; and helping a youngster with special educational needs to preparing a lecture for undergraduates. However, at times, it may appear as if the two sectors are merging closer together; 14–16-year-olds may now receive part of their compulsory education in a college, whereas vocational courses, previously associated with the post-compulsory sector, are now being taught in schools. This chapter will consider the original, quite distinctive, purpose of FE colleges. Through investigating why historical differences existed between schools and colleges, we can begin to understand some of the variations between the pay, conditions and expectations of teachers and lecturers that continue today. We can also reflect upon the gains and losses to staff, students and institutions of increased convergence. Current debates about the roles of lecturers will be considered, examining the extent to which we consider ourselves to be vocational trainers, academic instructors, pastoral counsellors or 'social includers'. Although statements in policy documents are far from clear or consistent, it will be argued that one ideological tendency is, through policies encouraging social inclusion in FE and safety in schools, to put safe participation at the heart of FE. This tendency is one that infantilizes both the FE lecturer and the FE student.

Cinderella sector or middle child?

Further Education, especially in its part-time forms, seemed to be the permanent Cinderella of educational provision for the 16–19-year-olds

(Brooks 1991: 147)

> *It's not a Cinderella but a middle child with huge potential that*
> *everyone has overlooked and it does itself no favours by moaning*
> (Sir Andrew Foster, quoted in Kingston, 2005b)

For years the Cinderella sector, most recently the moaning middle child, what the FE sector lacks in glamour it compensates for in breadth of purpose. Described by Kennedy as 'everything that does not happen in schools or universities' (1997: 1), the remit of FE is truly enormous: colleges may offer a range of undergraduate courses or even opportunities to study at post-graduate level while, along the corridor, classes are taking place in pre-entry level literacy and numeracy, as well as vocational training in alternative therapies or catering. According to the government, the objectives of FE are to bring about 'the dual and inextricably linked foundations of social justice and economic success' (DfES 2002b: 2). Looking at the history of this happy heterogeneity of striving for social justice and economic success, reveals a different and more depressing reality.

Guide to key events

Traditionally, the major difference between schools and FE colleges has been the relationship between the institution and the world of work: whereas colleges had close links to industry, and training skilled workers, schools were more removed, prioritizing the essentially academic skills. FE has its roots in the technical colleges of the twentieth century and, going back even further, in the Mechanics' Institutes of the nineteenth century. Mechanics' Institutes would have provided informal opportunities for youngsters with minimal schooling to learn new skills as and when deemed necessary by their employers.

The Technical Instruction Act of 1889, permitted local authorities to provide technical schools which would enable youngsters to pursue training for specific skilled professions away from the workplace. Elementary schools at this time served quite a different purpose, concentrating teaching upon 'the three Rs' – reading, (w)riting and (a)rithmetic – but this was no longer considered sufficient for a workforce expected to keep pace with rapid technological advances. Schools were expected to provide children with a basic level of general education in contrast to the more specialized training available in the technical schools. One eye was upon Britain's competitors and new forms of employment required a literate and numerate nation. Education was also expected to provide a civilizing influence upon the working class who needed to be educated into the mores of the elite. Schools often served a highly moralistic purpose and unashamedly promoted the values of church, empire, obedience and respect.

The distinction between general education provided by elementary schools and the skills training provided by technical schools persisted: the assumption was that technical schools offered students an entirely different educational experience. One basis for this distinction was that from 1870 onwards education, at least for the very youngest, was considered compulsory, whereas attendance at a technical school would be voluntary. Successive laws gradually increased the school leaving age, until the Butler Act of 1944 saw technical schools incorporated into compulsory education as part of the tripartite system of secondary, technical and grammar school education. Technical colleges catered for students past the age of compulsory schooling, and were praised in the Crowther Report of 1959 for providing a fresh start for those 'incurably tired of school'.

The eventual raising of the school leaving age to 16 in 1972 saw the constituency for FE colleges defined increasingly by 16–19-year-olds, although as unemployment increased by the end of the decade many adults also attended FE colleges. FE colleges were seen as providing a more adult environment than schools: students called lecturers by their first names, had access to a range of social facilities including smoking rooms, and mixed with other people of a similar age. More importantly, post-compulsory education was based on choice – not only were young adults choosing to attend courses, but the range of curriculum options provided exciting opportunities vastly different to those available at school. The 'adult environment' was further reinforced by the fact that many vocational courses were 'day release' with students spending three or four days a week in the workplace and only a day or two at college. Close formal and informal links between individuals in the various industrial sectors and the colleges meant that pay would be cut for non-attendance or poor performance at college.

FE colleges also met the demand among adults to study academic subjects either at a higher level or because they missed out at school. The tradition for academic studies departments within FE colleges emerged from the evening institutes of the 1920s and was consolidated with the 1973 Russell Report, which allowed for the expansion of non-vocational academic education. The academic year 1975/6 saw numbers of adults participating in locally available general education courses reach a peak (Stock 1996: 10). Adult education classes responded to a need from adults for self-expression, cultivation of personal interests and self-improvement. An informal team of educators were there to meet this demand for education. Many had their roots in the ethics of the Workers' Educational Association, founded to provide higher education for the working classes, and were enthusiastic about the transformative potential of education as well as promoting their own subject specialisms.

Today's reality

At first glance, today's FE colleges may not appear to be so far removed from the technical colleges of a generation ago. The emphasis on skills training appears reassuringly familiar. But scratch beneath the surface and what we have today is something quite different: an entirely new vocationalism. As responsibility for training workers has shifted from employers to the education system, the informal apprenticeships, day-release programmes and local specialist provision has been replaced by a highly formalized, regulated and inspected range of qualifications. From the launch of NVQs in 1986, and even more so with the launch of GNVQs in 1992, there has been a shift to providing vocational training based almost entirely in the classroom. Assessment, based on the ticking of boxes against skills and broken down into simple elements described as 'competencies', provided the certificates much in demand by job hunters who were now required to prove their attainment formally. More classroom time spent gathering and recording evidence of competencies met, meant less time for hands-on practical work.

Key policy initiatives, such as Dearing's *Review of Qualifications for 16–19-Year-Olds* (1996), attempted to establish parity of esteem between vocational and academic courses, creating a system of equivalent points for students using vocational routes to apply for further study at college or university. This increased the attraction for some schools to use GNVQs at first within their sixth forms and increasingly now at Key Stage 4. This has been encouraged since 2002 when the DfES proposed radical reforms to the national curriculum in which only a handful of core subjects (English, maths, science, ICT and, interestingly, citizenship) would continue to be compulsory, thus freeing up more time for vocational options.

Indeed, school sixth forms have provided FE colleges with a major source of competition for 16–19-year-old students, a trend enhanced by the introduction of teaching GNVQs in schools. As the numbers of students remaining in education after the school leaving age has increased, so too have the numbers staying at school to study: from 20 per cent of the age cohort in 1987 to 38 per cent in 2000 (Wolf 2002: 78). In 2005, of the 76.5 per cent of the youngsters in full-time education, only 29.3 per cent were attending FE colleges, with the remainder divided between schools or specialist sixth form colleges (DfES 2002c). Sixth forms are clearly no longer the preserve of a few elite grammar schools. Many comprehensive schools now offer discrete provision for 16–19-year-olds, thus retaining many of their pupils at school. These students are then lost from the pool from which the FE colleges would have traditionally recruited and there is a drift from FE. However, some teachers question the benefits of school sixth forms. They can often involve recruiting students onto courses with very low numbers; for example, just four students opted for AS English literature at a recently established sixth form at a school in Kent; or, alternatively, popular vocational courses are offered in schools that do not have teachers with sufficient industrial experience.

From 2002, the Increased Flexibility for 14–16-year-olds Programme (IFP) was introduced by the Department for Education and Skills (DfES) to provide vocational learning opportunities at Key Stage 4 for those young people who would benefit most, (Golden *et al.* 2005). The number of 14–16-year-olds in colleges is predicted to rise to 200,000 by 2007 (Unison 2004). Colleges have been encouraged to take on 14-year-olds deemed at risk of exclusion from mainstream education. At some institutions, such as Lewisham College in London, this has worked successfully. However, many lecturers raise concerns that FE institutions are being used to 'dump' children whose poor behaviour or ability makes them unsuited to school. This impacts upon more mature students, who do not always appreciate sharing their space with school children, and on lecturers who are often pushed into the role of disciplinarian.

A massive expansion of all 16–19-year-olds staying on in some form of educational institution took place from the late 1980s onwards, connected to the dramatic rise in youth unemployment at this time. The Dearing Reports of 1993 and 1994 begin to talk of a curriculum for 14–19-year-olds, 'based on the assumption that they would remain in education beyond the age of sixteen' (Barber 1996: 204). The notion of a continuous curriculum calls into question the voluntary nature of 16–19-year-olds' presence in FE. With few other realistic options available to them, the recently introduced educational maintenance allowance – offering up to £30 a week in assistance towards books, equipment and travel for young people staying on after 16 – and an education system that is entirely geared towards retaining students for as long as possible, few 16-year-olds have consciously decided that, as adults, FE is the right thing for them. The reality is that most students experience FE as being a direct continuation of school. This has no doubt been compounded in recent years by the numbers of 14–16-year-olds in FE colleges. Students lacking motivation or incentive to study beyond receiving the EMA payment may demonstrate a lack of discipline or commitment towards their programme of study. Much time of Certificate in Education (Cert.Ed.) courses is now taken up considering problems concerned with classroom management and dealing with behaviour problems.

As the EMA policy demonstrates, targeting young people aged 16–18 is a key priority as the government seeks to tackle the problem of youngsters not in education, employment or training (NEET). From September 2005, the Learning and Skills Council had to fund colleges to meet the needs of 16–18-year-olds first. The logic of this approach is that the more successful schemes, such as EMA, are IN attracting school-leavers, the fewer adult places there are that can be funded. Adults up to the age of 21 can study for a level 2 qualification for free; those hoping to study either as a leisure activity or for a higher (level 3) qualification will no longer receive subsidies. The thinking behind these funding cuts was made clear by the DfES in *21st Century Skills*, which argued that, 'we must target funding on those areas where skill needs are greatest' (DfES 2003a: 24) and goes on to warn that, 'The state cannot pay for everything' (DfES 2003a: 27). The reality of this funding policy, designed to push through the government's political goals of social inclusion and widening participation is that adult education, and especially the provision of leisure courses, may become increasingly rare. In an attempt to redress this problem, from 2007, adults up to the age of 21 will be able to study at level 2 for free and adults up to 25 will be able to study at level 3 for free, with subsidies available for older adults.

Many involved in FE are using the government's policy of promoting inclusive learning to challenge these funding changes. The National Institute of Adult Continuing Education (NIACE) argues,

> The future of adult education is important because the range and volume of opportunities that are supported, however modestly, from the public purse says something about the sort of society to which we aspire as well as to the sort of economy upon which it will be built.
>
> (NIACE policy briefing, 22 June 2005: 2)

The arguments for the 'sort of society' and 'sort of economy' NIACE want to see are an echo of the government's demand that FE be based upon 'the dual and inextricably linked foundations of social justice and economic success' (DfES 2002b: 2). In a similar vein, John Brennan, Chief Executive of the Association of Colleges (AoC) argues, 'The role of colleges is to meet the needs of their communities' (quoted in Hook 2005). His point is that FE cannot become successfully inclusive if it only serves what is in fact a small section of the local population. The government's manipulation of funding arrangements have met with a seemingly radical demand by some groups of lecturers to engage with socially excluded groups, and to push FE into meeting the political objective of inclusivity. They have had a considerable degree of success: college managers in particular have taken on board the widening participation agenda. However, the latest policies, even more specifically targeted at government priorities, are causing differences to emerge.

Lecturing or teaching? What really goes on inside classrooms?

The days of students expecting to turn up to a class and listen to a lecturer, who is an authority in the field share their subject knowledge are long gone. Today, the assumption of OfSTED and ALI inspectors is that students should be actively engaged in their learning and that this can only be demonstrated through seeing students involved in a myriad of group work activities; in preparing PowerPoint presentations or in differentiated, learning style-appropriate, individual learning projects. Students on PCET courses are taught that the lecturer is now the 'manager of the learning environment' and the co-ordinator of activities rather than the source of knowledge. In an attempt to become student-centred, lecturers are encouraged to follow the advice of contemporary practitioners, such as Geoff Petty, who propose 'silent teaching' and that lecturers should be encouraged to take a back seat in the classroom where students essentially teach themselves. However, concepts of lecturer professionalism are based upon subject knowledge and to deny we have such knowledge is both dishonest and a disservice to the students we teach. Many students, especially mature students, will assume the lecturer will be there to impart knowledge and despite the emphasis upon differentiated activities, there is still considerable scope for more didactic forms of pedagogy.

The shift away from lecturing to managing the learning environment came about, in part, as a result of the Tomlinson Report's proposals for a 'best match' between the needs of the learner and the teaching strategies employed, which has been codified in the principle of individualized learning (FEFC 1996). Until the mid-70s there had been little or no general provision for people with learning difficulties and/or disabilities within FE, with the exception of that offered in a few specialist and even fewer innovative colleges, and the expectation was that students would be both able-bodied and have reached a minimum educational standard. The Warnock Report of 1978, *Special Educational Needs,* recommended the creation of at least one special unit in a college in each region (DES 1978). Prior to 1980, the assumption in both schools and colleges was that any provision made for learners with disabilities would be quite distinct both in terms of the curriculum offered ('dressmaking for the handicapped' or 'crafts for the blind') and the physical location of the provision – this was the era of the special school. From the 1980s onwards there emerged a growing trend to question the separateness of special education. However, it wasn't until the 1992 Further and Higher Education Act that any major shift in the nature of special needs provision took place. The act called upon colleges to 'secure sufficient and adequate facilities' and 'have regard for the needs of persons with learning difficulties and disabilities. These moves were criticized for categorizing students in relation to their social position within a continuum of resource-dictated need. Today, all students are expected to have an individual education plan (IEP) or an individual learning plan (ILP). IEPs were initially developed for use with students with severe learning disabilities as a result of the 1981 Education Act. The theory was that learning could be demonstrated in a behaviouristic fashion and that the desired behaviour could be achieved by reducing the learning process down into even smaller behaviouristic steps. Since the Tomlinson Report, the use of IEPs with all students in PCET has become routine; the OfSTED *Common Inspection Framework for Inspecting Post-16 Education and Training* (2001) assesses how well teachers and trainers, with learners, 'develop individual learning plans, informed by initial assessment, that are reviewed and updated regularly' (2001: 8).

The development of individualized learning necessitated distinctive developments in pedagogy, drawing colleges closer in line with a model more akin to school teaching than andragogy. It is expected, more often from internal quality assurance departments than from OfSTED inspectors, that lessons will start with a clear statement of 'learning outcomes' and that all students will achieve these outcomes by the end of the session. This means lessons can not be left to develop in an open-ended manner as a result of issues emerging but need to be predetermined to avoid digressions. Likewise, learning outcomes cannot be concerned with understanding as this is too ambiguous to be demonstrated at the close of the lesson. Instead outcomes need to be framed in such a way as to enable students to prove a competency gained during the course of the teaching period: naming, listing, reciting, giving an example or showing. The emphasis upon predetermining the course of the lesson goes against the principles of andragogy, the discipline which studies the process of adult education and involves taking account of factors, such as the self-directed, experience-based, self-motivating nature of adult learning. In short, it looks at the process of creating independent learners. Instead of this, students are dependent upon the teacher who takes ultimate responsibility for ensuring learning takes place. Such responsibility often includes an emphasis upon differentiation; meeting the needs of students with a range of learning techniques appropriate to individual projects and small group activities rather than to whole class teaching; and portfolio building to demonstrate the learning outcomes stated in the IEP.

Alongside increasing awareness of the rights of disabled students, there developed an increased sensitivity to the needs of other students considered to be from 'disadvantaged groups'. Campaigners shifted their attention from a concern solely with youngsters with learning difficulties and/or disabilities to incorporate other marginalized groups excluded from educational services. Particular attention became focused upon the educational needs of students from ethnic minorities, female students and working class students. To give just one example from this period, it was in 1984 that the Women into Science and Engineering (WISE) project was founded to encourage girls and women into these subjects.

In Britain, in 1994, the Labour Party commissioned *Report of the Commission on Social Justice* alerted policy-makers to the issue of 'increasing alienation and disaffection among many people' (Commission on Social Justice 1994a: 82). The main concern of the report is with the 'equal worth of all citizens, their equal right to be able to meet their basic needs, the need to spread opportunities and life chances as widely as possible' (1994a: 1). These ideas were not translated into policy objectives until the election of the Labour government. In 1996, the Tomlinson Report's prime concern, as we have seen, was with students with learning difficulties and/or disabilities, but since then, ever broader definitions of special educational needs have been taken on board by institutions, encompassing obstacles to inclusion, such as poverty, race, gender, religion and disability. Government policy is therefore seen as politically radical, concerned with bringing about social justice, and is taken up enthusiastically by many of those within the post-compulsory sector.

Since coming to power in 1997, tackling social exclusion has been a stated policy focus for the New Labour government and much emphasis upon promoting an inclusive society has been placed upon education in general and FE in particular. The post-compulsory sector has been quick to take on board this political goal because it coincides with the ostensibly educational objective of inclusion. Inclusive pedagogy places an emphasis upon connecting individuals into the wider school community alongside a focus upon the feelings and self-esteem of students. A clear set of inclusive values begins to emerge; the national curriculum (DfEE 1999b) redefined the role of the teacher:

> Teachers create effective learning environments in which . . . stereotypical views are challenged and pupils learn to appreciate and view positively differences in others, whether arising from race, gender, ability or disability . . . all forms of bullying and harassment, including racial harassment are challenged.
>
> (DfEE 1999b: 20)

and the Further Education National Training Organization (FENTO) also stressed these more inclusive values in relation to developing better practice for teachers in FE:

> All learners should have access to appropriate educational opportunities regardless of ethnic origin, gender, age, sexual orientation, or

degree of learning difficulty and/or disability. Consequently, the values of entitlement, equality and inclusiveness are of fundamental importance to teachers and teaching teams.

(FENTO 2000, in Wallace 2002: 47)

Both organizations are making clear quite similar values, which focus on equal opportunities, tolerance and a celebration of what is now seen as 'diversity'. Many in PCET welcomed this focus on values, which is seen as in some way returning FE to its radical traditions through the politicization of work with marginalized learners. However, in the past, working with marginalized learners would have been either for a particular purpose: enabling individuals to gain employment opportunities, to compensate for earlier missed opportunities or to achieve intellectual enlightenment; or, to promote a particular set of values dear to the heart of that lecturer: feminism, anti-racism or socialism, for example. This is to misunderstand the new emphasis on learner participation in FE.

Participation and the new FE professional

Today, working with excluded groups is viewed as important for no other purpose than ensuring their participation. This new approach grows out of early work on widening access to non-participating groups. A good example is the Kennedy Report, in which participation in education and training is considered to be, by its nature, an inclusive act: 'the very process involves interaction between people; it is the means by which the values and wisdom of society are shared and transmitted across the generations' (Kennedy 1997: 6). Through education, the time of participants is accounted for; they have structure in their lives, routines and informal points of contact with the state. The act of participation, in and of itself, is further considered important in raising the self-esteem of students; even international bodies, such as the OECD (1997), claim: 'For those who have successful experience of education, continuing learning is an enriching experience, which increases their sense of control over their lives and society' (Field 2000: 102). The Kennedy Report likewise maintains that 'simply by engaging in the learning process [students'] self-worth and capabilities are improved' (Kennedy 1997: 7). Although the Tomlinson Report's concern was with providing students with the skills they need in order for them to 'contribute both to the economy and the community' (FEFC 1996: 7), there is little discussion within his report, which is entitled '*Inclusive Learning*', about the content of the curriculum or the skills students should be expected to acquire. The content of the curriculum is secondary to the act of participation by the students.

Alongside this ideological shift away from education and training to a concern with inclusion and the process of participation itself, was a parallel development with the professional approach of FE lecturers. In 1992, incorporation legislation was passed under the Further and Higher Education Act that saw FE colleges being taken out of local education authority control and being pushed into competing independently in a 'free market'. The effect of incorporation upon those working in colleges was considerable. Lecturers were made to sign new contracts which they saw as significantly worse than their previous 'Silver Book' conditions of service. The new contracts stated that teaching was only one aspect of the lecturer's role; this made the way clear for extra responsibilities relating to recruitment, retention, pastoral work, needs assessment and working with support and administrative staff, which would all be necessary parts of the inclusive learning agenda. Alongside new contracts came new forms of accountability, annual performance management appraisals, performance-related pay and a newly vigorous external inspection process under the control of the Further Education Funding Council (FEFC). It was from this point that the gulf between staff pay and course funding in the school and post-compulsory sector became significant – a situation that still exists today. There is a lesson here for the compulsory sector of education.

From 2000, all tutors and lecturers working within PCET were expected to have, or be working towards, a professional teaching qualification. Although it was initially welcomed for its potential in enhancing perceived professionalism, the mandatory qualification continued to be based on the prevalent instrumentalist and mechanical demonstration of specific competencies. It remains within the NVQ and GNVQ model of learning. Later, and in response to criticism, the demonstration of competencies was replaced by the requirement to meet 'standards' laid down by FENTO/LLUK. The difference is only in name. Indeed, such standards were used to judge the performance of all lecturers, not just those seeking qualification. The introduction of such general standards seriously undermined the professionalism of college lecturers. Whereas previously, professionalism was based upon the academic subject knowledge of the tutor or the technical accomplishment of high-level skills in a trade, now these achievements were judged as secondary to the mastery of the broad statements of what FENTO and now Lifelong Learning UK (LLUK) set out as professional standards. At one stage in the period, after FENTO developed into LLUK, there were over 200 that had to be met. However, it is what these standards will focus upon in terms of general professional requirements that is the issue. To understand the trajectory here, we need to look at what is happening in compulsory schooling.

In the school sector, the era of *Every Child Matters* (ECM) and the subsequent Children Act 2004, completed a process which redefined professionalism to place child protection concerns as secondary to specific subject knowledge. The Children Act covers young people up to the age of 18 or beyond if they were classed as 'looked after' (in care) on their 16th birthday or if they have a learning difficulty. With this remit, the vast majority of tutors in PCET will be directly affected by the demands of the legislation to work alongside external agencies in reporting any concerns and placing the social, emotional and economic welfare of students central to their teaching. Their teaching will come to be dominated by the five outcomes, ensuring that young people are healthy, safe, enjoying and achieving, making a positive contribution and achieving economic well-being. Organizations, such as NIACE, already see the post-compulsory sector as playing a further role in relation to the ECM agenda. They argue in their response to the green paper that ECM is a holistic approach to fulfilling potential. It builds on adult and family learning that 'improving the confidence and abilities of adults/parents will have a lasting impact on children – and on their educational success in particular' (NIACE 2003). This fundamentally alters the role of the FE lecturer – not only is building confidence, seen as a crucial objective, but this is to be done not with an eye to the students in the classroom but to future generations outside the direct personal contact of the lecturer.

Conclusions

Convergence is rapidly taking place between the once quite distinct school and FE sectors. This coming together occurs in a number of ways. Perhaps most obviously, there are no longer the distinct separations into constituent age groups. Likewise, the choice of subjects and vocational options available to those remaining at school or entering a college may be roughly similar. However, these changes can be seen as relatively superficial in comparison to the more fundamental areas of convergence. The teaching styles of those working in a school and a college are no longer dissimilar. A pedagogic model that only a generation or so ago was associated not just with schools but with primary schools in particular, individual and small group project work, an emphasis upon activity and 'busyness', learning through 'discovery', to say nothing of 'circle time', is now the accepted and expected norm within FE. This should cause concern for anyone serious about providing quality education for young adults in either sector. Linked to this infantilization of pedagogy is a fundamental shift in the purpose of both the FE lecturer and school teacher – both are now expected to play a broader political role and tackling problems of social exclusion. As workers in both sectors seek to promote inclusive values and place child protection strategies to the fore, the passing on of knowledge and skills becomes relegated. An irony with sectoral convergence is that the government uses FE to promote social inclusion through exploiting its veneer of adulthood and the radical sense of purpose associated with the sector. The more convergence takes place the more difficult it will become to sustain this image. Convergence is doing neither sector any favours as education, specifically the acquisition of subject knowledge, loses out in both school teaching and college lecturing.

Chronology of key policy initiatives

March 1996   Dearing's *Review of Qualifications* for 16–19-year-olds. Dearing notably commented upon the 'long tail of under-achievement', arguing that the education system had let down a significant proportion of youngsters who were not suited for academic qualifications; which included both students with learning difficulties and/or disabilities as well as students from disadvantaged backgrounds. One remedy Dearing put forward to tackle this under-achievement was promoting the idea of 'parity of esteem' between vocational and academic courses: GNVQs would now have an equivalence with GCSE's and A Levels, allowing GNVQs to be used as a route into higher education.

June 1996   Tomlinson's *Inclusive Learning*, Report of the Learning Difficulties and/or Disabilities Committee. Tomlinson investigated the provision available for students with learning difficulties and/or disabilities after leaving compulsory schooling. He moved away from a 'medical model' of viewing special educational need as a defect within the individual to a socially constructed model of disability which placed the defect with the institution. The role of lecturers, he argued, was to find the 'best match' between the needs of the learners and the provision on offer, which was to be considered 'best practice' for *all* learners and resulted in a trend towards individualized learning programmes.

June 1997   Kennedy's *Learning Works: Widening Participation in Further Education*. Kennedy explored ways in which the constituencies recruited into FE could be

cont.

---

increased through colleges reaching out to those in disadvantaged groups. She makes the connection between qualifications and employment, arguing the disadvantaged risk exclusion from the workplace because they lack skills. An FE sector geared towards training disadvantaged young people for employability could help to bring about both economic prosperity and social cohesion.

September 1999   *Learning to Succeed: A new framework for post-16 learning.* This White Paper enshrines many of Tomlinson's 1996 proposals stating that, 'Everyone should have access to education, training and skills opportunities – systems should be equitable and inclusive'.

September 2000   Introduction of *Curriculum 2000.* Formal implementation of Dearing's 1996 proposals, including the introduction of key skills as a compulsory component of all courses; records of achievement for all students; standardization of entry and foundation level courses; and the broadening of the academic route through dividing A levels into AS and A2 qualifications.

November 2002   *Success for All.* Outlines the reform strategy of the Learning and Skills Council, which aims to bring the FE sector into the mainstream of the education system and use FE to ensure that 14–19-year-old learners have 'greater choice and higher standards'. It also argues that lifelong learning should be 'enshrined' into people's daily lives and the culture of the country.

January 2003   *14–19 Opportunity and Excellence.* Proposes the creation of a more coherent 14–19 phase with greater flexibility and choice and an increase in vocational learning to tackle the number of learners leaving full-time education at 16 and create a parity of esteem between academic and vocational education.

July 2003   *21st Century Skills: Releasing Our Potential.* Sets out a 'skills strategy', which emphasizes the importance for individuals, the employers and the nation of a more highly skilled population, and outlines ways in which this can be achieved.   *cont.*

September 2003	*Every Child Matters*. In response to the Victoria Climbie inquiry, the ECM report forms the basis of the Children Act 2004, which enshrines in law child protection concerns as being central to the teacher's role.
October 2004	Tomlinson *14–19 Reform: Report of the Working Party*. Proposed abolishing GCSEs and A levels in favour of a diploma as part of a continuous curriculum for 14–19-year-olds. Diplomas would cover both vocational and academic disciplines, combining them wherever appropriate.
November 2004	Children Act. The general impact of the Children Act is to focus everyone's work on the ECM outcomes and to improve the children's well-being in five areas: (1) physical and mental health and emotional well-being; (2) protection from harm and neglect; (3) education, training and recreation; (4) the contribution made by them to society; and (5) social and economic well-being.
February 2005	*14–19 Education and Skills*. A White Paper in response to the Tomlinson Report of 2004. Aims to ensure that every young person masters functional English and maths before they leave full-time education, that vocational options are improved, that academic qualifications offer a suitable 'stretch' to motivate disengaged learners.
November 2005	Foster Review – *Review of the Future Role of FE Colleges*. Foster argues the need for a clearly recognized and shared core purpose among FE colleges that focuses on the needs of both learners and business. He makes clear the purpose of post-compulsory education as being directly linked to the needs of the economy. But he adds

> The need for an outstanding FE college network is not just about national prosperity. It is also about how far countless individuals in this country value themselves, enjoy being who they are and have fulfilling and enjoyable lives. The appalling figures for the number of people who lack basic literacy and numeracy skills suggest great reservoirs of
>
> *cont.*

> disappointment and poor self-esteem. And it will
> surprise no one that many of those in that
> predicament come from the most disadvantaged
> parts of the community.
>
> (2005: 9)

Key readings

Armitage, A., Bryant, R., Dunnill, R., Hayes, D., Hudson,k A., Kent, J.,
   Lawes, S. and Renwick, M. (2007) *Teaching and Training in Post-
   Compulsory Education*, (3rd edn). Maidenhead: Open University Press.
Brine, J. (1999) Economic growth, social exclusion and the European
   discourse of equality: pathologizing the unemployed, *Research Papers in
   Education*, 14(1): 93–105.
Field, J. (2000) *Lifelong Learning and the New Educational Order*. Stoke-on-
   Trent: Trentham Books.
Furedi, F. (2004b) *Where Have All the Intellectuals Gone? Confronting 21st
   Century Philistinism*. London: Continuum.
Hyland, T. and Merrill, B. (2003) *The Changing Face of Further Education:
   Lifelong Learning, Inclusion and Community Values in Further Education*.
   London: RoutledgeFalmer.
Levitas, R. (1998) *The Inclusive Society? Social Exclusion and New Labour*.
   Basingstoke: Macmillan.
Raggatt, P., Edwards, R. and Small, N. (eds) (1996) *The Learning Society:
   Challenges and Trends*. London: Routledge.

2 The McDonaldization of further education
Jon Bryan and Dennis Hayes

McDonald's has been described as the 'hate brand' of all time. If you want to denigrate something, it's easy to prefix it with 'Mc' and people get the idea. To take a popular example, a 'McJob' would be a low status, low paid job with little prospect for career progression of the sort McDonald's employees are supposed to have. McDonald's have tried from time to time to use copyright law to control the label 'McJob', but it has entered into common usage. The 'Mc' prefix is unstoppable and there are references to everything from speed dating as 'McDating', to western political systems as 'McDemocracy', to voters as 'McCitizens', to employment as 'McWork', to doctors as 'McDoctors', to the university as 'McUniversity', to newspapers as 'McPapers', items of news as 'news McNuggets', and to the process of globalization as creating 'McWorld'. These appellations are often vague but there are serious treatments of the McDonaldization of the church, of sexual relations, of the family, the Internet, the university and most state institutions, including the police, the courts, and even prisons. It seems that there is nothing that isn't, or isn't said to be, McDonaldized.

Another way of looking at this is to say that 'McDonaldization' is so widely used that it has lost any specific meaning. The term is mostly used in a negative manner, as shorthand for cheap, processed, easy, convenient, unhealthy and mass-produced. If this was all there was there would be no point in writing about the McDonaldization of FE and merely adding it to the demoralization of the 'Cinderella sector'. There are lessons to be learned from examining the applicability of the concept and whether or not lecturers need to resist the creation of McColleges.

McDonaldization as a 'McDonaldized' concept

The term 'McDonaldization' was coined by the American sociologist George Ritzer in 1983. He has been described as the living embodiment of a concept that, like McDonald's restaurants, goes from strength to strength.

This is not because of a universal distaste for McDonald's but because the term 'nicely points to the exemplary role of one of the most successful contemporary practitioners of Weberian Rationalization' (Kumar 1995: 189). It has been argued that, although it's *neat*, the power of Ritzer's conceptualization is in its simplification (McDonaldization) of Weber's idea of *rationalization* (Alfino *et al.* 1998: xvii–xxvi; Hayes and Wynyard 2002a: 1–9). Ritzer's explanation is certainly formulaic, and relies on four fundamental features: efficiency, calculability, predictability, and control.

Applying them to the area of McWork, a McJob will be efficient because it will involve simple routine repetitive tasks that involve no creativity or judgement so that more can be produced. It will be calculable in terms of time spent on each task. It will be predictable as every item to be produced will be the same size and shape. There will be control of every action and everything said. The result is dehumanizing. In the end the employee is potentially or actually replaced by a machine.

The McLecturer teaches routine repetitive sessions – to say gives 'lectures' would be an archaism. These sessions are repeated year after year and across each year. The handouts and notes help the students get through. The teaching is formulaic, objectives are stated, the teaching is delivered and student learning is assessed. All session are alike. Not only the hours taught, but the timing within each session is structured. The content of all sessions is predictable and stated in the learning objectives of the course/programme handbook. The teaching is controlled explicitly by management and peer observation as well as external inspection, and implicitly through teacher training, appraisal and staff development.

A McManager's job consists of simple administrative tasks, such as keeping student and examination records, and drawing up schedules and timetables. Their role is to ensure that the system of getting students through to the successful completion of their awards is smooth. This usually involves completing proforma documents, often online. The work is calculable as it must meet fixed annual deadlines. It is predictable, as what must be done is set out by the LSC and OfSTED. It is controlled externally by OfSTED inspections. Internal controls are operated by various 'quality' monitoring departments.

McStudents demand that McLecturers efficiently spoon-feed easily digestible McNuggets of knowledge and skills, so they can fill their portfolios and get through their exams. They calculate the hours they need to attend and keep them to a minimum. They keep close account of the number of words they have to write and divide them by the topics they have to cover, 300 words on X, 300 words on Y. Their work is predictable, as what they have to do is clearly set out and there is no room for judgement before the 'pass' or 'fail' box is ticked on the mark sheet. They are controlled through 'learning agreements' and registers of attendance.

All this seems real enough. A mature sociology student once complained: 'I don't like these questions that make us work out what they mean. Your job is to tell us what to say so we can write it in the exam.' In one small bite, here is the essence of what we call McDonaldization or getting carried away with the McDonaldization game: what we'd call McThinking. Is it any wonder that plagiarism is on the increase, when it is getting through that matters rather than understanding?

The 'McDonaldization' of FE is not something that is always imposed on lecturers or on the sector. One lecturer we know who was entirely committed to a humanistic education philosophy was unable to cope with student demands for help. Her solution was to issue them with 'Tutorial Tokens' of 30 minutes in value to the sum of their tutorial entitlement. *Ad hoc* 'McDonaldization' of this sort is a creative response to the McMassification of FE. The question is how far has the process gone. Can we now talk of the 'McCollege'?

Towards McCollege?

A 'McCollege' would be an FE college run technically like a McDonald's restaurant.

Many of them already have that look, heavy on the foyer and the charming receptionist in the 'Reception' area. Would it be a bad thing if they were? From the time the McDonald brothers opened their first restaurant in Pasadena, California, in 1937 they were on to something. Ray Kroc who built the empire, from 1954, through franchises saw this. What did he see? Production lines with tasks broken down. All food portions the same, what employees did and said tightly controlled. The result is fast food served by smart, polite young people in neat uniforms.

You only have to contrast McDonald's with what went before: the traditional 'greasy spoon' restaurant in which the food was of uncertain quality, fatty and overcooked. The service was slow, often indifferent and the environment often dirty. Anyone who doubts this should read John Caputo's account of his first visit to Canterbury when there was no McDonald's there (Caputo 1998: 40–2). Eating in college canteens still is, to this day, often that sort of experience. Wouldn't they be better if franchised to McDonald's? It's the whole college curriculum rather than the canteen that matters and it's ironic that there is probably more progress in the of curriculum than the canteen.

That the head of Human Resources and Training at McDonald's was, for a time, a member of the Tomlinson Review of 14–19 qualifications is a clear recognition that McDonaldization may have something to offer. To establish over 31,000 restaurants worldwide since the entrepreneurial Ray

Kroc opened his first franchise in 1955, you have to be doing something right. It is important to say in the face of environmental criticism and anti-American feeling, that the modernizing process that McDonaldization represents is a good thing. From Pizza Hut to Starbucks and from the Body Shop to Waterstone's bookshops the process is the same, and most of us are, to quote McDonald's latest trade mark, 'lovin' it'.

FE is equally successful and efficient with some 4 million people, including 1.27 million adults improving basic skills and 1.5 million young people in learning and loving it: 120,000 14–16-year-olds now attend college for part of the week; 176,900 young people are on apprenticeship schemes; and 69.8 per cent of 19-year-olds now have a level 2 qualification. The outcomes are also much more predictable and calculable then they were a decade ago: 555,010 – or over half of all – vocational qualifications achieved are by trainees in FE. The national 'skills gap' has also declined from 22 to 16 per cent according to employers. Working in FE is now much more of a controlled experience with lecturers having to be qualified teachers. There are 246,000 employees working in FE, 132, 626 of them are teachers and it was predicted that by 2007 over 95 per cent of full time lecturers will be teacher qualified along with over 60 per cent of part-time lecturers. FE is also more cost-effective than school education, undercutting it by £400 per student or 13 per cent overall (LSC 2006, Staff Individualized Record (SIR) Data 2003/4, 2004/5). It's not all about quantitative success, there are qualitative achievements, such as a customer service ethos and a 'student-centred' curriculum orientation in every FEC.

It's exactly the efficient, calculable, predictable and controlled experience we value and find comforting. But is easy, comforting, safe and unchallenging all that we want from food? Perhaps we do want just this for much of the time. But is this ever what we want from a college? Isn't education, by its very nature, something that undermines the possibility of more than a veneer of McDonaldization? Don't we just have McDonald's style college foyers and endless statistics that are irrelevant to the real education and training that goes on? A case can be made that these educational aspects of FE contradict Ritzer's fundamental features of McDonaldization.

The inefficient college

In 1961 McDonald's opened a Hamburger University that awarded degrees in 'Hamburgerology'. It no longer exists in that form, but we could imagine what it was like. Superficially FECs today look McDonaldized. But do we recognize our colleges from this description we've adapted from Rizter's *The McDonaldization of Society?*

The modern [college] has, in various ways, become a highly irrational place. Many students and faculty members are put off by its factory-like atmosphere. They may feel like automatons processed by the bureaucracy and computers or feel like cattle run through a meat-processing plant. In other words, education in such settings can be a dehumanizing experience

(Ritzer [1993] 2000: 143)

This does not describe the reality of the 'learner-centred' FEC of the 21st century. FECs today, with some dismal exceptions, are friendly welcoming places with signs and people everywhere offering support and help. There are the endless 'learner' services, such as counselling, student support, and careers and guidance. It would be cynical and misleading to see this as the customer service aspect of McDonaldization. It is based on a genuine philosophy of support for young people and adults. Talk to any lecturer and they will defend FE for its ability to widen access to people who need a second chance, a different curriculum or special support. The commonest defence of FE is that it meets the needs of certain people, who are not academic, who have learning, behavioural or psychological difficulties, or who, because of their background, lack self-esteem. The popularity of 'social inclusion' arguments of this sort suggest that New Labour have provided a philosophy which most clearly expresses the new ideology of FE. Lecturers rarely celebrate the efficient way in which FE is said to be saving the economy, something which was always a managerial myth (Bryan 2004). This approach to defending the role of FE has a profound problem contained within it but it does seem to be something that cannot be argued on the basis of the 'McDonaldization' thesis.

Teaching FE students, if this characterization is right, cannot be done in ways that are 'efficient' in a business sense. They are always unpredictable.

The bureaucratization of FE

We have suggested that FECs go beyond McDonaldization and actually clog up a potentially efficient, calculable and predictable system by over-calculating: attempting to predict everything through absurd systems of complex 'risk management'. This process of 'bureaucratization' can be illustrated by what is now known as the problem of student 'retention'.

If we consider the monitoring of attendance of students in an FE college, this was once a task probably taken on solely by the subject lecturer, or perhaps the course tutor who oversaw the whole experience of the student. Colleges now have a variety of staff involved in the task of monitoring and improving the attendance of students. The system and type of staff involved will vary from college to college depending on the latest fashion, but what used to be a task performed by one is now performed by more. In some cases, one member of staff is responsible for phoning the student, another for writing to them with a letter or postcard, while the lecturer deals with the problem in the classroom.

In what is perhaps a strange twist, one of the purposes of rationalization is to make the job easier to do. In many FE colleges, what was once a simple task of chasing up poor attendance and dealing with it has been broken down into more tasks than were ever done in the first place and which are unnecessary. One FEC 'Teaching and Learning' director even suggested that staff make attendance or 'retention' an objective in every lesson. This is McDonaldization gone mad. It is what Ritzer called an 'irrational' outcome of the McDonaldization process.

Controlling the controllers

Those of us who have worked in an FEC for a number of years will not have failed to notice the aspect of McDonaldization, referred to earlier, as 'control'. New lecturers coming into the sector can sometimes see this as normal, but nonetheless, are often perplexed at the extent to which their activities are increasingly measured and monitored. Ritzer, speaking in Canterbury in 2001, commented on how much more control there is in British post-compulsory education compared with the situation in the United States.

Of course, control is often experienced to different degrees depending on the nature of the management and the institution that lecturers work in, but some of the following will be familiar with those who work in a College:

- weekly checks on attendances in classes;
- regular reports on the number of students leaving (retention);
- collecting 'achievement' data – either in year or following the publication of final exam results;
- observations of lessons – either by internal or external inspectors; and
- gathering data about student satisfaction.

In one of the worst cases, a vice principal monitored the time students left classes to ensure that they got their exact entitlement of time.

In some cases, the control which managers seek to exert over lecturers is too much and leads to disputes between the staff and the college. Where industrial action used to be almost solely around pay, hours of work and redundancies, increasingly there are disputes across the country over attempts by college managers to stamp their mark in the battle for control where the local University and College Union (UCU) branch view this as an attack on their members' professionalism.

But it is not the human clocking in and increasing data collection that are the major concern on this list. Much more worrying is the use of the 'softer' forms of control, such as teaching observation, which may appear supportive. Since 2000, for example, union branches that have declared disputes over how and when lesson observations should take place and the level of scrutiny of newly appointed teachers, led to a large number of teachers leaving the profession. Ask almost any union representative at an FEC if the pressure of lesson observations has led some lecturers to leave – you will almost always get an affirmative answer. This is because helping lecturers to be better teachers is no longer the aim of these interventions. It is merely a disciplinary visit with a checklist.

While 'control' is one of the aspects of McDonaldization, which is clearly evident in FE Colleges, this should not give us a sense of fatalism about the process. The very fact that the methods employed are so obvious makes them vulnerable. Part of their obviousness at the moment is that they are applying to the control of what happens in the classroom, the lecture theatre and the workshop. At the moment lecturers experience this as being a challenge to their professionalism and an unnecessary questioning of parts of their job which were often beyond questioning. Whether this will continue with the introduction of the new professionalism is questionable (see the Introduction by Hayes, Marshall and Turner in this book).

It seems that FE has necessary inefficiencies, bureaucratized management systems and intrusive control methods that are being resisted. Is this a basis for re-enchanting FE?

Resisting the McDonaldization of FE

There are three stages in Ritzer's thinking about McDonaldization (Hayes and Wynyard 2002b). In his earlier work, as illustrated by his characterization of the college as a meat-processing plant, he saw the process of McDonaldization as inevitable. It would eventually apply to all aspects of cultural and personal life as well as to industrial and commercial activity. He was frequently challenged on this and increasingly looked at ways of 'resisting McDonaldization'. In a second phase he thought that the absurdity and irrationality it produced would simply undermine McDonaldization. Clearly influenced by post-modernism, he thought that

McDonaldization would suffer from imperial over-stretch and collapse into multiple irrationalities. Both these approaches are mechanistic and in his more recent writings Ritzer has become more combative. He now seeks to re-enchant the McDonaldized cultural institutions, primarily by arguing that we should seek, consciously and actively, to reverse the four fundamental features of McDonaldization. Applied to McColleges this would mean that an argument should be put forward for a further education that was inefficient, incalculable, unpredictable and uncontrolled.

The accidental contradictions of the process of McDonaldization of FE we have identified, do not show that it is still enchanted or is easily re-enchanted. The learner-centric support for students, with its caring humanistic philosophy is merely the padding on the iron cage of rationality and in no way challenges the McDonaldization process. In fact it is complementary to it. However, we have claimed that it is not the superficial and insincere 'Have a nice day!' approach. What it is premised on is a real belief that the average student in FE, not just those with special needs, needs special help. There is behind this caring concern a therapeutic culture (Hayes 2003, 2004b, 2006e; Ecclestone *et al.* 2005b; Ecclestone and Hayes 2007). What this means for FE is that students are not offered courses in therapy, but therapeutic language and approaches dominate the curriculum and the thinking of managers, lecturers and the students themselves. Of course they may well be offered counselling and other therapeutic support. Even tutorials now concentrate more and more on the 'personal' than academic or work-related issues.

The language that we use – such as 'empowerment', 'enabling', 'sharing', 'open', 'non-judgemental', 'listening (to the learner's voice)', 'inclusive', 'safe learning experience' – is therapeutic. To this we can add the current obsession with student 'self-esteem' and 'emotional learning', forgetting how new and faddish these concerns are.

The way we teach often resembles activities from the therapy room rather than the traditional classroom. Whether we label it 'circle time' or not, teaching in FE increasingly reminds you of the nursery carpet more than the industrial workshop (see Chapter 8). If you are on a certificate in education course, see how much of the training you are going through uses therapeutic language and techniques. The presence of 'flip charts' and the playing of learning games are reliable clues that amateur group therapy is on offer.

The facts, numbers and outcomes that seem to characterize the McDonaldization of FE are complemented by the new therapeutic approach. The McDonaldization of FE is more of a reality because of its therapeutic aspect.

Therapy culture in FE is the antithesis of a humanistic culture. It may seem that it is a modern form of the old approach that was expressed as 'treating students as adults', but it treats them as essentially hopeless adults. When there was a wider, more robust, culture of autonomy and independence the approach was humanistic. Now, when students are seen as isolated and vulnerable it becomes therapeutic and damaging. It is damaging because it re-enforces the feeling that support is always necessary and so more and more 'therapeutic' courses, or courses delivered in therapeutic ways, are provided. This is mutually rewarding for lecturers, students and the FE sector. We are seeing the creation of a self-sustaining therapeutic economy in FE.

Fatalism, therapy and the future

Ritzerian fatalism is not our conclusion. Not in relation to the general McDonaldizing tendency in FE or its particular therapeutic form. The McDonaldizing process has lead to a stifling bureaucratization and the therapeutic approach has lead to a damaging culture of victimhood. Fortunately both have been and are being resisted. Unfortunately this is not a simple two-fold resistance and the forces resisting the McDonaldization and bureaucratization of FE often support the victim consciousness that gives rise to therapeutic forms of FE and those few, often academic, voices opposed to the therapeutic culture of FE have not made much headway in the FE sector. One reason why the suggestion that it is necessary to oppose therapeutic FE is resisted, is that the funding that may ameliorate conditions of working and the bureaucratization of the system is often allocated in support of therapeutic initiatives.

Lecturers, managers, support staff and their professional associations have an interest in promoting therapeutic FE. Opposition to this, and any sustained defence of education and training, may come as a wake-up call from outside the sector. To understand why this is the case requires a short survey of resistance to McDonaldization and its historically narrow focus on the creation of 'McJobs'.

Guarding the Ark of the Covenant: the 'silver book'

Guides and textbooks for teachers in FE are written as if its development has been a long line of uncontroversial and uncontested events. For example, the incorporation of FE colleges on 1 April 1993, which removed them from local education authority (LEA) control is often mentioned as something that was merely a change rather than a fundamental shift towards a market mentality in which FEC principals saw themselves as running businesses rather than as being academic leaders. Even a balanced account of the 'radical change and development' that has affected FE 'more than any other sphere of educational provision', never mentions a strike or a protest (Hyland and Merrill 2003: 4). Resistance in the form of campaigns, protests and strikes is hidden from popular FE history.

Like any successfully McDonaldized sector, what was there before McDonaldization was, at best, variable in quality. FE suffered from neglect by LEAs who showed an almost total inability to develop it. For many staff, employers and students, incorporation was not an unwelcome development and there were many myths about the positive developments it would bring (Hayes 1993). But, as a perceptive leader in the *Times Educational Supplement* (*TES*) declared on 26 March, just a week before vesting day, it was lecturers who would 'pay the price' for change. Over the next seven years 22,000 full time lecturers left FE as a result of that change and the imposition of new contracts and the disparity in their pay compared with that of teachers.

This 'change' was consciously resisted and the 1990s were marked both by confrontation and strikes, but also by something that no one predicted, widespread mismanagement and corruption.

The National Association of Teachers in Further and Higher Education (NATFHE) was initially optimistic about the possibility of 'partnership' rather than conflict. The newly formed Colleges' Employers' Forum (CEF) led by its Chief Executive , Roger Ward, proved not only determined to turn lecturers into McWorkers, but to be so enthusiastic about the new corporate freedom from local authority control that they threw themselves into entrepreneurial activities. Management-speak was universally adopted and subsidiary companies were often set up to offer various forms of training.

Six years of disputes over pay and the imposition of new contracts began even before incorporation, although many colleges were slow to abandon traditional educational practices and preferred to work by agreement. The main issue was the ending of the first ever national agreement on salaries and conditions of service that had been in place since February 1975. It was known as the 'silver book' after the silvery grey clip binder that contained the 94, A5 pages of detailed information covering all aspects of pay and conditions. The binder was a feature of every staffroom and management office in FE. Dust-covered copies may still be found.

The 'silver book' specified working hours and the new contracts simply increased these from 30 hours a week to a minimum of 37 and contact teaching from 20 to 26 hours a week; a fixed holiday period of 35 days, some to be taken at management's discretion; weekend and bank holiday working; abolition of 12 month redundancy notices, and clauses restricting freedom of expression and intellectual property rights.

NATFHE organized a series of strikes in the month before the new corporations came into being. Over 266 of the 392 colleges came out on strike in defence of the 'silver book' and nationally agreed conditions of service. It was clear that, in the spring of 1993, the colleges had not been McDonaldized and some 260 principals signed the NATFHE 'pledge' not to pre-empt national negotiations. This was a clear defeat for the newly formed CEF. Paul Mackney, who became general secretary of NATFHE in the aftermath of the 'silver book' campaign, reflecting on this period, said, 'If anyone doesn't believe unions can be effective, just look at this campaign.'

This narrowly focused campaign was relatively successful, and ironically unsuccessful. Not for the reasons some activists think, who try to keep the 'silver book' campaign alive today as if it were the Ark of the Covenant. An informal survey (we undertook for this chapter) indicated that there were one or two lecturers, now nearing retirement, in many colleges who remained on the old 'silver book' contracts and in some cases had not received pay rises for ten years. The personal tragedy of these individuals constantly reflects the reality that conditions have gradually worsened, often by agreement. What it detracts from is the abandonment of further *education* for new and purely economic aims for the sector.

The years of the locust: corruption and mismanagement

The message was clear that all was not well because of the degree of corruption and mismanagement that followed incorporations. College principals became 'chief executives' and the majority of college governors were now from business and knew nothing about education or training. The CEF was a keen advocate of a new approach to staffing, particularly the use of 'agency lecturers' through a single agency, the Education Lecturing Services (ELS). The Further Education Funding Council (FEFC) was responsible for both funding and inspection, which was a recipe for disaster. Unlike a truly McDonaldized sector this one was inefficient, not subject to any honest calculation, unpredictable and out of control. Here is just a summary of many of the newsworthy examples of what was going on in FE at a time which Mackney called the 'years of the locust':

Years of the locust

1994 Wilmorton College, Derby. Many allegations about a bullying management style, and dubious financial arrangements, brought about an official inquiry. Subsequently, there were senior management resignations.

1997 Stoke-on-Trent College. A long running series of scandals, at what was Britain's second largest college, led to a cash crisis of £8 million and the dismissal of the Principal who was said to be running a pub in Wales while on long-term sick leave.

1997 Gwent Tertiary College. This college in South Wales had a deficit of £7 million which led to a crisis that saw the Principal suspended. He then resigned.

1997 Doncaster College. The College sacked whistleblower and NATFHE Branch Secretary, John Giddins. The subsequent furore inspired Paul Foot to produce *Private Eye*'s column 'High Principals' (Bright 1999). An Employment Tribunal found Giddins to be unfairly dismissed.

1998 'Rogergate'. The Chief Executive of the CEF/AoC resigns after a tangle of claims about financial irregularities and his relationship with the ELS.

1998 Cricklade College. At one stage the police were investigating trading arrangements (Coughlan 1998). An inquiry into the running of the college by the FEFC found mismanagement and recommended better training and regular evaluation for college governors.

1998 Halton College. The Principal and Vice-Principal were suspended pending investigations into the college's finances.

1999 Bilston Community College. The college was forced to close after the worst inspection report in college history. The Principal resigned. Accumulated debts, due to heavy reliance on franchising and subsidiary companies, are said to be £10 million. Unravelling the finances of this crisis were estimated to cost £1 million (Slater 1999).

(*Sources*: UCU Archives; NATFHE 2004; Education Select Committee Reports 1997, 1998 www.parliament.uk/pa/cm/cmeduski.htm; Coughlan 1998; Midgley 1998; Bright 1999; Slater 1999; Beckett 2006).

This was just the most extreme aspect of introducing what Denham calls marketization 'as a context for crime' (2002). The result of the new conditions of service and widespread mismanagement and corruption was that demoralization became a feature of the FE sector, with the loss of 22,000 lecturers over these years. A survey in 1996 revealed that 35 per cent of lecturers were actually seeking to leave FE, 60 per cent were considering leaving and 80 per cent would seriously consider early retirement (Midgley 1998). Strange as it may seem, the corruption and mismanagement of the sector was as a result of the inability to do for FE what McDonald's had done for fast-food. At least McDonald's knew, and continue to know, what they were doing. FE managers then, and perhaps even now, couldn't run a McDonald's!

The second Great Training Robbery?

The 1990s was the decade that saw the highpoint of what we have called the 'Bilston College Fallacy'. The name refers to the works published by members of that college propounding the idea the FE can save the economy (Bryan 2004). The fallacy was a mixture of a social vision and what appears to be the lure of straightforward commercial profiteering. The vision was a simple and much welcomed one of freeing FECs to develop and meet local, regional and national needs. The subsequent mismanagement was possibly predictable but the scale of corruption wasn't.

It certainly wasn't predictable to New Labour. Individualizing responsibility for learning through customer choice was their equivalent to Tory marketization. The main vehicle for this was their flagship programme of providing over-18s with individual learning accounts (ILAs). Launched nationally in September 2000, they were quickly abandoned following police advice in November 2001. The scheme allowed individuals to claim £100–£200 towards the training of their choice, to which they contributed £25. By the time it was shut down there were 6000 complaints about the scheme, almost 300 providers were under investigation and 98 had been referred to the police. Of the 2.6 million accounts opened only 58 per cent were ever active. The government and tax payer lost over £100 million of which little was recovered. The sorry tale is told in a National Audit Office report which contains a useful chronology of events (NAO 2002: 39–41). Despite the obvious corruption there is still thought of the LSC reviving the scheme.

Lessons do not seem to be being learned by New Labour, and the idea of freeing colleges from LEA control to serve the needs of the economy has returned with more vigour than before. In 2006 the DfES's FE White Paper and the subsequent FE bill, put forward proposals to offer whole sections of the FE sector up for privitization. There may be, as there are for the health sector, no 'arbitrary limits' to private sector involvement in the FE. As we have said, we do not believe, on the basis of the evidence that private bodies, anymore than FE managers, can run the sector as well as McDonald's. Past experience also suggest that the locusts may be gathering for another feast.

A bit of relish on the FE burger

The problem that FE faces is not primarily about the need for regulation and restriction of private sector involvement. The NAO report makes good suggestions about this. The real problem is that FE has lost its way and doesn't know what it should be 'producing'. That is why management and private sector involvement won't work: they do not know what they are supposed to be doing. This explains the endless production of college 'mission statements'. The government does not know what to do with FE either, save to let it accredit work-based 'foundation degrees' (DfES 2006b) and to encourage more employer involvement (Leitch 2006). FE is at a turning point.

The campaign launched by the Women's Institute in 2006 to save adult education should remind us of what FE should be about – education, as well as skills. The WI reminds us that education is not just the relish on a 'skills burger' but should be a major part of FE. However, with no exceptions, the Women's Institute and other campaigners all defend FE, not as providing education but as something that helps develop skills, confidence, self-esteem and social inclusion. There is no defence of education for its own sake. Education is not a means to an end but an end in itself. If we can only defend FE by attaching it to the latest policy fad, then our defence will be weak and unconvincing when policy priorities shift. If the current directionless and chaotic state of FE is to end, it requires as a minimum that education is defended for its own sake. Otherwise fragmentation and privatization will happen, and we may see the end of FE as a distinct college-based form of community provision and its dissolution into the school and HE sectors, with work-based training run by businesses.

A Chronology of Resistance

1904   The Association of Teachers in Technical Institutions (ATTI) is formed on the 27 October at Birkbeck College.

1964   ATTI starts to look at 'protecting and promoting' members' interests rather than having purely educational objectives.

1975   First national contract secured in February 1975, after over a decade of campaigning. Known as the 'silver book', the press and employers often called it the 'Skivers' Charter'.

cont.

1976	NATFHE formed from the merger of ATTI with the Association of Teachers in Colleges and Department of Education (ATCDE) on 1 January.
1984	The Great Training Robbery begins as private agencies milk the cash cow of MSC money aimed at the new YTS initiative.
1993	Incorporation of FE Colleges. On the 1 April FECs left the control of local education authorities to become independent corporations. Throughout March lecturers in 266 of the 362 FECs came out on strike against proposals to implement local changes to the 'silver book'.
1994	New Contracts dispute continues. One hundred colleges strike over imposition of new contacts and the abandonment of the 'silver book'.
1994/99	The 'dash for cash' stories of corruption and mismanagement in the colleges become commonplace – Bilston Community College, Cricklade College, Derby College (Wilmorton), Halton College, Wirral College and many others are named.
1997	Paul Mackney, well-known for his exposure of corruption in colleges and on training schemes, is elected General Secretary of NATFHE.
1998	'Rogergate'. Roger Ward, Chief Executive of the Association of Colleges, the man once known as 'Mr FE UK plc', resigns after a 'tangle of claims' about his relationship with the employment agency ELS.
1999	On 1 March, NATFHE and the AoC sign a statement ending six years of dispute over pay. FE had lost over 20,000 full time lecturers since incorporation.
2000	All FE unions strike on 5 December to defend national conditions – the employers agreed to maintain them in 2001.
2001	FE lecturers came out on strike – 290 colleges were hit by strike action on 22 May as part of a claim for a £3000 'catch up' with teachers' pay.
2001	In December, after another 'dash for cash' caused losses of £100 million, the government's flagship individual learning accounts (ILAs) is abandoned. Only £1.5 million was recovered.

cont.

2002	In May 2002, 30,000 lecturers took part in a two-day strike, and on 5 December NATFHE and UNISON went on strike together for the first time over FE pay.
2003	'Fund the Future'. NATFHE's campaign to keep up the pressure to restore services included a further strike day on 4 February.
2006	University and College Union, formed on 1 June from the merger of the AUT and NATFHE, is the largest post-compulsory education union in the world.
2006	Campaign for adult education. Further cuts in the decimated adult education service are announced. The opposition to them is led by the Women's Institute and NIACE. Train to Gain (T2G) rolled out in September as a national project to fund adult training through the services of 50 regional 'Skills Brokers'.
2007	The new freedom for FE. The focus of the 2006 Education Bill is more privatization and partnership with business. Government control and oversight will be slimmed down and strategic; inspection by OfSTED will be 'light touch'. The '157 Group' of FE colleges held its launch event on 15 January. The 157 Group is named after paragraph 157 of the Foster Review that suggested that the principals from the largest and most successful colleges should have a bigger role in policy-making. The 157 Group had 22 members at the time of the launch. Trials of 'Learner Accounts' (LAs) began in September – a pale shadow of the failed New Labour flagship ILAs.
2008	The second Great Training Robbery? FECs have to bid for the majority of their funding for employment-related courses in open competition with private providers.

Key readings

Hayes, D. (2005) Diploma? Is that with fries? *TES FE Focus*, 2 September.

Hayes, D. and Wynyard, R. (2002a) Whimpering into that good night: resisting McUniversity, in G. Ritzer (ed.) *The McDonaldization Reader.* Thousand Oaks, CA: Pine Forge Press. 116–25.

Hayes, D. and Wynyard, R. (eds) (2002b) Introduction, *The McDonaldization of Higher Education.* Westport, CT: Bergin and Garvey, 1–18.

NATFHE (2004) *NATFHE 100 Years On.* London: NATFHE.

Ritzer, G. ([1993] 2000) *The McDonaldization of Society,* New Century edn. Thousand Oaks, CA: Pine Forge Press.

Ritzer, G. (ed.) (2002) *The McDonaldization Reader.* Thousand Oaks, A: Pine Forge Press.

Williams, S. (2004) Accounting for change in public sector industrial relations: the erosion of national bargaining in further education in England and Wales, *Industrial Relations Journal*, 35(3): 233–48. Available at: http://eprints.libr.port.ac.uk/archive/00000026/01/FEBARG4.pdf# search =%22Ward%20new%20CEF%20formed%20in%201992%22

3   What's motivating students?
Patrick Hayes

Retorts in answer to the lecturer's question, 'Why aren't you paying attention?' could well soon include, 'I'm only here for the free iPod', or 'Because I just need you to sign my Education Maintenance Allowance (EMA) form at the end of the week'. Someone unfamiliar with the post-16 sector may be forgiven for thinking that the issue of motivation among further education (FE) students pales in comparison to motivation for compulsory school courses that pupils have to attend. It's true that students have chosen to attend FE college courses. Through the introduction of various bribes to attend, however, reasons for attending are unlikely to be just an interest in the course. It is understandable that many in FE are starting to consider strategies to motivate students.

The issue of motivation is now covered in all the major introductions to lecturing in the post-compulsory sector. Popular as the topic 'motivation' is, however, it is probably better not to deal with the issue of student motivation at all. Why? Simply because once a lecturer begins to ask questions about students, such as 'Why are they here?' or 'What do they want out of the course?' their confidence levels go down. Worse still, as these questions are routinely posed to students, they will inevitably lose confidence in and respect for their teacher. What students want is for lecturers to have the confidence to explain clearly to them what they are going to be doing in the course and the reasons why and then, through the successful delivery of the course to prove to them that the reasons given were sound.

Confidence in the value of the course and the importance of the knowledge and skills transmitted within it will more than likely prevent any major motivational issue from arising. Unfortunately, however, motivational strategies are all the rage at the moment. The irony is that the teaching of motivational strategies on training programmes is more likely to undermine confidence than build it.

This chapter gives an outline of the various tactics and strategies used to motivate students and will suggest that there are good grounds to be wary of adopting them. Through this process of criticism an alternative approach to 'motivating' students will be suggested.

Everyone seems to agree that students being 'motivated' towards learning is a good thing. What there is less agreement on is what this actually means. This is clear from the analysis of people talking about motivation throughout this chapter. However, before we go on to look at ways of motivating students, it's important to consider two things: first, what motivation actually is and, second, what is unique about motivation in FE?

What is motivation?

One of the most familiar definitions of motivation, as it relates to FE, is that of Curzon: 'a person's aroused desire for participation in a learning process' (Curzon [1976]: 195). When we are discussing how to motivate students, then, we are discussing how this desire to participate in a learning process can be aroused. What is now becoming commonplace, however, is, instead of trying to arouse the desire of the student to participate in the learning process, the very learning process itself becomes altered in order to arouse desire. Motivation in the classroom becomes prioritized over the very learning process that students, we assume, are there in the first place to participate in.

Motivation is typically divided into two categories (Armitage *et al.* 2007: 69). The first is intrinsic motivation, which is the idea that students are naturally disposed to have an aroused desire for the learning process and that this comes from within, rather than from external stimuli. Students who possess intrinsic motivation will be driven to learning for its own sake rather than for particular rewards. The second is extrinsic motivation, which is basically to offer incentives or rewards to students in order to get them motivated to participate and achieve in lessons. This distinction, while potentially useful in the abstract, may cause a false dichotomy if applied too literally. No student will be completely internally driven and, likewise, extrinsic factors will never be entirely what motivates a student.

What is unique about motivation in FE?

In early 2006, a reader wrote in to the *Times Educational Supplement* (*TES*), concerned about the announcement that principals will be helping with the 3Rs in schools where pupils were failing. The reader made the following complaint:

One would assume that MPs can interpret raw data and not attempt to make direct comparisons between two disparate groups.

Post-16 students have different motivations to those of school children.

There is no legal compulsion to attend, therefore the motivations will generally be intrinsic as opposed to extrinsic. Colleges have no uniform policies, have no need of exclusion rooms, behaviour bases or discipline systems.

(*TES*, 10 February 2006)

The argument here is presumably that, as it isn't compulsory for students to attend FE colleges after the age of 16, their motivations for being there are entirely different to those of younger students still participating in compulsory education. The evidence used in support of this is the absence of disciplinary mechanisms. The assumption here is that as FE colleges contain self-motivated students who are there of their own free will, then no discipline is required.

Let us leave to one side the fact that, as the 14–19 skills agenda looks set to be implemented, a significant proportion of FE lecturers are likely to be teaching younger students who are still in compulsory education. Is it actually the case that as students aren't legally required to be in an FE college, they are more likely to be self-motivated to be there?

Certainly Susan Wallace (2002) in *Managing Behaviour and Motivating Students in Further Education* sees fit to dismiss such 'idealism' in the first paragraph of her book. According to Wallace, those interviewing such idealistic candidates for places on an initial teacher training courses, should 'take the opportunity to explain some of the realities of teaching in FE in the 21st century' (Wallace 2002: 1). Wallace gives two main reasons for this reality check. First, it's harder to find jobs after leaving school than in the past and therefore FE is less of a choice than one might think. Second, a number of students are likely to be in FE because they either didn't do well or didn't enjoy school, and have reluctantly turned to FE as an alternative way to gain qualifications (Wallace 2002: 7).

In fact, as we will consider shortly, with the introduction of EMAs and other incentives to undertake courses, such as iPods, laptops and free driving lessons, the reasons for students wanting to attend these courses probably now have less to do with the content of the course than ever before. However, even if we accept Wallace's arguments as true, there is still another argument that the *TES* reader could have made: that is the lack of uniforms, compulsion and formal school discipline systems mean that the student has a far greater opportunity than ever before to be treated like, and to act like, an adult; that being treated like an adult is something that all students, even if they may be initially resistant to the responsibilities this entails, will respect lecturers for doing; that it does require a certain faith on behalf of the lecturer, however, that this is possible.

Motivating students to sign up to FE (and stay there)

Working as a researcher for the *TES*, I quickly became familiar, from the FE Focus archives, with the array of accounts of colleges trying to motivate students to sign up and stay on courses. These concrete examples of what happens in FE colleges can give a fascinating insight into on-the-ground motivational and recruitment strategies.

In January 2006, it was reported that Bournemouth and Poole College had to counter criticism for offering free laptops or driving lessons to students under 19 who attended their six month 'Fresh Start' course. This scheme followed on from one the previous summer that had offered iPods and £100 if 16–18-year-old students completed a day-a-week 'Step Up For Summer' course. Students would also be given £50 a week while they were attending the course. The Executive Director for the local LSC argued that such an 'innovative' scheme was necessary, as 'one of the biggest challenges facing the learning and skills sector is to find ways to engage with young people who are currently not involved in any kind of education, training or employment' (Richardson 2006). The summer campaign was seen to be a great success. The College attracted 58 students and 41 completed the course. A spokeswoman for the College claimed that 37 students were 'continuing in education or starting work'. It was claimed that 'the kids are very motivated'; however, whether or not this was linked to the fact that the students were being paid above the minimum wage to attend a course was not mentioned.

Similar schemes are not uncommon. The previous year, Bedford College offered £1000 to any student who regularly attended and completed a level 3 course. This was non-means tested, although students needed 5 A*–B GCSEs. The college principal claimed that the initiative was rolled out after the success of the EMA scheme at boosting retention rates through meeting travel and other expenses.

And what about lifelong learners? If money no longer has its allure, then according to a survey undertaken by the LSC in 2002, part-time study courses are second only to the pub as places that lifelong learners find love. An LSC spokeswoman at that time told the *TES* that 'People in search of romance or friendship should enroll on part-time study courses . . . Courses are regarded as social events as well as a chance to learn new skills' (Hook 2002).

It's telling that social events are prioritized over the actual learning of skills. Indeed as with all of these incentives, it appears that the priority is to encourage students to sign up for courses and remain on them. The problem is that actual achievement on the courses doesn't seem to get anywhere near as great reward. Indeed, as Susan Wallace points out, 'we can no longer say with any conviction to students on "vocational" courses, "work hard and there'll be a job at the end". We know this will not necessarily be true' (Wallace 2002: 35).

A creeping trend in HE is for lecturers and students alike to view the role of the student as being that of a consumer. One of the common reasons given for this is the introduction of tuition fees. The contradiction in FE is that the students really do get to have their cake and eat it. They are increasingly being paid to be on the course and are treated as consumers as their regular attendance on college courses carries, to paraphrase Susan Wallace, 'a unit of funding'. However, it is questionable how nutritious the cake is that the students are given to eat, especially as courses are now being designed to motivate students to sign up. Take, for example, the Learning and Skills Development Agency (LSDA), (which has now evolved into the Quality Improvement Agency (QIA) and Learning and Skills Network) (LSN), pamphlet *Get Up Stand Up: Citizenship Through Music*, which encourages students to become more active citizens through the use of music and poetry. James Barber, the co-author of the pamphlet, has set up classes in writing and performing rap music. This course, which also has a section on the history of protest music, encourages students to write their own rap songs, 'to motivate young people into expressing their views and making a difference in their communities' (Clancy 2005). Andrew Thompson, the then Chief Executive of the (LSDA), made the following statement:

> I have an empathy with young people and the world they are going into, and I am concerned about helping them to make it a better world . . . Music can be very positive. It affects people's moods and states of happiness . . . It requires enormous intelligence to produce any type of music. It is a celebration of what they are capable of doing.
>
> (quoted in Clancy 2005).

I recently discussed this article with a small group of sixth form and FE college students. One remarked that there was 'something pretty sinister' about the idea that institutions would be encouraging them to protest. Another found it very strange to equate the idea of rap and protest music with the idea that it affects people's states of happiness, saying, 'you're not going to get anywhere rapping about your college canteen. If you want to rap, you go out onto the streets. College is where you go if you want to learn stuff'.

The paradox of this sort of attempt to 'motivate' young people is that in trying to get 'kids' off the streets to widen participation in FE, colleges seem to be attempting to recreate the street in the very place that should be giving students the opportunities to achieve far greater things in life. Furthermore, alarm bells should ring when Thompson argues that simply producing 'any type of music' should be regarded as something that requires 'enormous intelligence' and be celebrated. There is no doubt that college students do have an enormous amount of intelligence, but it's what they achieve when that intelligence is applied that should be celebrated, or criticized, depending on its merit. If simply possessing intelligence is grounds for celebration, then why bother learning 'stuff'?

A course in rap music, however, is simply the tip of the iceberg. Colleges run courses from ice hockey to video game design to boxing NVQs. Although the intentions of those individuals setting up and running the courses are usually genuine, the official reasons justifying them are invariably along the lines that it is important to have courses that are 'relevant to young people's lives'.

The obsession with relevance in the FE sector is epitomized by the fact that the LSC is currently undertaking a five year survey of 110,000 students asking them what they think of the education and training offered to them. This exercise, estimated to cost in the region of £2 million, was the brainchild of LSC chairman Bryan Sanderson, who used to be the chairman of BP. Questioned about the relevance of his previous post by FE Focus Editor, Ian Nash, Sanderson drew many parallels between FE and his work for BP. He expressed a desire to learn from his successes with a major market research survey about how consumers perceive BP. This survey resulted in the realization that women, who make up 6 out of 10 of BP's customers, saw the BP shield logo as being 'aggressive and hard'. A subsequent re-branding exercise resulted 'in a 10 per cent rise in sales' (Nash 2002). Targeting the 'bottom 20 per cent of the population', a similar survey is being planned for FE. Sanderson argues that the five year survey is fundamental as, 'without a clearer idea of what motivates people to learn and where they want to learn it, we cannot shape policy to meet our targets' (Nash 2002). At the highest level in FE, then, the motivations of students are seen to be of paramount importance to the shaping of policy. At a more local level, courses are being structured to be more relevant to students and incentives are being given to motivate them to sign up. And certainly recent statistics show that the FE sector is growing at a phenomenal rate (see Chapter 2). However, as has been noted, what is lacking in the discussion about motivating students to sign up is any real discussion about the quality of the education the students will be getting.

The truth is that students are actually very shrewd when it comes to gimmicks, such as free iPods. They'll be looking for the catch. The group of students I interviewed immediately responded, 'Can we just sign up and get the iPod and not turn up?' Without undertaking a major research study, it's a fair bet that such responses would be commonplace. The students were all swayed by the idea of the financial incentives to go on the course though. One said, 'If I didn't have much to do for a few months over the summer, why not? It pays well and it might be a laugh.'

Gimmicks may get the attention of students, but if it's going to require a lot of time and effort to get the promised rewards, they soon weigh up whether they can be bothered or not. Once they sign up for a course it becomes the responsibility of the FE lecturer to prove to them that it was worth bothering to do so. We'll now take a look at this in more detail.

Are you sitting comfortably? Creating the right learning conditions

A popular grumble of FE lecturers is that students lack any motivation to work and yet they still have to sign their EMAs at the end of every week. Susan Wallace sees this as one of the effects of widening participation in FE, 'If we widen participation without addressing motivation, we end up with a lot of participants who aren't necessarily enthusiastic or willing' (Wallace 2002: 7).

Refusing to teach courses that one thinks will not benefit the student, or campaigning for their abolition is something that should be encouraged. Regardless, any FE lecturer will almost certainly have to face students who have been recruited for reasons other than the fact that they are enthusiastic about the course content.

How to motivate these students is a perennial topic that features in all FE training courses. In almost all cases the psychology of motivation is treated in FE training guides and on courses in a very mechanistic and uncritical way. There is no better example of this than the use of Maslow's hierarchy of needs that is a staple in the motivation section of almost all FE training guides. Maslow's influential work is increasingly popular on business and training courses although his most important book, *Motivation and Personality*, was first published in 1954. The basic idea behind the use of Maslow's ideas is to outline the so-called 'preconditions to learning'. In a tick-box fashion, various factors are outlined that are supposed to be in place before the conditions are ripe for learning, or 'self-actualization' as Maslow calls it. At the bottom are hunger and thirst, next is physical and psychological well-being, then love and belonging, followed by self-esteem, with self-actualization at the top. This is the outline of Maslow's hierarchy of needs that is often given in no more detail than that which is contained in the famous graphic showing the triangle or pyramid of needs. As is highlighted in the companion book to this, *Teaching and Training in Post-Compulsory Education*, it's important to realize that 'moving to a higher level is dependent on the level below' (Armitage *et al.* 2007: 67). It's also important to note, as the book points out, that the highest level of Maslow's hierarchy is open-ended, 'because human potential is not finite' (Armitage *et al.* 2007: 67).

Certainly some people seem to take a very literal interpretation of Maslow as regards motivation in FE. This was clear in an article written by Mark Haysom, the Chief Executive of the LSC, in which he claimed, 'I believe passionately that when you walk through the door of a place of learning, you should feel proud, uplifted and motivated. On visiting those colleges, far from feeling uplifted it was difficult to stop my heart from sinking' (Haysom 2005). It would appear that Haysom believes that FE students derive their motivation from the physical conditions in which they find themselves. It must be added, however, that this is despite the fact that a major 2001 study, by the management consultancy firm PriceWaterhouseCoopers, showed that improving school buildings had little effect on test results (PriceWaterhouseCoopers 2001).

Susan Wallace takes a similar approach arguing that if a classroom was too 'chilly' then it is fundamental that the radiators be turned on as, 'Any other strategy we use – such as encouragement, or devising fascinating activities for them to do – will only have limited success until their basic need for a tolerable temperature to work in is met' (Wallace 2002: 65).

The great strength of Maslow's arguments derives from his very positive view of people. All people, according to his theory, are able to reach the point at which they can begin to realize their potential as long as certain conditions are met. Maslow's belief in the ability of people to be self-actualizing is something that should be adopted, if it's not already, as an antidote to the cynical views of students' capabilities held by many FE managers and lecturers today.

There are, however, two major dangers in the application of Maslow's approach, whether such an application takes place consciously or not. The first one of these also applies to the theories of extrinsic and intrinsic motivation briefly mentioned earlier. This is that it is easy to get so bogged down in trying to understand the barriers that students have to overcome before they can start learning that this very process of understanding becomes a major obstacle to learning in itself. The related danger is that, in trying to overcome the hierarchical barriers that students have to overcome before they can start learning, their attempts to do this become a major obstacle to learning itself. These two dangers will now be considered in more depth.

Getting to know the motivations of students

In addition to having to prepare courses, FE colleges across the country are now starting to encourage lecturers to undertake courses in emotional intelligence (EI) in order to gain a better understanding of what motivates their students. This shows the widespread influence of books like Daniel

Goleman's *Emotional Intelligence* (1996), but the fad is much more widespread. For example of the broader spread of these ideas, take lecturer David Martin, who undertook courses in behaviour management, counselling and motivational techniques. As a result, he claims of his students, 'we have this relationship now. You understand who you're working with, why they're shouting, not complying, why they're being silly' (Whittaker 2003a).

A more structured experiment in emotional intelligence is taking place on a much larger scale at Farnborough College in which all 2500 students have had an EI test. All of the lecturers are required to get students to 'examine their emotional responses to college life' (Kingston 2005a). Peter Kingston reports that one lecturer will sit down with each of his students and regularly ask them how they feel about his sports lessons, 'whether they are having fun but also how they are feeling in general' (Kingston 2005a) The Principal, John Guy, cites the success of EI in corporate organizations and the fact that the world's great leaders have good EI as a reason for implementing it. He claims that, 'EI is about self-awareness, awareness of others, self-motivation and motivation of others. Those have always been things that people have tried to improve' (Kingston 2005a). This may be the case but these things that were not traditional aims of FE. Something different is going on that focuses students more on their internal lives.

There is no doubt that the students have become very fluent in the language of EI but it is by no means evident that this gives students a greater drive. One of the students quoted suggests that EI has had some uses however as, 'Teachers have become much more understanding about why work hasn't been given in' (Kingston 2005a).

In some cases attempting to understand students better is a commendable thing. David Martin managed to increase achievement from 34 per cent to 89 per cent the year after he implemented his new strategies. Martin's strategies included greeting all new students with a one-to-one discussion of why they were on the course, saying to them at the end, 'I will look after you, but if you mess about I will tell you straight – we don't do bad behaviour . . . forget the past – this is an opportunity for you to make a fresh start' (Whittaker 2003a).

Martin's hard-line seems to have earned the respect of the students. How much is this to do with emotional intelligence, however? The introduction of EI training for lecturers in Cardonald College, led Assistant Principal John Laird to remark that, 'In many ways this is what good teachers have always done – encouraging quiet youngsters to speak, putting students into groups and checking the interaction between them' (Munro 2002). Indeed. The difference now is that these practices of good teaching are being formalized and couched in the language of emotional intelligence. Such formalization inevitably makes students wary of staff.

One of my lasting memories of being a student at a college is a lecturer who was always trying to ask us how we were doing and how we felt about the course. I remember a canteen discussion in which fellow students on the course described this approach as being 'creepy', 'slimy' and 'paranoid'. One of my friends was really concerned at the time that the feedback to coursework was formulaic and unhelpful and there was a real sense that his time could be better spent talking to us about our work, rather than about how we felt. He was contrasted with another journalism lecturer, who was friendly, but very firm and critical, and would keep a professional distance from the students. We looked up to him as a result. With hindsight the creepy and paranoid lecturer was probably only trying to hone his emotional intelligence skills. It's a shame that, in the process, we lost all respect for him as a lecturer and actively avoided him when we saw him coming down the corridor.

Attempting to overcome the obstacles to learning

At least 'learning through laughter' hasn't yet been introduced on FE courses – although it may be the time this book is published. In 2001 Alan Tuckett, Director of the National Institute of Adult Education (NIACE), wrote an account of Singapore's 'Manpower Learning Festival' where he describes Bombay doctor Madan Kataria's laughing exercises which, 'help people explore conflict through laughing'. According to Tuckett, 'Madan reduced a thousand deeply serious people to helpless laughter within a few minutes' (Tuckett 2001). This is somewhat unsurprising. More surprising, however, is the extent to which various gimmicks are being tried out in an attempt to motivate students in FE college classrooms. As can also be seen in recent government schemes to try to get young people to vote, new technology is often seen as a way to motivate young people to participate in FE. The favourite seems to be mobile phones. In 2003, the LSDA held an international conference on mobile learning. The *Guardian* cited Jill Attewell, the m-learning programme manager, who claimed that, 'Making learning attractive and fun for young adults is important. There appears to be the potential to engage and motivate, hopefully encouraging some students to progress to more substantial learning' (Hiscock 2003).

Initiatives have included lecturers texting multiple choice questions to students with the promise of prizes if they respond. Cynicism about the use of mobile phones abounds, however. The *Guardian* reported a random selection of comments from 16–19-year-olds, which are worth quoting in full:

I couldn't be bothered to use my phone for anything other than speaking to friends or texting. If I wanted to learn something I'd rather sit down at a computer.

It seems to me like another way to keep up with young people. What would you be able to fit on the screen anyway? I don't think it's an appropriate way to learn. It seems patronizing.

It could work, but it depends on whether you take it seriously. I'd rather interact with a teacher. I don't associate my phone with work; it's my own personal thing, separate from anything else.

(Hiscock 2003)

These views are telling, both about mobile phone initiatives and other similar attempts to engage young people. Students are hardened to gimmicks to try to motivate them and will inevitably adopt a detached cynicism when such measures are adopted. This cynicism, when entrenched, is a far greater barrier to try to overcome than the barriers that could potentially be lifted through mobile technology.

Another attempt to motivate FE students is through trying to entertain them in the classroom. An extreme example is the 2005 'STAR' award winner Matthew Wilson, a biology teacher from Bede College. The 'STAR' awards were established by the DfES to recognize outstanding 'stars', be they managers, lecturers or support staff, working in the learning and skills sector. One of his students claimed at the time, 'You're never bored, never dictated to. He has you up and dancing to music all the time. There's a dance for everything. He has so many different ways to make the information stick in your mind' (Whittaker 2005). Other strategies used by Wilson include bingo, snakes and ladders and wheel of fortune. But does a lecturer have to turn himself into a clown and his classroom into a funfair in order to motivate students? Wilson is a novelty and it appears that students do engage as a result, hence his pass rate is 'well above average'. It's likely, however, that if students had to go from class to class singing and dancing and playing bingo, the novelty would wear off pretty quickly.

Some suggestions about how students can really be motivated

Students hate to be patronized. While talking about a motivational mobile phone pilot, one of the lecturers made the claim, 'Students like the fact that their tutors are engaging at their level' (Whittaker 2003b). She couldn't be further from the truth. I read a paragraph of D. S. Grant's *Motivation for Teens* to the group of students I interviewed:

> Teenager, think about the percentage of time where you are non-productive at school. It really is far too high! But let's not be doom merchants here. I'm glad to say there are students who work diligently. Special commendation to those students, and to you if you are one of those. Try to positively influence all your friends to do the same. Why? Because it will be worth it.
>
> (Grant 2002 cited in Barton 2004: 17)

According to the description on the book cover, Grant is supposed to have 'a finger on the pulse of teenage angst, teenage culture and psychology'. Instead, after initial baffled looks, it had this group of students rolling round laughing in a way that Dr Madan Kataria could only dream of achieving!

If a lecturer starts telling students that their work is 'nang', writing in text-speak or pretending they like 50 Cent as much as their students do, rest assured: students will be laughing at them and not with them. And those cynical expressions will be locked onto their faces.

Students like to be treated like adults

A report published by the LSDA, in February 2004, found overwhelmingly that FE students like to be in mixed classes with adult learners. Stephen McNair, Professor of Education at Surrey University, claimed that students argued that, 'Being in an adult environment made us behave better than if we had been on our own. We learned better and performed better' (Kingston 2004). I recently had the opportunity to ask the best lecturer I had about his motivational strategies. The response was that he had none, 'except a firm resolution that all students should be treated like adults as much as is possible'.

What does it mean to treat students like adults? Fundamentally, it is to take them seriously, what they have to say should be critically engaged with and clear reasons should be given for any praise or criticism given to them. I often think back to things my old philosophy lecturer said and, when engaging in situations, try to think how he would approach things. I'd trade a thousand singing and dancing lecturers for that one role model of what it is to be an adult.

Students are resilient

Treating students like adults means, in short, that lecturers should not be afraid to criticize them for fear of damaging their self-esteem. In the adult world such criticism is important and necessary in order to develop. This should also be the case in the classroom. Here we should take note of Dr Raj Persaud, who was a difficult student:

> Assessment that appears arbitrary or unjust is demotivating, and if teachers cannot justify grades, a lot of kids just stop bothering. I used to drive my teachers mad because I would frequently take bits of homework more or less identical to my own and say, 'this is the same as mine, but this pupil has obtained a higher mark'. I wanted teachers to give reasons for their judgments
>
> (Persaud 2006)

The point is not that students should whinge about marks, but that they should be allowed to engage in both constructive and destructive criticism about assessment. The trouble with Persaud's example is that most teachers today would just give in to such criticism and up the marks and college managers would support the students!

Praise for good work is only valuable if clear reasons are given for awarding it and the same is true of criticism. Even if student self-esteem takes a blow in the short-term, a more genuine confidence can be gained in the long-term because only criticism of their work ensures that students don't make the same mistakes again. Criticism, even harsh, if justified makes development possible. Not pointing out flaws in students' work for fear of damaging their self-esteem means the lecturer is effectively responsible for them repeating the same mistakes again and again.

Students are wary of lecturers who try too hard to find out what motivates them: the QUEST paradox

Research published by QUEST (Quality of Experience in Schooling Trans-Nationally) comparing English and French attitudes towards schooling yielded a very interesting result:

> Paradoxically, it is in England where teachers try hard to develop positive relationships with pupils that a negative sub-culture opposed to teachers' values emerges. In France, where teacher–pupil relationships are more formal and based on greater inequality in authority, children express a stronger liking for

teachers, a greater degree of consensus with teachers' values, and more positive feelings about school

(Osborn 1997)

In addition one of the students in the group I interviewed made an interesting parallel:

You know when you get in one of those relationships where the other person is very keen and tries too hard, endlessly asking you what you're feeling and wanting to know everything about you and stuff? You end up going 'Woah, intense!' and getting suffocated and dumping them. It's sad because they obviously wanted to make it work, but they just went over the top. It can be a bit like that with lecturers sometimes – obviously with them there's no physical stuff – but it's worse because they're supposed to be teaching you, not going out with you.

Perhaps the QUEST paradox isn't so surprising. The actual process of trying to build relationships with students, which we've observed in the numerous examples of lecturers, in order to find out what motivates them is more than likely going to generate cynicism among students. No student is going to see a lecturer who tries too hard to build relationships as a role model. It's understandable that, as a result, students become detached and will generate 'negative sub-cultures' opposed to their values.

Students like lecturers to tell them what they should learn, not the other way round

Even if they're only there for the free iPod, students have chosen to enter into the classroom. The battle, according to Susan Wallace, then begins:

The battle – if we're going to call it that – is for the hearts and minds of the students. It is one that is fought to motivate them and develop their potential. And one of the ways we can win it is to let them know we have great expectations of them; not necessarily in the sense of high achievement, but rather an expectation that we can enjoy working together toward whatever goals are appropriate to them.

(Wallace 2002)

While letting students know that they are capable of great things is very positive advice, accepting that the goals of the course are whatever is 'appropriate to them' is to let students down. As has been argued above, setting a strong model for students and not being afraid to criticize them – while perhaps less enjoyable in the short-term – is far more rewarding in the long-term.

As we can see from the QUEST research, being authoritative is more likely to generate a positive response from students than otherwise. After all, surely a lecturer knows more than the students about what they're studying? Surely the reason a lecturer is in front of the class is to pass on knowledge and skills to them? Otherwise why be a lecturer?

A chronology of the death of motivation in FE

1972   Raising of the School Leaving Age (ROSLA) to 16. ROSLA focused educationalists' attention on the need to motivate pupils whose extended education was now compulsory in a period of economic crisis.

1976   The Great Debate. Prime Minister James Callaghan launches a great debate about education that invited industry and business to influence the aims and content of education.

1977   Young People and Work (Holland Report). The Holland Report set out the philosophy and plans for new youth training programmes.

1978   Special Educational Needs (Warnock Report). Warnock sensitized FE to the need to make provision for students with special needs.

1979   Youth Opportunities Programme (YOP). The MSC begins to make major inroads into colleges with large numbers of ill-motivated students.

1993   Years of the locust. After incorporation a period of financial and other scandals that rocked the sector.

1997   Defeat of effective union organization. Four years after incorporation the lecturers' union NATFHE was in disarray not simply because of the seeming failure of the campaign to defend 'silver book' conditions, but because of a loss of potential and actual members and internal political faction-fighting.

1998   Further Education National Training Organization (FENTO) is established. The significance of FENTO is that it marks the real beginning of the quangocracy impact on professional life and the bureaucratization of professional life in FE.

2001   Mandatory teacher training qualifications for new entrants to FE. FE lecturers are, from 1 September, subject to professional regulation of the sort familiar in schools.

cont.

2006   *Loud and Clear.* The NUS launches a campaign to give students a say in all aspects of college life, from appointments to curriculum development. The decline in motivation, from seeing students as a problem, to de-motivation of lecturers through bad management and bureaucratization, has a solution; power is given to the students and adults abandon control of the classroom.

Key readings

Many lecturers will be familiar with discussions of motivation in the standard works: Curzon ([1976] 1990) and Armitage *et al.* (2007) and Wallace (2002) which all draw on Maslow's work ([1958] 1970). Popular accounts of motivation in the education press are useful in understanding the fads and fashions of motivation in practice. Both the *TES* and the *Education Guardian*, allow free access to their archives online at: www.tes.co.uk and http://education.guardian.co.uk

Here are a few of the articles mentioned in this chapter:

Clancy, J. (2005) Protest is fully rapped, *TES FE Focus*, 30 September, p. 7.

Haysom, M. (2005) Make spaces fit the future, *TES FE Focus*, 1 April, p. 39.

Hiscock, D. (2003) Could text messaging be used to engage new students? *Education Guardian*, 25 February, p. 45.

Hook, S. (2002) Brush up flirting skills with adult learning, *TES FE Focus*, 13 September, p. 35.

Kingston, P. (2004) Mix and match: research shows teenagers like learning with adults, but is there enough evidence to convince MPs, *Education Guardian*, 24 February, p. 17.

Kingston, P. (2005a) Hello. How are you? *Education Guardian*, 18 January p. 14

Munro, N. (2002) Emotions are key to focus on learning, *TES Scotland*, 20 December, p. 32.

Nash, I. (2002) Pump the punters or lose business, *TES FE Focus*, 8 March, p. 3.

Osborn, M. (1997) When being top is not seen as best, *TES*, 10 January, p. 14.

Richardson, L. (2006) iPods lure students back to college, *TES FE Focus*, 6 January, p. 1.

Tuckett, A. (2001) You've got to laugh in lifelong learning, *TES FE Focus*, 14 December, p. 44.

Whittaker, M. (2003a) Learning from the listener, *TES FE Focus*, 11 April, p. 48.

Whittaker, M. (2003b) I'm on the training, *TES FE Focus*, 15 August, p. 30.

Whittaker, M. (2005) Dancing feat earned award, *TES FE Focus*, 8 April, p. 3.

4 Educating the digital native
Toby Marshall

Practitioners working within further education (FE) are commonly exhorted, and sometimes compelled, to make greater use of information and communications technology (ICT). Often the process of introduction is fraught with both conflict and frustration. New devices, such as virtual learning environments (VLEs), e-registers or interactive whiteboards (IWB), will be promoted on the basis that they can be used just like old technologies, or can be learned within minutes.

Experience demonstrates that these claims are rarely true. Launching e-registers will reveal problems of network capacity. Practice will demonstrate that staff VLE training was ineffective, or non-existent. Sometimes, the most minor design flaw in a user interface will bring the forward march of a new teaching technology to a disorderly halt.

At this point senior management teams will often become impatient. Frustrated by poor investment returns and, believing that the fault couldn't possibly be at an executive level, their adoption strategies will become draconian. Old media will be withdrawn and the use of the new will begin to be tracked centrally. Warnings will be issued to middle managers, who will cascade the resulting anxiety downwards. Internal memoranda will then be distributed, reminding staff of the requirement to use X technology by Y deadline with Z consequence for non-compliance. Finally, directors will call meetings to resolve the crisis.

ICT and the beasts of FE

At meetings of this type the concentration of collective pressure will sometimes result in a disturbing, and most unseemly, metamorphosis. Once rational, sentient and for the most part fully human practitioners will find that the mere mention of e-learning will result in the adoption of one of four beastly postures: the intransigent mule, the myopic bull, the obsequious toad or the indifferent cat.

Typically, a toad will be the first to address the meeting. One of their slimy number will croak on about the need to, 'fully embed digital beast practice' or, 'hoof-proof our enablement strategies'. On a very good day, they might even suggest that providers of the future should, 'develop learner-centric knowledge architectures'. The words will be meaningless, but the sentiment will be clear: the awkward mules and feckless cats should do the manager bulls' bidding immediately, and without question.

FE lecturers might have also observed respected colleagues responding to provocations of this type in the most mulish of fashions. 'A moratorium on all change should be called for at least forever and one day', you may have heard a grizzled mule declare. 'The bulls', another mule will often add, 'have failed to consult the beasts over change, and in doing so have lowered the morale of the already overworked and undernourished. Have they even considered the health and safety implications?'

At this point a manager bull will typically weigh in. If they feel that the meeting is going to swing their way, goring will be avoided and sympathy might even be expressed. 'But all beasts should be clear', a director level bull will often add gravely, 'there is no alternative to adoption. Our masters, the *Lords of Slop Cut*, have threatened to reduce our feed and redirect our stream [a rather miserable rivulet the beasts call Funding]. They may even send in their wrangler, ALI, and we all know he will take great pleasure in branding UNSATISFACTORY on our hides.'

At this point the response of the largest section of the audience will often be unclear, at least to the unseasoned observer, as the numerous FE cats rarely contribute to meetings. In private, however, they will be working through a thought that runs something like this:

1   Manager bulls can easily gore me
2   If I give off the appearance of adoption then the more obviously non-complaint mules will be attacked first
3   If ALI ever arrives he will be most likely to brand the bigger, and more slow moving, bulls.

Departmental meetings will usually be closing by the time that the cats have reached point three. Nowadays, mules often retreat after an initially aggressive charge, for they lack the certainty that youth, and greater numbers, once provided. Sadly, this means that manager bulls too often end such events with a victorious snort. But as we all know, their victories are of the hollow sort as, while the bulls of FE have the muscle to ensure beastly quiescence, they lack the wit and intelligence to build real commitment to change. Still, at least the resulting inertia keeps the grim-faced ALI in regular work.

Explaining the fable

If you have seen ICT bring out the mule, toad, bull, or cat in your colleagues, you will be happy to know that this chapter hopes to explain, and perhaps even moderate, these unnerving transformations.

It has four sections. The first sketches out the ideas of some of the key theorists of the 'digital learning revolution'. In doing so, the author aims to draw the reader's attention to the important positions within the debate, and to help them situate their own responses to ICT.

The second section examines the discussion of ICT in education and training policy, with particular reference to FE. It will also outline the principle carrots and sticks that are being used to encourage practitioner adoption. At the very least, this should make it clear why the management of your college is so desperate for you to use ICT, or to be more precise, to *evidence* usage.

The third section offers some highlights from the vast and ever growing field of empirical studies that have examined the impact of ICT. These show that there is a considerable gap between the effect claimed of ICT and that evidenced by large-scale studies. Perhaps lecturers are right to dismiss the hyperbole that surrounds e-learning.

Finally, my thoughts on how ICT might be more effectively promoted within FE are summarized in the concluding fourth section. Here I will explore the following paradox: ICT really does magnify, extend and diversify our pedagogic powers, yet characteristically practitioner experiences are that it reduces, limits and restricts their agency.

ICT and education in theory: automated pedagogy as dream and nightmare

Anxieties, aspirations, and theories relating to educational impact of communications technologies are no doubt as old as the notion and practice of education itself. The various positions that have been developed in relation to the impact of educational media can be located using Figure 4.1. Applying this to your own thinking might help you to understand why you have, or have not, chosen to engage with ICT.

The vertical axis corresponds to positive or negative attitudes towards ICT. The dominant response of today's policy-makers is overwhelmingly, and perhaps uncritically, positive. The reasons for this are explored in more detail in the second section.

The horizontal axis relates to factors that influence patterns of ICT usage. Some theorists believe that ICT determines the ways in which users behave. Others stress the inverse: the use of ICT, they argue, is shaped by wider cultural forces, such as the values of the institution in which a technology is based, or the agency of its users.

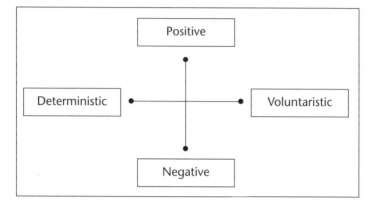

Figure 4.1   Perspectives on the Impact of ICT on Education and Training

Actual theorists, and lecturers, will of course have viewpoints that are considerably more nuanced and sophisticated that this simple diagram allows. It is possible and entirely sensible to adopt different positions on different technologies. One might reasonably assume that television access within the home has a broadly negative effect on the literacy of learners but believe that exposure to the Internet is positive.

Equally, it could be argued that while the efficacy of ICT is usually dependent on contextual factors, specific packages can have a consistently positive and context-independent impact on the achievement of students. Technologies that support the visually impaired, for example, often work in a wide variety of contexts.

We should also note that views on ICT usually reflect a practitioner's wider philosophy of education and training. Traditionalists, whose pedagogic creed stresses the importance of cultural transmission and the primacy of a lecturer's subject-knowledge, are unlikely to be sympathetic to a teaching technology with which students are said to be able to construct their own understanding of the world. Similarly, progressive educators will often be the most vocal critics of software that employs traditional didactic methods of instruction, or what is sometimes referred to as 'drill and kill'.

The theorists whose ideas will be examined in this section, illustrate the extensive range of such thinking. They include writers who are alternatively positive and negative about the impact of ICT, as well as those that argue for both voluntarist and determinist perspectives. A contrast can also be drawn between those that foreground the impact of ICT on teaching, and those that are more concerned with the opportunities it provides for learning.

Teachers as programmers

The first theorist to be considered is B. F. Skinner. Skinner is known more broadly for his contribution to a psychological school of thought called behaviourism, so called for its emphasis on the external and measurable behaviour of the subjects it studied. Skinner's theory of education and training, which sought to uncover the scientific principles by which these services might be delivered more efficiently has been, and remains both influential and controversial, primarily for its alleged objectification of humanity.

Skinner's work on instruction technology is not discussed so frequently, which is surprising given its prescience. At the time of writing the *Teaching Machines* Skinner was a professor of psychology at America's Harvard University (Skinner 1958) and automated computation was, for the most part, a mechanical, rather than electronic, exercise. Yet he anticipated much of the contemporary debate.

His essay begins by drawing our attention to the growing social demand for education, a demand that cannot be met by 'building more schools and training more teachers'. Instead of allocating more resources, Skinner suggests that America should develop its delivery and assessment technologies. Existing mediums, such as film, could replace teachers in terms of standardized lectures, he argues, but they do not interact with students, both in terms of the matching of content to student need, or the assessment of their understanding. The solution, he argues, is to develop the teaching machines that were first invented in the 1920s.

A variety of teaching machines are then discussed by Skinner. These required that students read and respond to a series of carefully ordered and progressively more challenging frames of information. Incorrect answers trigger remedial frames, while correct responses allow students to progress. Feedback is immediate and respondents can set the pace of progression. Anticipating his critics, particularly those within the humanities, Skinner then goes on to provide illustrations of these technologies working across arts, languages, science and social science disciplines. He also describes early examples of what would now be called multimedia technologies, in which auditory, as well as visual and verbal stimuli, were a feature.

Finally, Skinner addresses himself to the question on the mind of the increasingly anxious teacher-reader: will I become redundant? The development of teaching machines does not signal the demise of their fleshy counterparts, argues Skinner, but their coronation. Teaching machines, like assembly lines, will force a new division of labour. Within this, teachers will concentrate on complex and high value-added activities, such as programming the machines, and analysing the information generated, 'In assigning certain mechanizable functions to machines, the teacher emerges in his [*sic*] proper role as an indispensable human being.

He may teach more students than heretofore' and in return 'for his greater productivity he can ask society to improve *his* economic position' (Skinner 1958: 8).

It is clear that Skinner believed that technology would amplify and extend the agency of practitioners. His contribution is important in that it provides an early example of technology being positioned as a means of solving an educational problem, in this case the growing demand for resources required to expand provision. It also raises an issue that will continue to be a feature of instructional technology discourse, which is the question of productivity.

In principle, the aspiration to raise levels of productivity is a healthy one, as nobody gains from the squandering of human resources. If pedagogy could be reliably automated in part, or in whole, this would significantly lighten the associated costs. This, in turn, would enable provision to be extended, diversified or deepened.

It is notable, however, that Skinner's prediction regarding the potential gains of applying technology to education is nearly half a century old. In the first decade of the twenty-first century we are still waiting for examples of teaching and training being effectively automated on the mass scale he envisioned. Indeed, as we shall see in the third section of this chapter, the empirical evidence of ICT-based strategies raising productivity is mixed, in spite of the considerable sums of public money and practitioner time expended.

There are many possible explanations for this delay. To be fair, instructional technology was in its infancy when Skinner was writing. In the intervening years computers have developed significantly, and it is possible that the rate of technical development, coupled with the institutional inertia that characterizes the education and training sectors, has delayed the predicted productivity gains.

Alternatively, it could be that Skinner overlooked, or discounted, the important interpersonal dynamics of educational and training. Those that work within FE will recognize that students in fact require significant levels of personal contact and feedback. Interaction with another more knowledgeable human often provides them with both the inspiration and discipline they need to engage with their studies. Lecturers, for better and for worse, are usually the principle mediums of instruction. For this reason it may be that the claim that ICT can systematically facilitate autonomous, resource-light, learning is mistaken. Time will ultimately tell. In the interim, however, it seems likely that overall staff–student ratios will remain constant.

Contemporary thinking in relation to ICT would seem to be moving in this direction. In the recent period few sensible advocates of ICT suggest that lecturer numbers are going to be significantly reduced by machines.

Rather the discussion is of 'blended provision', which combines both ICT and real, not virtual, lecturers.

Sadly, too many learning technologists and policy wonks continue to promote ICT on the false premise that it can provide an immediate solution to the resource problems of FE managers. In doing so, they do a disservice to the technologies they advocate. ICT, as the American critic Clifford Stoll has noted, is too often sold as if it were 'Silicone Snake Oil'. One immediate consequence of this is that lecturers often dismiss the technology on the mistaken grounds on which it is promoted.

Technopoly and the end of education

The writings of the cultural critical Neil Postman provide a dramatic dystopian counterpoint to Skinner's positive, if perhaps overly metallic, vision of education's electronic future. In *Technopoly* (Postman 1993) he offers a wide-ranging critique of new communications technologies, updating positions on the electronic media that were outlined in the more commonly read *Amusing Ourselves to Death* (Postman 1987).

Where Skinner sees ICT positively enhancing the pedagogic agency of practitioners, Postman offers a more darkly deterministic account. According to Postman, America is a society characterized by both a deification and a glut of information and technology. In his view it is no longer a 'tool-using' culture, but has become the world's first 'technopoly', a society ordered around information generation.

Postman suggests that one effect of this is that traditional cultural gatekeepers, such as schools and churches, have lost their purchase. He notes that:

> When the supply of information is no longer controllable, a general breakdown in psychic tranquillity and social purpose occurs. Without defences, people have no way of finding meaning in their experiences, loose their capacity to remember, and have difficulty imagining reasonable futures.
>
> (Postman 1993: 72)

New communication technologies, Postman argues, shift the ways in which we frame and act on the world. They: '. . . alter the structure of our interests: the things that we think *about*. They alter the character of our symbols: the things that we think *with*. And they alter the nature of the community: the arena in which thoughts develop' (1993: 20).

For Postman, one important consequence of this is that alternative means of communication become marginalized. With particular reference to schools he notes that a fine balance has historically been struck between oracy and literacy, as 'Orality stresses group learning, cooperation, and a sense of social responsibility', whereas 'Print stresses individualized learning, competition and personal autonomy'. ICT, he argues, upsets this balance, encouraging students to adopt an egocentric orientation to the world (1993:17).

Postman's point is that communications technologies both encourage and discourage certain forms of mental and social activity, both within schools and beyond. In particular, ICT discourages forms of communal discussion that are central to the process of democratic deliberation and action. The elevation of ICT within American culture, or to be more precise its displacement by ICT, results in information, rather than values, becoming both the means and ends of existence.

The ideas of both Postman and Skinner represent different ends of the Figure 4.1 axes. For Skinner, ICT is a tool that constructively amplifies the agency of practitioners. Postman, by contrast, views technology as having both a predetermined and destructive impact on the core functions of schooling. If Skinner is open to the charge of being overly technical in his approach, Postman could be said to be equally one-sided. His is ultimately an essentialist view of technology, insofar as he believes that the functions of ICT are fixed.

But there are problems with this perspective. Certainly, it may be true that ICT can be used in the ways described, but need this necessarily be so? Surely technologies, such as the Internet, can facilitate, if not stimulate, the desire for new forms of sociability? And if people no longer desire social interaction, then our account of this trend must include a far wider range of factors than communications technology, as where there is a will there is a way. Perhaps Postman's identification of technology as the determinate agent of social change mirrors the technolopolists he seeks to critique.

With this qualification, Postman's notion of technopoly, of a society that has come to deify technology, and to elevate its techniques over content, is a useful idea. It may not describe the whole process, but it will provide a useful starting point in our analysis of New Labour's approach to education and training.

Digital natives and digital immigrants

Interestingly, computer consultant Mark Prensky shares much with Postman, but where Postman sees negatives, Prensky sees positives. Like Postman he believes that the emergence of ICT gives rise to distinct information processing strategies. Those that are conversant with these he terms 'digital natives', while those who are not he dubs 'digital immigrants' (Prensky 2001).

Prensky's theory has captured the imagination of many learning technologists, because it positions them as superior to those they instruct, so you may well have encountered his ideas during staff development sessions. It has also travelled beyond the confines of educational technology discourse, being referenced by no lesser authorities than Ken Boston, the Chief Executive of the Qualifications and Curriculum Authority (QCA), and Rupert Murdoch, Chief Executive of international media conglomerate News Corporation.

Prensky's argument is that today's 'students are no longer the people our educational system was designed to teach' as they 'think and process information fundamentally differently from their predecessors'. Indeed, Prensky goes so far as to argue that 'our students' brains have physically changed' (2001: 1) as a consequence of the media environment in which they were raised, with the result that, 'our Digital Immigrant instructors, who speak an outdated language . . . are struggling to teach a population that speaks an entirely new language' (2001: 2).

His analysis of the distinct information processing strategies of digital immigrants and natives is summarized in Figure 4.2.

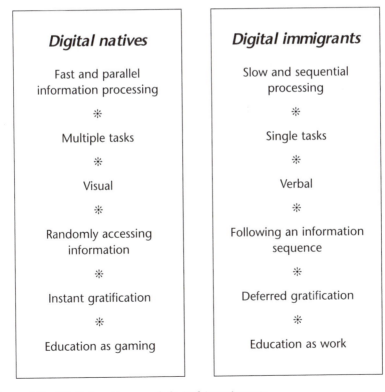

Digital natives	*Digital immigrants*
Fast and parallel information processing	Slow and sequential processing
❋	❋
Multiple tasks	Single tasks
❋	❋
Visual	Verbal
❋	❋
Randomly accessing information	Following an information sequence
❋	❋
Instant gratification	Deferred gratification
❋	❋
Education as gaming	Education as work

Figure 4.2   Digital natives and digital immigrants

Like Postman, Prensky believes that the development of new communications technologies is having a profound impact on the ways in which some of us are processing information. His theory, like Postman's, essentializes technology, insofar as it conflates the potential, and actual, uses of ICT. Conceptually, the consequence of this is conservative, in that it restricts our appreciation of that which might be achieved with ICT. By essentializing technology Prensky and Postman also tend to erase the agency of users. However, routine examples illustrate that ICT usage in fact contains a large volitional component.

For many years domestic computers have provided interfaces that enable users to engage with a number of streams of information simultaneously. To your irritation, you may have found 'digital natives' in your class or workrooms searching the Internet, while answering their email and listening to audio files. Hence Prensky's identification of parallel information processing as a method associated with the digital native.

In fact there is no good technological reason why computers must be used in this way. It is users who have decided to open various windows, and the interface designers who have provided the technology that makes this possible. Learners are equally free to process information sequentially via one window. Parallel information processing is a choice made by humans, not a fixed function of the technology. Understanding why it is that the 'digital natives' might choose parallel, over sequential, processing is therefore a question that takes us beyond technology and into the wider field of learner agency and its relationship to broader cultural values.

Keeping agency at the forefront of our minds also means that we avoid the defeatist belief so often propagated by the apostles of the 'digital learning revolution'. This notion suggests that, because 'digital natives' often process information in parallel in their leisure time, we need to ape them in our lecturing practice. This view is mistaken for a variety of reasons. Most importantly, it assumes that learners lack the ability to adapt to the methods of information processing that our work requires of them. In fact, experience demonstrates that learners consistently evidence the capacity to adapt, although at different rates and by different routes, providing we as practitioners make our expectations clear. Indeed, surely the very notions of education and training assume the developmental capacity of learners.

Computers as Mind Tools

While Prensky's notion of digital natives and immigrants has a certain rhetorical appeal – there's nothing like a catchy metaphor to ensure the rapid adoption of an idea – an arguably more substantive case for the transformative impact of ICT on our thought processes has been articulated by David Jonassen and his colleagues.

In *Computers as Mind Tools* (Jonassen *et al.* 1998) it is argued that in conceptualizing the role of ICT within education and training, it is important to recognize that these technologies can do more than simply convey information. Rather, ICT should be understood as a set of technologies 'that students learn *with*, not *from*'. Reorienting our understanding in this way enables us to recognize that, 'learners function as designers, and computers function as Mind tools for interpreting and organizing their personal knowledge' (1998: 1).

Jonassen continues by citing a range of commonplace packages, such as spreadsheet, database and word-processing software, which enable students to interrogate critically and represent their own understanding. Examples include 'semantic networking tools', or digital brainstorming software, which facilitate the visual representation of ideas and require that 'learners analyse the structural relationships among the content they are studying' (1998: 4).

Admittedly, a cynic might reply that a pencil and paper are sufficient for this purpose, but Jonassen suggests that this is more than a case of old wine in new bottles. Thinking with computers, he argues, brings about a qualitative shift in the mental operations of users because it provides a dynamic 'scaffold' for their thinking. Jonassen makes a particularly strong case for this when discussing 'microworlds', or simulations as they are more popularly known. Microworld software, he argues, gives rise to new thought patterns because it enables users to control the variables that structure the programmed environment. In doing so, they allow students to analyse factors in ways that would not be practicable, and in some instances possible, in non-virtual situations. Microworlds, Jonassen concludes, provide 'perhaps the ultimate example of active learning environments' (1998: 7), and in case there was any confusion over the direction of causality, he adds that 'Mind tools are *un*intelligent, relying on the learner to provide the intelligence, not the computer' (1998: 14).

Jonassen's notion of ICT acting as a 'mind tool' offers a useful contrast to the thinking of Skinner, Postman and Prensky, insofar as it draws our attention to the agency of the learner. Like Skinner he views technology as potentially positive in its effects, but unlike Skinner, he is more concerned with the volitional activities of students rather than instructors. He also makes an intriguing case for ICT influencing and stimulating our thought processes. Perhaps an interesting question to consider is the extent to which ICT-related changes in the process of thought impact on its content.

Overall, it is also clear that the 'active' method of instruction, he describes, bears more than a passing resemblance to currently fashionable constructivist theories of learning, which are in turn influenced by the work of the American philosopher John Dewey. This illustrates the fact that discussions of ICT are intimately bound up with far broader debates over the ends and means of education, even if the discussion appears technological. Deciding if one supports the learning activities proposed by Jonassen is, therefore, more than a technical issue.

Towards a theory of instructional technology?

The theorists surveyed in this section illustrate the range of thinking that has been developed in relation to the educational, and wider cultural, impact of new communications technologies. We have engaged with thinkers who variously believe that ICT makes possible new forms of thought, or destroys important pedagogic practices. It has also been argued that computers amplify the pedagogic powers of the teacher, and by contrast, the learning capacity of students. Hopefully, this brief overview of the theory has enabled readers to reflect on their own thinking.

Assessing the various claims that have been made in relation to ICT is a task with which the seriously minded lecturer, and the educational research community, should engage. Key questions that have emerged include:

- Does ICT enhance the productivity of lecturers?
- Can the use of ICT displace important alternative modes of learning?
- What is the relationship between the medium and the content of instruction?
- Can all contents be delivered with equal effectiveness via all mediums?
- Are the spontaneous information processing strategies of students different from their tutors? If they are, can they adapt, or should we?
- If ICT provides new thinking tools, does this enable new thoughts?
- Does ICT change the relationship between lecturer and student?

It is unlikely that there will be any simple answers to these questions in either the short- or medium-term. Theory, in this instance, poses more questions than answers. Indeed, as both the technology and our awareness and use of it develops, so each one of these questions will need to be reappraised. The relationship between theory and practice is complicated still further by the variety of contexts in which we all operate, and the diverse contents we are employed to deliver.

Given this complexity, it is clear that mono-factoral theories of e-learning, and approaches derived from them, are unlikely to serve us well. ICT is only ever one aspect of any given learning situation, and its effective usage will always be a synthesis of individual, cultural and technical determinants. In other words, we need to move beyond ICT theory to understand if we need to use ICT.

The inherent variability and complexity of learning situations also means that it is practitioners, rather than theorists or managers, who are best placed to assess if ICT should, or should not, be used within their workrooms. In order to make the right decisions, it is important that lecturers both think about their practice and are given operational freedom to decide on the most appropriate course of action. Enforced practitioner adoption, which is often justified by theories, such as Prensky's, is unlikely to have the intended outcome. First, it is likely to demotivate lecturers, by restricted their space for creative engagement in their work. Second, it is likely to encourage indiscriminate, tokenistic and consequently ineffective usage. As we shall see, enforced adoption is too often the order of the day in FE.

ICT in education and training policy: the technopolist monopoly

For some years, ICT has been a feature of national debates regarding the future of state-funded education and training. Schools began experimenting with ICT in the 1960s, and in the early 1980s the government made funds available so that they could purchase hardware produced by Acorn and Research Machines. Labour's 1987 Manifesto talked of an education system in which students, 'can exploit the advantages of science and technology with confidence and in safety' (Labour Party 1987), and while the Conservative Manifesto of 1987 made no explicit reference to technology, Margaret Thatcher's Education Reform Act of the following year established it as a mandatory component of the soon to be introduced national curriculum. By 1992 the Labour Party's manifesto made it clear that it would support the continuation of technology as a subject, and would invest heavily in the equipment required to ensure its effective delivery (Labour Party 1992).

It was in the 1997 election, however, in which investment in ICT would become an issue of national significance. Following the report of the Stevenson Commission, which had been established by Tony Blair to investigate the future of schooling, the Labour Manifesto included six education pledges, one of which related to 'access to computer technology' (Labour Party 1997). Following this, some 187 words of Manifesto space were give over to elaborate New Labour's views on the contribution of technology to education and training, equal to the combined space allocated to their higher education and broadcasting strategy, and just shy of that devoted to national defence.

Interestingly, under the headline of 'Realizing the potential of new technology' it was claimed that 'Labour is the pioneer of new thinking'.

While the principles of this thinking were not made clear, specific commitments were given in terms of school Internet connectivity, establishing a website to host teaching resources, providing a grading system to facilitate the purchasing of software, as well as funds that would be made available for training teachers in the use of ICT.

At the time, these proposals were not especially remarkable. Each one, taken in its own terms, was sensible, as teachers and lecturers, like any other group of professionals, obviously require access to the communication technologies being used by the rest of society. What was remarkable, however, was the level of significance that New Labour had attached to ICT relative to other aspects of education policy, not least to the content of the school curriculum. New Labour's political investment in the educational potential of these technologies was, arguably, illustrative of a technopolist approach to education, in that a question of means was taking priority over ends.

For New Labour the elevation of ICT also served a number of important functions in terms of political positioning. First, and perhaps most importantly, the promotion of ICT was non-controversial as who, except perhaps arch traditionalists, such as Sir Rhodes Boyson, would be likely to argue against the provision of new technologies for schools. Consequently, the elevation of ICT provided a contrast with the more overtly morally contentious, ends-focused agenda of John Major. By extension, the promotion of ICT offered the easy appearance, if not the substance, of educational modernity, innovation and foresight.

New Labour: in the Microsoft Office?

The promotion of ICT has been a consistent theme of New Labour's education policy in the years that have followed, although its approach has developed. As we have seen, their initial focus was on questions of infrastructure and training. More recently, however, attention has shifted to the actual application of ICT. In the intervening years New Labour has also developed a more coherent view of its education policy, centred in particular around the notion of 'personalization'. Consequently, New Labour has become more prescriptive in terms of how it believes teachers and lecturers should actually use these technologies, with the result that the autonomy of practitioners tends to be undermined. Today, teachers and lecturers are in the invidious position of being judged by both the means and the results of their actions.

Make 'em laugh, make 'em laugh

Harnessing Technology (DfES 2005b) is the key document in which the government's current ICT strategy is encoded. In its foreword the former

Secretary of State for Education, Ruth Kelly, elaborates the idea of 'personalization', by which she means the notion that provision should be matched to the particular needs and interests of students. She, like Skinner, frames new technologies as a means of realizing this objective, while avoiding prohibitive additional funding. For Ruth Kelly, 'the effective use of interactive technologies is absolutely crucial' in bringing about personalization. ICT provides 'easy and efficient ways of keeping in touch, giving feedback on students' progress, and managing marking and assessment'. And by networking, provision learners will access a diverse virtual curriculum, enabling the consumer-student to make the choices that New Labour believes are so necessary.

According to Kelly, recent developments in ICT also address the problem of student motivation. Echoing Prensky she argues that,

> imaginative use of ICT should help engage more learners in the excitement of learning. Borrowing ideas from the world of interactive games, we can motivate even reluctant learners to practice complex skills and achieve much more than they would have through traditional means.
>
> (DfES 2005b: 3)

There are good reasons to question the wisdom of the approach advocated by Kelly. Ultimately, the idea that education might be more effective if it resembled a video game represents a defeatist approach. It may be true that learners, particularly within the compulsory sector, find their education tiresome, but it doesn't follow from this that we should use this sentiment as an organizing principle. Instead of accommodating to them, practitioners might alternatively consider how the case for education and training might be made more convincing.

The notion of personalization might also be questioned for its misrepresentation of the actual content of education and training. While effective lecturers do indeed deal with the distinct learning requirements of those they are instructing, they do so not as an end in itself, but in order to lead them to skills and bodies of knowledge that are in fact impersonal, or suprapersonal, insofar as they represent agreed social standards. The notion of personalization, by contrast, seems to position education as a form of self-expression.

The promotion of ICT within further education

While New Labour's main focus, in terms of policy, has been schools, FE colleges have not, in spite of the nominal independence granted by incorporation, been immune to the trends discussed above. The government's post-16 e-learning strategy is, as one might expect, remarkably similar in content and tenor to its pre-16 e-learning strategy. It outlines four strategic objectives: to transform teaching and learning; to reach out via ICT to groups of 'hard-to-reach' learners; to facilitate co-operation between organizations so as to enable the 'personalization of provision' and to bring about greater efficiency within FE (BECTA 2005a).

Attached to these are six priorities by which those who are responsible for implementing the strategy will measure their success. Of most relevance to practitioners is priority 4, which includes a series of sub-targets. By 2008, for example, the strategy intends that 85 per cent of post-16 practitioners will be 'confident in using ICT and e-learning to deliver learning' and these skills will be embedded in lecturer training. Similarly, the strategy states, without irony, that 'All practitioners *will choose* to access online e-learning resources and guidance' (BECTA 2005a: priority 4, italics added).

ICT and lecturer training

A similar concern for ICT is in evidence with the Lifelong Learning Sector Skills Council, (LLSSC) the body responsible for training lecturers. Its specification of the capacities required of those who are entering the profession includes a willingness to apply these technologies. It states that FE lecturers should have,

> ... domain-wide knowledge and critical understanding [of] information technology and how it can be used to extend and enhance learning [as well as] generic knowledge of ... the information and learning technology support available to learners.
> (LLUK 2006: 5–13).

In addition to this, they are required to 'offer a range of flexible opportunities for learning including learning facilitated through information learning technology' (LLUK 2006: 15). Those that wish to be certified as qualified lecturers are also required to demonstrate an understanding of 'the role of information learning technology in creating new modes of learning that are attractive to potential learners' (LLUK 2006: 15).

ICT and inspection: non-adoption is not an option

As you might expect, ICT characteristically plays an important role within inspection. While OfSTED's key inspection instrument, the *Framework for Inspecting Colleges* (OfSTED 2006a), makes no explicit statement on ICT, its more weighty 36,000 word companion volume, the *Handbook for Inspecting Colleges* (OfSTED 2006b), makes a number of direct references to it. When describing what it believes to be effective practice, OfSTED makes the point that institutions will be judged on the extent to which learners use ICT resources, and that one of the criteria by which a lesson will be judged as good is evidence of 'interesting and relevant use of ICT'. Equally, at a course level, institutions will be evaluated according to the extent that 'ICT is used by learners as an integral part of their courses, where appropriate' (OfSTED 2006b: 57–8).

In a key section, it is argued that e-learning, 'should form part of the overall teaching and learning strategy for courses'. Furthermore, managers and practitioners are expected to take responsibility for this being tracked, signalled and reviewed in 'schemes of work, lesson plans, assignments, course reviews and staff development plans' (OfSTED 2006b: 59). While little in terms of justification is offered for this practice, OfSTED, echoing New Labour, declares that institutions must provide evidence that e-learning is being used to 'improve learners' understanding of topics or activities . . . their skills and their knowledge of the technology' and 'interest in their programme' (OfSTED 2006b: 59).

Taken together the policy framework detailed above, exerts significant and unproductive pressure on those who work and manage others in FE. While there is nothing wrong with expecting trainee lecturers to critically engage with new technologies, compelling the qualified has the immediate effect of undermining their sense of control, ownership and, indeed, responsibility for that which takes place in the classroom. In reality, it is clear that adoption is the only option. This heavy-handed approach is likely to engender tokenistic engagement, as it encourages practitioners to orient their energies to ensuring compliance with an externally imposed regulatory code, rather then considering and exploring how ICT might be integrated into their practice. This approach might have justification if there were clear evidence of ICT usage raising standards. As we shall see in the following section, the evidence is less than clear.

The actual impact of ICT on education and training: beyond the hype

The research literature relating to the impact of ICT on education and training is extensive in range and diverse in approach. It includes many detailed, small-scale, qualitative studies that have considered the impact of particular software packages in specific contexts. It also features large-scale quantitative studies, which have attempted to measure the overall impact of ICT across entire learning sectors.

Given the volume and complexity of this material, this chapter will not attempt to provide a comprehensive literature review. Rather, it will summarize and comment on four studies. These have been included for two reasons. First, they are all relatively large-scale in terms of their respective datasets. Consequently, they enable us to evaluate the often large-scale claims that are made in relation to the 'transformative' impact of ICT. Second, the studies illustrate the range of issues that are raised when one tries to answer this deceptively straightforward question: Do practitioners work more efficiently and effectively when they use ICT?

The first study to be considered was produced by the learning technologies research team at King's College, London, on behalf of BECTA (BECTA 2003). It usefully surveys the international literature, while also providing an overview of the BECTA's long-running *Impact* project. This has tracked the use of ICT in England's schools for more than a decade. After this, the work of the antipodean educational researcher, John Hattie, will be explored (Hattie 1999). Over a period of many years, Professor Hattie has attempted to draw together and summarize our collective knowledge of those factors that improve teaching and training. His method is termed 'meta-analysis', which is essentially the process of collating and synthesizing existing studies. By using this approach, Hattie has been able to put the various methods of raising teaching and lecturing standards, including ICT-based strategies, into an illuminating rank order of effectiveness. Following this, we will explore the work of Thomas Fuch and Ludger Woessmann (2004). Like the *Impact* projects, their study examines the effects of ICT on the delivery of school age core curriculum subjects, although their frame of reference is wider, including all participants in the Organization for Economic Co-operation and Development's Programme of International Student Assessment (PISA). Finally, we will end with a study produced by Cardiff University. This relates most directly to the work of practitioners in FE, as it explored the impact of ICT on the formal and informal educational experiences of adult learners (Selwyn *et al.* 2005).

The impact of ICT on attainment in England's schools

The BECTA report argues that studies of the impact of ICT on education generally report a positive correlation between access to ICT in schools and educational attainment. However, it adds that this generally optimistic picture needs to be balanced by an awareness of the fact that the most robust positive evidence relates to a small number of academic disciplines – English, maths and science – which have been most intensively resourced and studied at school level.

Even at this level, the report argues that the impact of ICT is uneven. In some subjects and at some levels there is indeed a statistically significant correlation between access to ICT and examination performance, but in some instances this is not significant. Indeed, one of the studies in the

Impact series notes that many institutions do exceptionally well without making extensive use of these technologies (BECTA 2002).

Usefully, the report also notes a tension between the scale and quality of the available data. Often those studies that are most robust in terms of sample size tend to be less useful in terms indicating which particular methods and applications have been effective. Consequently, studies of this type often provide little by way of direct guidance as to how ICT should be applied.

In addition to this, the report notes the difficulty of assessing any independent ICT effect, as this factor is just one of many variables in any given teaching or training situation. According to the team at King's there is a need for the research community to give greater attention to a range of factors beyond the simple provision of equipment, including the underlying methods employed by practitioners and the influence of the wider institutional context in which they operate.

All of this indicates that considerable caution should be exercised when making simplistic claims regarding the positive impact of ICT. There is indeed some evidence of ICT making a positive contribution to learning, although this depends on the context in which it is applied.

Key influences on student learning

In 1999, John Hattie was inaugurated as a Professor of Education at the University of Auckland (Hattie 1999). At this event he presented a lecture that usefully summated his analysis of 180,000 studies of those factors which influence student learning. Interestingly, he found that almost all educational initiatives have some positive effect, such as those that are designed to enhance the quality of lecturer feedback, which registered the most significant impact, through to approaches that individuate teaching provision, which scored among the lowest.

Hattie's overall point is that when making judgements about the impact of any educational initiative, it is important to consider the question of magnitude. According to his study the average effect size of all initiatives is 0.4. Without going into the intricacies of what this represents statistically, this indicates that almost all educational initiatives have been shown to have some positive impact on student performance.

In his lecture Hattie also looked specifically at ICT. On the basis of 31 separate meta-analyses of some 17,952 studies of technology-related initiatives, he concluded that the average impact of ICT initiatives is below average. In relative terms, promoting ICT may therefore be counterproductive in that resources might be productively invested in other more important aspects of learning.

As the BECTA report makes clear, studies that operate at such high levels of generality risk losing sight of the arguably more important specific details that enable us to consider how practice might be improved. Nevertheless, Hattie's work usefully draws our attention to the importance of considering the relative efficacy of one approach over another. When considering how standards of lecturing might be raised, we must ask ourselves if the strategies being proposed are those that are likely to have the greatest possible return on the resources invested.

Computers and student learning

The next study to be considered was produced by Thomas Fuchs and Ludger Woessmann in 2004. Like the *Impact* studies, it paid particular attention to compulsory education. It used data that had been generated as part of the European-wide PISA study of literacy and numeracy. For numeracy it sampled 96,855 students in 31 countries, and, for literacy, the results of 174,277 students in the same number of countries were considered.

On the basis of their analysis two key conclusions were drawn. First, there was a negative correlation between students' home access to ICT and educational performance, although this became positive when it was used for educational purposes. Second, there was a negligible positive association between access to ICT in schools and examination results, and performance in fact decreased when ICT was used excessively.

Fuchs and Woessmann are clear about the limitations of their findings. They argue that their study does not indicate how ICT might be used effectively. Rather, their evidence demonstrates that ICT as it is currently applied across the schools of the European Union is not significantly enhancing results. They also point out that use of ICT can be a proxy for more important determinants. It may not, for example, be the case that excessive ICT usage lowers performance, rather that low performers are drawn to use ICT more frequently than the more able.

One clear message that can be drawn from this study is that there is nothing inherently positive about the provision of ICT resources: access does not necessarily improve results, if we are to judge this in terms of examination performance.

Adult learning and ICT

The final empirical study that will be considered was produced by Cardiff Universities' Adults Learning @ Home research group (Selwyn *et al.* 2005). This investigated the extent which ICT, within FE, has transformed the adult population's engagement with both training and education. Surveys were completed with 1101 adults, and were complemented by 100 semi-structured interviews.

The findings of this study would seem to indicate the current impact of ICT provision within FE has been minimal, at least in the south western locales in which respondents were based. It found that 46 per cent of respondents had engaged with formal learning after leaving school. Within this, the key determinants of engagement was not access to ICT, but the affluence of the families into which the respondents had been born. ICT access, the researchers conclude, had a 'non-effect' on 'patterns of partici-pation' (Selwyn *et al.* 2005: 22).

In terms of ICT usage the report found that 48 per cent of respondents had not used a computer within the past year, and of those who had, word-processing was the most popular activity. Twenty-one per cent indicated that they had used a computer during a post-compulsory learning episode, although very few had been taught via ICT. Only 6 per cent indicated that they had used the Internet more than rarely for 'participation in educational courses' (Selwyn *et al.* 2005: 22–23).

From all of this, two things become clear. If this evidence is indicative of the national picture, it is clear that for many learners ICT is being used superficially. Equally, the study makes it clear that ICT is not in itself a stimulus to learning. As the reports authors argue, for: ' . . . most of respondents who were informal learners there was little evidence that ICTs had create a new-found desire for learning – rather it was building on previous learning behaviours and disposition' (Selwyn *et al.* 2005: 25).

So does ICT transform learning?

These studies enable a number of conclusions to be drawn. First, it is clear that there is no simple association between ICT provision and improved performance in examination results. In some academic subjects at some levels there is a correlation, but it is not always clear *how* the use of ICT has raised performance. Equally, there is evidence of ICT use being associated with low levels of performance. For this reason, studies suggest that decisions made by practitioners continue to be important. Second, studies of the impact of ICT suggest that this may not always be the most effective strategy for raising standards, relative to other possible approaches. Finally, it appears that, at this time the provision of ICT within FE is not yet feeding through to learner experiences, or stimulating a 'desire for learning'.

Admittedly, these empirical studies relate to how ICT has been used, which does not tell us how ICT might be used. We know from these studies that, on its own, ICT does not transform standards of provision. So it seems that any strategy for change within FE must account for the wide range of factors that contribute to quality in learning. Considering how we might attempt to do this within FE is the topic of the final section.

Whither the digital learning revolution?

ICT is, as is often said but rarely understood, nothing more than a tool. It can be used in many ways, but it has no essential, fixed or predetermined use or effect. As soon as we see ICT as the solution, we can be sure that we have a problem. If we take this proposition seriously, it follows that the provision of ICT does not, in itself, constitute a strategy for change within FE. In other words, ICT cannot substitute for our pedagogic thinking.

This argument will not persuade many managers within the sector, who too often reach for the silicone snake oil. They have a variety of motives. The dull-witted and bullish among them do so because they have adopted the government's fetish: they really do believe that ICT will transform lecturing. Weaker managers promote ICT because it is easier to put new computers and software into workrooms, and in doing so to *appear* to manage, than it is to convince their colleagues of the need for change. Survivors do so to ensure that they are compliant with the code of the quangocracy.

Whatever the motives, the manner in which ICT is promoted within FE tends to be sub-rational and, as a result, draconian. Rarely is a convincing case put for using ICT. One reason for this is that advocates of ICT often rely on ICT theory. We should be clear that there can be no discrete, stand-alone, theory of instructional technology, as any act of instruction includes more factors than ICT. Consequently, the case for ICT can only ever be as secure as the wider pedagogic framework in which it is located. And because we live in a technopoly, our appreciation of, and engagement with, these wider frameworks is often feeble.

As result of this, ICT is for the most part imposed on staff: often through monitoring, sometime through hectoring, occasionally by more aggressive disciplinary procedures. This approach has perverse outcomes. Most immediately, it depletes the most powerful and pivotal resource at a manager's disposal: their staff's capacity and desire, to engage with, or experiment, and take responsibility for their work. Enforced adoption also results in tokenistic application. The use of ICT becomes just another item of quangocratic code with which practitioners need to evidence compliance.

What this means is that ICT is rarely used effectively, let alone with conviction and daring. As a result, the returns on ICT investment are characteristically meagre which confirms, and spreads, cynicism in relation to the technology.

There is an alternative. Managers working within the sector should bin all adoption strategies that seek to erase, or minimize, the decision-making capacity of their staff. Instead of using ICT as a technology of control, as a mechanism for teacher-proofing their institutions, it should only be used in ways that maximize practitioner autonomy. Commitment and engagement from staff requires that lecturers are the masters of their own pedagogy.

At the same time, lecturers have adjustments to make. ICT might not be transforming FE, as New Labour and its quangocracy often claims, but it really does extend its means. Virtual learning environments and microworlds offer exciting new possibilities. For this reason, practitioners have a responsibility to rise above the positions of aloof, feline disinterest or mulish rejection. The technology, if not the hype, demands and deserves our serious, creative and sustained attention.

It is hoped that this chapter has provided a convincing critique of the 'digital learning revolution' and that it has been clear that the author does not extend this to the technology itself. It is the social practices that are at fault. None of this should be taken to mean that more mundane questions related to technological access are unimportant, or have been resolved. A recent BECTA report makes it clear that levels of provision have not matched the recent growth in student numbers in FE, with the result that the ratio of computers to students has in fact decreased in the past two years (BECTA 2005b). If Senior Management Teams spent more time addressing these issues and less time meddling in the classroom decisions of practitioners, then perhaps there would be less beastliness in the Kingdom of FE.

A short chronology of ICT

1920s	Sidney Pressey develops the teaching machine.
1940s	During World War Two the American military responds to the need to train new recruits by developing an extensive range of audio-visual teaching materials.
1958	Skinner publishes *Teaching Machines* and initiates a related research programme at Harvard University.
1960s	International Business Machines (IBM) develops the IBM 1500 Instructional System, the first purpose built multi-user teaching computer.
1973	University College London is one of the first international connections to ARPANET, an early version of the Internet.
Late 1970s	IBM and Apple develop the personal computer (PC); basic drill and practice programmes are developed for schools.
1980	Government launches the Micro Electronics Program, which will enable schools to purchase hardware developed by Acorn and Research Machines, and software developed by teachers.
1980s	More computer-based tutorials and learning games begin to be developed by commercial software manufacturers.

cont.

1984	Joint Academic Network (JANET) is built to connect UK universities to each other.
1988	*Education Reform Act*: ICT will now formally become part of the modified technology section of the national curriculum.
Late 1980s	Early versions of what will come to be called virtual learning environments are developed.
1990s	Multimedia PCs are developed and are increasingly used in schools and colleges.
1997	The Stevenson Commission publishes its inquiry into ICT in UK schools.
2000	Interactive whiteboards and virtual learning environments begin to be adopted by schools and colleges.
2001	99 per cent of secondary and 96 per cent of primary schools are connected to the Internet.
2005	BECTA publishes its *Post-16 E-Learning Strategy*.

Key readings

BECTA (2005a) *Post-16 E-Learning Strategy*. Available at: http://becta.org.uk /post16elearningstrategy/overview.cfm

BECTA (2005b) *ICT and E-Learning in Further Education*. London: BECTA.

DfES (2005) *Harnessing Technology*. London: DfES.

Fuchs, T. and Woessmann, L. (2004) *Computers and Student Learning: Bivariate and Multivariate Evidence on the Availability and Use of Computers at Home and at School*. Available at: http://papers .ssrn.com/sol3/papers .cfm?abstract_id=619101

Hattie, J. (1999) *Key Influences on Student Learning*. Available from the 'Papers to Download' section at: www.arts.auckland.ac.nz/staff/index .cfm?P=3694

Independent ICT in Schools Commission (Stevenson Commission) (1997) *Information and Communications Technology in UK Schools: An Independent Inquiry*. Available at: http://who.ultralab.anglia.ac.uk /stevenson/ICT.pdf

Jonassen, D., Carr, C. and Yueh, H-P. (1998) *Computers as Mind Tools for Engaging Learners in Critical Thinking*. Available at: www.coe.missouri .edu/~jonassen/Mindtools.pdf

Postman, N. (1987) *Amusing Ourselves to Death*. London: Methuen.

Postman, N. (1993) *Technopoly: The Surrender of Culture to Technology*. New York, NY: Vintage Books.

Prensky, M. (2001) *Digital Natives, Digital Immigrants.* Available at: www.marcprensky.com

Selwn, N., Gorard, S. and Furlong, J. (2005) *Adult Learning @ Home.* Available at: www.esrc.org

Skinner, B. F. (1958) *Teaching Machines.* Available at: www.bfskinner .org/teachingmachines1958.pdf

5   Key skills or key subjects?
Alec Turner

'Today', the teacher announced as he pressed the play button on the tape recorder, 'We are going to listen to a rather unusual, contemporary, musical composition.' We listened to four minutes of silence.

'Today', the teacher announced as he pressed the play button on the VCR, 'We are going to witness the attempts of a family to bury their son.' The students watched, mesmerized.

'Today', the teacher announced, 'We will be doing some exercises on sentence structure and, particularly, the correct use of the comma.' 'Whatever', came the only response.

Key skills lessons? Not exactly. In the first example, I was a 17-year-old business studies student in a liberal studies class at my further education (FE) college, 35 years ago. There were Wednesday afternoons when our teacher must have despaired as he bravely attempted to open our eyes, and other senses, to areas of human activity we knew little or nothing of. Equally, he often caught us in a receptive mood, and that afternoon was one of those occasions. The discussion soon switched from one of speculating over the composer's intentions to rich and vivid accounts of what had gone through individuals' minds during those four minutes. An hour and a half flashed by.

Twenty years later, I was the trainee teacher pressing the VCR button in the second example. By this time, liberal studies had disappeared from vocational curricula in colleges and had been replaced by general and communication studies. The syllabus I was presented with involved completing application forms, compiling a CV, writing letters of complaint and other assorted banalities. I was confronted by a class of level 3 mature motor mechanics aged 25-plus who derived much greater pleasure in hurling racial taunts at each other than in attending to the finer points of their CVs. In desperation, I showed them footage of the attempted funeral of an IRA volunteer, which involved three days of mass confrontation between the Nationalist community in West Belfast and the RUC, as the family struggled to get the coffin, draped in IRA regalia, out of the house and up the road to the cemetery. Given that these lads had grown up on North London housing estates during the Thatcher years, they were no strangers to a bit of civil disobedience, but the video opened their eyes. The arguments over self-determination and civil rights then raged. Measured in terms of progressing their CVs, the lesson was an abject failure. In terms of communication, it was a resounding success. The final example comes from a communication key skills class at Anytown FE college this year and should, more accurately, have been labelled a basic skills or adult literacy class.

In 2006, just about the only elements on the timetable of an average 17-year-old FE student, in addition to their main vocational classes, are three weekly sessions in each of the key skills of communication, application of number and ICT. In terms of content, the newly qualified lecturer will be told the byword is 'relevance'. For anyone whose brain has not been totally hollowed out by current educational jargon, they will realize that the concept of relevance is actually the antithesis of everything education stands for. Relevance belongs to the realm of who we are and what we do. Education is about developing lines of enquiry and critical thinking into what we are not and what we know not. Education, then, should be concerned with the unknown and with stretching boundaries, while relevance necessarily limits us to the everyday and the street in which we live.

Key skills became a curriculum component for many 16–19-year-old, full time FE students as a result of the inception of Curriculum 2000 and are the subject of this chapter. What will undoubtedly be of concern to the lecturer entering FE for the first time, will be the systems and processes associated with key skills and what is expected of them. To simply take them as read would represent a failure in terms of understanding; an understanding which can only be reached in conjunction with an appreciation of the historical development of skills-based curricula and associated critiques. That policy-makers have been successful in driving these curricula into a dominant position is not in question. A wider understanding of the consequences of that fact is both helpful and illuminates how the very notion of skill has been diminished as a result. What follows is a brief account of the ascendancy of skills in post-16 vocational curricula from a historical perspective.

Although the acquisition of employability skills by pupils at the lower end of the achievement scale has long been a (perhaps not so) discreet concern for governments, that concern was made absolutely explicit by the then Prime Minister, James Callaghan, in his Ruskin College speech of 1976 in the face of British economic decline, which was noted by many commentators (Benn and Fairley 1986; Holt 1987; Hodgson and Spours 2002). As youth unemployment rocketed to unimaginable levels in the 1980s, concerns over both vocational and academic curricula post-16 in terms of their ability to deliver employability mounted, leading to a skills debate which is still ongoing and, from which, key skills emerge. If we understand key skills as a partial settlement of that debate, then, in my opinion, it is a flawed settlement.

A report by the Further Education Unit (FEU), *A Basis For Choice* (1979), led to the development of core skills in a range of vocational courses for school under-achievers, including the Unified Vocation Preparation (UVP), the Youth Training Scheme (YTS) and the Certificate of Pre-Vocational Education (CPVE). 'They were for those who did not have sufficient qualifications, skills or experience to enter the labour market directly . . . In the first stage of their development, therefore, core/key skills were associated with an idea of remedial education' (Hodgson and Spours 2002: 30). While this does go some way to expressing what was happening, it would have been useful to add that this teenage labour market was shrinking to the point of non-existence and the schemes in question were commonly understood to be exercises in youth containment. At this stage, core skills focused on the supposed lack of communication, personal, social and life skills of the young unemployed moving some to conclude that, '. . . our official conceptions of skill became loosened from their traditional moorings and were allowed to drift more freely' (Hayward and James 2004: 56).

As economic recession continued throughout the 1980s, leading industrial and educational bodies were noting differences in vocational education and training with mainland Europe. For instance, in France, '*culture generale*' denoted a system whereby a core, general education played a significant part in vocational curricula, while, 'The Germans have a concept of "formation", of combined education and training of the whole person' (Maclure 1986, cited in Holt 1987: 168). While these concepts and practices were being played out at a higher level, the point to understand was that these examples pointed to a more thoroughgoing vision of vocational education requiring broader learning, over a longer period rather than some quickfix thrown-together skills agenda.

In 1989, at the behest of Education Secretaries, Ken Baker and, subsequently, John MacGregor, a host of bodies, including Her Majesty's Inspectorate (HMI), the National Curriculum Council (NCC), the Schools Examinations and Assessment Council (SEAC) and the National Council for Vocational Qualifications (NCVQ) published reports recommending the inclusion of a range of core skills into post-16 curricula, while the Confederation of British Industry (CBI) published its own document, *Towards a Skills Revolution* (1989), advocating much the same within vocational training (Halsall and Cocket 1996; Hodgson and Spours 2002). Such a coalescence of opinion among this number of organizations was, perhaps, quite unprecedented. However, it must be noted that there were several different agendas at play related to ideology and interest, as well as differing definitions of core skills (Kelly 2001). Additionally, despite many references to all post-16 curricula, many pointed to the difficulties of implementation in such a well-established curriculum as that for A levels, to the extent that, 'These practical issues, together with the traditional fear of diluting A levels ensured that . . . the main developments in this area continued to be taken forward in the vocational track throughout the 1990s' (Hodgson and Spours 2002: 31).

With the introduction of General National Vocational Qualifications (GNVQs) by the NCVQ in 1993, core skills finally took their place on full time courses of education within FE colleges, taking the form of three mandatory skills: communication, application of number and IT, with three optional skills of: problem-solving, working with others and improving own learning and performance. The early years of the growing, new vocationalism in the form of GNVQs and work-based training in the form of National Vocational Qualifications (NVQs), raised many concerns over low completion rates in the case of the former and variable quality and standards in the latter, provoking the Department for Education and Employment (DfEE) to call for reviews of both: first, Beaumont's *Review of 100 NVQs and Scottish Vocational Qualifications* (SVQs) in 1995, and Ron Dearing's influential *Review of Qualifications for 16–19-Year-Olds* in 1996. Dearing's focus during the review was to create parity of esteem between the three pathways of academic and vocational education and vocational training, leading him to delineate National Awards at Entry, Foundation, Intermediate and Advanced levels embracing the three pathways. At every level, he emphasized the essential nature of key skill development and suggested that national awards could not be achieved at intermediate and advanced levels unless competence had been demonstrated in those skills. Although not all Dearing's recommendations were taken on board by the Government, under the aegis of Curriculum 2000, the three key skills would be offered to all post-16 students but without the element of compulsion.

Although undergoing minor revisions to their specifications in 2004, these are the animals we are now dealing with. Having sketched their development over a period of time, it may seem appropriate, at this stage, to consider what it means for those of us charged with their delivery. However, to do so would suggest an acceptance of their logic and validity within their own terms, which is far from the case.

Many commentators (Gregory 1997; Hyland and Johnson 1998; Hayward and James 2004) have developed substantial arguments regarding the coherence or value of key skills and, indeed, whether they are in fact key or skills at all. It would be useful, at this stage, to offer some definitions of key skills:

Key skills are described as skills that can be applied (and assessed) in a variety of settings which are relevant to an individual's circumstances. They are assessed at four, progressively difficult levels

(NFER 2003: 51)

Key skills are defined as generic and transferable skills that people can learn and develop in a wide variety of situations, whether in education or in the workplace

(Kelly 2001: 21)

The possession and development of sufficient knowledge, appropriate attitudes and experiences for successful performance in life roles. This includes employment and other forms of work; it implies maturity and responsibility in a variety of roles; and it includes experience as an essential element of competence

(Reece and Walker 1997: 204)

Many more examples could be given but it can be seen clearly from this small sample the different emphases placed upon learning and assessment, attitudes, skills and knowledge, and an apparent lack of consensus upon genericism and transferability.

Notwithstanding, significant differences in interpretation of what key skills actually are, all post-16, publicly funded learning providers, were exhorted to offer them and encourage their charges to participate and seek accreditation under the scheme. It would appear timely to unravel justifications offered by various individuals and bodies for contributing to the occurrence of such a blanket approach. 'Core Skills exist at each level of the NVQ/SVQ framework. Employers believe they should be defined as part of competence . . . There is a widely-held view that Core Skills are key to transferability' (Beaumont 1995: 15–16). Dearing is more explicit in linking key skills to a post-Fordist, globalized economy, in which the UK's competitive edge is seriously questioned. Referring to the National Targets for Education and Training, (NTET), in which 75 per cent of 19-year-olds should achieve level 2 in the three key skills and 35 per cent of 21-year-olds level 3, he says, 'These targets, for the year 2000, have already been surpassed by Germany and Japan. The Report also recognizes that in the future, relevant comparators will increasingly include the nations in the Far East . . .' (Dearing 1996: 3). Additionally, we find in the final report of the National Skills Task Force that, 'Employer survey confirms that employers continue to seek the key skills originally established by the National Council for Vocational Qualifications' (DfES 2000c: 3).

On the basis of such statements and the definitions previously outlined, it would appear to be the case that if young people are not given the opportunity to develop the three key skills, which are claimed to be both generic and transferable, they will be irresponsible, unable to contribute to adult society and the world of work, and the UK will become a third-rate nation as its economy declines. Clearly, the awesome impact of a deficit of key skills bears closer scrutiny.

Many academics and commentators take serious issue with the all-pervasive 'skills-talk' invading every aspect of FE curricula, a sector now dominated by sector skills councils (SSCs), the Learning and Skills Council (LSC) and the Department for Education and Skills (DfES). At the heart of these discussions vital questions are raised about the meaning and purpose of education. First among these, is that all students are entitled to an element of general education if they are to become active citizens, capable of exercising human and moral agency. Only through a deeper and broader understanding of the social and work worlds in which we operate, that is to say by developing a core of knowledge, can we critically assess situations and make reasoned and informed choices. It is interesting to note that both conservative and radical educators share this view. Smithers, for instance, is quite specific in terms of a general education content for vocational courses: 'Maths and English, certainly, science probably, civics, a foreign language, and the social sciences perhaps' (Smithers 1996: 13). Gregory, in his powerful argument for liberal education encompassing the arts and humanities, suggests that, '. . . students in a skills-based curriculum are not worth society's investment of any kind of education longer, broader or more liberating than the skills needed for an immediate job. The lesson here is profoundly undemocratic . . .' (Gregory 1997: 4). Sieminski, in a thorough exploration of the growing instrumentalist and competence-led changes of the 90s reminds us that, 'Until recently, students who worked towards a vocational education had opportunities to build on their general education and explore a range of issues through General and Communications Studies. Such subjects were seen to aid personal development . . .' (Sieminski 1993: 97).

Many more illuminating comments could be added here, but, in order to move the discussion forward, several strands of thought emerge: first, that a breadth of education is essential and a core of general education should be common to both academic and vocational pathways, or as Gregory neatly summates, 'the best education for any of us is the best education for all of us' (Gregory 1997: 4). Kelly edges us towards the notion of parity of esteem between both pathways by suggesting that Tawney resolved two contrasting models of education: the utilitarian and functionalist, sociocentric model geared to economic prosperity and the liberal, individualist model (education of the whole person), regarded as a resource for community and a benefit for the individual. His illustration for this resolution is that of French engineering schools in which there is, 'The belief that those with technical knowledge should be capable of good expression and communication, provided by a minimum of general, non-vocational education' (Kelly 2001: 23). Holt goes rather further in suggesting that established models of education in the UK generally fail to meet everyone's needs in that, 'Neither a purely vocational nor a purely epistemological approach can constitute a basis for an educational approach' (Holt 1987: 172). Hayward and James, in their deconstruction of the new skills talk and the introduction of core skills into mainstream curricula by the National Council for Vocational Qualifications (NCVQ) note that, 'In effect, NVQs downgraded knowledge in favour of competent task performance, while "core skills" acted as an impoverished surrogate in English vocational programmes for the general education normally available to European vocational students' (Hayward and James 2004: 59). Rather surprisingly, lead bodies in this country often refer to the UK's poor standing in OECD data relating to the proportion of the population that is vocationally qualified, and then appear to suffer a blind spot when examining the reasons why.

Having established the importance of a general education for all and the damaging consequences of it being sidelined for vocational students, we can now turn to a second emerging strand in the form of a critical questioning of the key skills concept. What constitutes skill, which are key and, by implication, are they transferable?

An examination of these questions is instructive as it serves to unravel terminology which, today, is widely accepted in an unquestioning fashion. In reference to the indiscriminate use of skills-talk, Hayward and James assert that, 'Indeed, it is hardly an exaggeration to say that "skill" has now become a universal grab-bag for any attribute that employers and policy-makers deem desirable in their ideal-typical, flexible employee . . .' (Hayward and James 2004: 69). Williams takes the political allusion a stage further,

> However, 'Skills For Employability' represents a major ideological shift. In the past, high unemployment or poor job opportunities would have been interpreted as a political problem, failure to invest or the mismanagement of the economy. By putting the focus on skills, the 'blame' for poor employment prospects is clearly shifted away from governments and on to individuals'
> (Williams 2005: 185)

Here we see justification for skills-talk being given economic, political and ideological expression. In practical terms, Hyland and colleagues (Hyland and Johnson 1998; Bolton and Hyland 2003; Hyland and Merrill

2003) go to great lengths to ridicule the increasing use of the term 'skills' to describe dispositions, attitudes and abilities, and indeed the very notion of key skills; summarizing,

> If key skills are meant to pick out general, transferable skills which are domain-independent (and clearly such wide-ranging applicability is exactly what much skill-talk is wanting to prescribe) then such skills can be shown – on both logical and empirical grounds – to be entirely illusory.
>
> (Hyland and Johnson 1998: 164)

Others point to simplistic, competence-based assessment within narrow, prescribed standards as relatively worthless in the absence of values or ethics. Gregory, the arch-advocate of liberal education, expresses the coalescence of skills and knowledge as lying, '. . . not merely in knowing how to do this or that as a skill but lies instead in knowing why this or that skill is important and why it is worth doing well in the first place' (Gregory 1997: 14).

Given the necessarily brief account of these arguments, readers might be forgiven for assuming that I am simply pursuing my own agenda in claiming that key skills are a vacuous construction, serving no recognizable educational purpose. There is, in fact, a mass of evidence to suggest that the claims of government, and various lead bodies, for the elevation of key skills into a position of centrality within the education system for the benefit of the national economy and individuals alike, is a myth.

At the level of employment, a skills survey reported that 27 per cent of the workforce did not require a qualification in their jobs: more than double the number of the economically active population who were without a qualification. Additionally, the proportion of employees reporting a great deal of choice over the way they do their work, fell from 52 per cent to 39 per cent between 1986 and 2001 (Hayward and James 2004: 64). Meanwhile a survey of skill gaps, conducted by the DfEE in 1998, reported results in terms of ten work-based skills. Ninth and tenth were literacy and numeracy, both coming in below 20 per cent, while the other eight ranged from managing own development at 37 per cent to technical/practical skills at 64 per cent (DfEE 2000c: 24). These employers were, first and foremost, recording deficits in particular job skills and not underdeveloped 'skills' somehow overlooked in the classroom.

A similar overview of reviews in the educational field is equally contradictory. Notwithstanding the existence of core skills in communication and application of number, a national survey of GNVQs found that, 'Only a minority of GNVQ students are taking or retaking GCSEs in maths and English . . . However, the absence of formal programmes in maths and English may create problems in the future, especially given the numbers aspiring to higher education' (The Nuffied Foundation 1994: 55). Remarkably, in the workplace, where core/key skills are supposedly essential and reap benefits, Beaumont noted that as employers are the ultimate customer, they must decide whether these skills are included in NVQs/SVQs, on the basis of whether they are required to perform the occupation. 'Care needs to be exercised. Making them all mandatory could affect access' (Beaumont 1995: 15). With the onset of Curriculum 2000, Dearing must have been quite perplexed to find many of his recommendations regarding key skills rejected. Having suggested that national diplomas should become an overarching qualification bridging academic and vocational pathways, he went on to suggest that the level 3 diploma would only be awarded to students who had achieved the three key skills by means of standalone NVQ units or an AS key skills qualification, and similarly appropriate achievement would be required at level 2. Both the aspect of compulsion and the AS award were dismissed. Little noted was his recommendation that, 'Below A level it should be accepted that the GCSE develops general education as well as the practical application of skills, for example, in communication and application of number' (Dearing 1996: 9). Echoing the earlier GNVQ review, this eminently sensible proposition was dead in the water. Finally, a review of the working of key skills refers to ministerial guidelines supporting the view that, 'Where students are starting on advanced levels . . . they should be supported to gain at least one key skill at level 3' (QCA/ACCAC/CCEA 2003: 7). Clearly, key skills are not quite so essential if one out of three hits the mark.

What these quotes really reveal is the limiting nature of 'key skills' and the fact that they are not about a progression of learning at all but rather a system of certifying low achievement and failure at GCSE. Several commentators have validated this point in strong terms, '. . . the Curriculum 2000 agenda was likely to be flawed in these three respects: the emphasis on remediation skills and a deficit agenda; the role of assessment in the search for credibility; and the issue of external recognition as a voluntarist system' (Hodgson and Spours 2002: 35). This conclusion was reached on the basis of an historical analysis of the key skills agenda, while another writer makes the logical point,

> If key skills are so important, surely they should be embedded in the curriculum from infants school onwards . . . policy-makers have allocated responsibility for key skills mainly to the post-16 sector, accentuating the belief that the key skills project is a deficit-oriented policy
>
> (Eraut 1999: 5)

In a both perceptive and timely analysis of DfES documents relating to the skills agenda, Williams notes the heavy emphasis on excluded groups

and the way in which skills can be utilized in the enhancement of participation and social inclusion noting that,

> This targeting of education at a particular audience, those without
> a level 2 qualification, has a considerable impact upon the
> classroom practice of FE lecturers. It leads to an inevitable focus on
> basic skills . . . The problem here is not with teaching basic skills,
> but the fact that teaching anything beyond basic skills is called
> into question
>
> (Williams 2005: 189)

An overview of the data available on key skills nationally completely
substantiates the view already expressed that the key skills agenda is one of
remediation almost entirely conducted at the level of basic skills, if we
accept that level 2 key skills are somewhere around a GCSE D grade, a view
supported by ministerial guidelines previously referred to. By far, the main
take up of key skills has been in the FE sector with 51 per cent of recorded
achievements between 2001 and 2003 (DfES 2004). The remainder are
accounted for in schools, sixth form colleges, private training providers and
within NVQs in the workplace. The figures are far from complete, but my
analysis suggests the following. For each of the three academic years
between 2000/1 and 2002/3, there were approximately one-third of a
million learners enrolled on level 2 and 3 vocational, full time courses in
the FE sector aged between 16 and 18, i.e. one million in total. A total of
297,000 key skill awards were made to FE students over the three years, with
92 per cent equally divided between levels 1 and 2, and just 8 per cent
awarded at level 3. A total of 188,000 students achieved awards, with just
34,000 achieving awards in all three. Please do not blink, just in case you
miss the economy collapsing. Clearly within the FE sector, take-up is
uneven as universal take-up by students on vocational courses would leave
success rates in single-figure percentages. National key skill performance
data informs us that success rates vary between 18 per cent for level 2
application of number and 27 per cent for level 1 communication. There is,
perhaps unsurprisingly, a wringing of hands in response to the fact that less
than 50 per cent of 16-year-olds achieve GCSE grade C in maths and
English. I have yet to witness a similar response to the dismal results in
relation to key skills.

The foregoing has looked at key skills historically, theoretically and by
viewing available data, leading to the conclusion that they are a
problematic and unnecessary intrusion into our students' increasingly
limited learning time and, as yet, nothing about the practice of delivering
key skills. This is partly because a consideration or discussion of delivery is
not a straightforward task. Nevertheless, I will now examine issues relating
to delivery and practice which will, of necessity, be largely experiential.

I should, first of all, lay my cards on the table. While I clearly have difficulty with the very concept of key skills, the fact that communication, application of number and ICT have been bracketed together only adds to these difficulties. The first are modes of expression, ways in which we convey information, ideas and meaning. The latter is simply a means of transmission. While a PC can transmit articulated ideas and expressed feelings, only we can give articulation and expression to those ideas and feelings. ICT is a tool like pen and paper or an abacus, however infinitely more complex that may be. As a key skills co-ordinator in my own college, I have argued that time devoted to ICT key skill would be far better spent on basic literacy and numeracy. It is difficult to see what value there is in students producing wonderfully presented, ICT-generated reports, which are quite incoherent in terms of content. An argument for retaining it for lower achieving students is 'they enjoy computers'. Frankly, if the content of education is to be primarily determined by whether or not something is enjoyable, then forget any further material advance in human societies. In fact, pandering to the notion that the focus of education should, first and foremost, be about how enjoyable it may be is, in many cases, the very reason for low achievement. It would seem far more appropriate that ICT should be harnessed as a tool in the development of basic skills. As a major literature review of basic and key skills concludes,

> Computers appear to be utilized in the provision of basic skills in three main ways:
> * to draw people into basic skills;
> * to overcome traditional barriers; and
> * to aid tuition/instruction.
>
> (NFER 2003: 23)

The assumption underpinning key skills and their delivery, is that candidates are in possession of a body of knowledge relating to language and its uses, and number-handling techniques and mathematical methods. Based on this assumption, the way in which candidates are assessed is on whether they are able to demonstrate their ability to apply this knowledge in various ways, either by way of verbal communication in a discussion, or by presenting data in an appropriate graphical form. This model is illustrated in Figure 5.1.

The accompanying text suggests that, '. . . key skills begin towards the middle of the continuum' (DfES 2002a: 10). It is at this point that the whole key skills edifice comes tumbling down. Closer scrutiny tells us that key skills level 1 is a contradiction in terms. At this level, students are lacking in basic skills and do not possess the necessary knowledge required for application. At level 2, this point is rather more contentious, being dependent upon one's own particular understanding of the meaning of

Led by the teacher	Guided by the teacher	Independent

What you need to know:	What you need to do:	What you must be able to demonstrate:
basic techniques and underpinning knowledge	practise and build your skills	that you can apply your skills in different contexts

Assesssed in the tests	feedback and advice from teacher	Assessed in your portfolio

Relates to Part A of the key skills units	Relates to Part B of the key skills units	

Source: DfES (2002a: 11)

Figure 5.1   Developing your key skills

'basic skills'. However, since in my experience many students with GCSE D grades, who should by implication be level 2 key skill candidates, find it difficult to structure sentences correctly or undertake, say, long division, then they are also suffering a basic skills deficit to some degree.

An acceptance of the above as an accurate reflection of reality presents the key skills practitioner and, theoretically, the providing institution (although this is not normally the case) with hugely challenging questions. The onus on the key skills practitioner to deliver stand-alone key skills sessions is to ensure that acceptable numbers of candidates complete their portfolios at level 1 (the vast majority, if not all, will have proxy exemption from external examination) and their portfolios at level 2, also passing relevant external examinations (the majority of candidates will not have exemptions). Inevitably, practitioners spend much time, on an assessment-led basis, highlighting errors as they occur, and insufficient time on teaching in order for students to acquire an adequate knowledge base. The time constraints can be formidable and teaching and learning is often compromised, not unsurprisingly, since the key skills doctrine implies no teaching whatsoever – *reductio ad absurdum*.

I can give this better expression with a recent example from my own teaching. Delivering key skill application of number to an intermediate level group, I had delivered several weeks of underpinning knowledge (quite insufficient given the ability of the students) before setting the students to work on a substantial assignment. Kathryn (a pseudonym) had not said a word during this time and, week after week, she refused to make a start. One day, she called me over for assistance. Sitting with her, I began to explain how to calculate actual measurements from a scale diagram. She burst into tears and exclaimed, 'I've always been bloody useless at this.' I spent the rest of the lesson with her, during which time she made progress. Since then, she has been very demanding, enthusiastic and hard-working. I know that if she does not get the attention she demands she will shut up shop as she appears to have done for substantial periods of her school days. I spend about one-quarter of the group's time with her, as she desperately tries to catch up. Can this be fair? What would you do? There are no easy answers.

There are clearly major questions regarding educational value as well as structural and institutional issues to be addressed if we are to move our students out of darkness. I would suggest that any practitioner new to FE should be asking searching questions when instructed to deliver key skills. While this may seem daunting, any curriculum manager with a genuine interest in students' progress will listen sympathetically to the raising of valid issues by a new and enthusiastic member of staff expressing interest in and concerns about their practice. Think about the following:

- Students should be streamed into key skills groups according to relevant GCSE grade rather than simply staying with their vocational studies group.
- English and maths specialists should be consulted over appropriate delivery modes and times.
- Detailed schemes of work should be available for different key skill levels, drawn up in consultation with appropriate subject specialists.
- Wherever key skills groups embrace students who do not speak English as a first language or who have statemented learning difficulties, then an ESOL specialist or learning support tutor should be available as required.
- Substantial training should be available from subject specialists in techniques, strategies and methods in delivering language and number (we are all sentient beings with thoughts and feelings, but that does not lend us an innate ability to teach psychology).

This last point is crucial as it does challenge the key skill doctrine. Notwithstanding the fact that the need for training is widely recognized, hence, 'The most successful organizations ensure that they develop the capacity to deliver key skills through promoting the professional development of their teaching staff' (NFER 2003: 82–3), the problem that you are likely to face is that any training you are offered will be related to portfolio-building, cross-referencing, assessment, opportunities for integration and methods of tracking progress and achievement. Key skills delivery takes on the appearance of a bureaucratic and technical exercise, devoid of any content. I and colleagues recently attended training on entering students for online external examination. Training has never been offered on how we might prepare students for those examinations.

In general, then, at levels 1 and 2 key skills, their delivery (teaching) should be seen, essentially, as the development of basic skills. This is vital at level 1, otherwise students progressing to level 2 without the inconvenience of having to pass an external examination will find themselves a country mile away from understanding the level 2 examination, let alone completing it. Interestingly, application of number key skill examinations were recently extended from allowing one hour for completion to one and a quarter hours, presumably because of the appalling failure rate. It didn't seem to occur to anyone deciding this that prolonging the time allowed did not represent a solution to the knowledge deficit of students entered for the examinations. Basic skills instruction at the level 2 phase is equally essential, then, if students are to achieve.

It is possible, however, to approach delivery rather differently when working with level 3 vocational students. The majority of students at this level will be enrolled on level 2 key skills (there are very few offers of level 3 around, clearly) and many will be exempt from the examinations by virtue of prior achievement at GCSE. At this point, we can perhaps return to the seemingly outdated notion that education is something capable of transforming young people's lives rather than simply a process of churning out phalanxes of young adults destined to take up their predetermined, relatively low-status roles in society with the requisite number of boxes ticked and accompanying certificates. We must, therefore, view key skills as a part of that process and take the opportunities that exist to engage with subject matter that goes beyond the banal and narrow boundaries of their vocational courses. This is not necessarily going to be an easy approach but, in much the same way that education should not be easy for the student, why should it be any easier for the classroom practitioner?

It is certainly more straightforward to apply the principle of broadening knowledge and understanding to the key skill of communi-cation, rather than to application of number. At level 2, a student is required to research two documents as information sources, which will be used as a basis for undertaking one or more of the other tasks, which are to participate in a group discussion, make a presentation and produce two pieces of written work. The subject matter is not specified and the common temptation (if not instruction from on high) is to stick with the students' own life experiences or what they should know for their vocational studies – a situation where students learn absolutely nothing and leading to an abundance of portfolio work on rap music and health and safety at work. The dogma of relevance is the antithesis of education. On the contrary, there are opportunities to examine major contemporary issues, such as the invasion of Iraq, the pros and cons of promoting multiculturalism or questions of individual liberty, such as a public smoking ban or the increased use of anti-social behaviour orders (ASBOs).

Similarly, within the key skill of application of number, the utilization of official data can open up an understanding of the world of which the student would otherwise be blissfully unaware. Domestically, data can lead to an understanding of health inequalities and income differentials, raising questions about poverty, gender, ethnicity and so on. Internationally, data on life expectancy, fertility rates and GDP, can raise understanding and awareness of the range of conditions in which people live and development (*sic*) issues. There is no shortage of the number-handling techniques that can be derived from and applied to data sets in order to meet specified criteria. With an imaginative and creative approach along these lines, bridges from narrow vocationalism can be made with culture. Questions of historical development, social power, morality and ethics, can be aired and discussed in order to lift students out of and beyond their present, limited world view.

Within the narrow confines of the notion of transferability espoused by the likes of the DfES and QCA, these suggestions do not, of course, sit easily. However, I would argue that the student who can make sense of competing claims for the advantages or otherwise of multiculturalism and critically analyse-related documents, or who is better able to understand the key determinants of poverty, is far better placed to understand and analyse a range of other different situations and settings than the student who has drawn up a health and safety policy for a residential care home and can calculate the cost of a carpet and underlay. What do you think?

If key skills are, as I would contend, a flawed concept requiring a remedial approach, which is most certainly what they are not supposed to be, then that leaves practitioners to make the best of a bad job. We are left in a situation where we wish to develop our students' knowledge and understanding but the dominant ethos requires us to aid our students' completion of minimal portfolios and rehearse for multiple-choice tests which, in fact, test very little in a meaningful way. These contradictions and banalities are widely understood by providing institutions, with practitioners and students marginalizing them or, at best, paying lip service to their demands.

It would appear that there has been a somewhat belated understanding of this within the corridors of power and the successors to key skills are about to make an appearance. Mike Tomlinson's report on the 14–19 qualifications framework (DfES 2004d) has moved through an Implementation Plan (DfES 2004e) to its final incarnation in the *Further Education: Raising Skills, Improving Life Chances* White Paper (DfES 2006a). From 2008, vocational education will take the form of specialized diplomas designed around 14 occupational groupings. At levels 2 and 3, some 30 per cent of learning will be 'core' learning as opposed to 'specialized' learning and will include an extended project, core knowledge, skills and attributes, and three functional skills: mathematics, communication and literacy, and ICT. By the time all specialized diplomas have been launched in 2010, key skills should, thankfully, be dead in the water.

However, whether or not the emergence of functional skills will present greater opportunities for practitioners to help their students to develop and acquire knowledge and understanding of essential material, is a matter for conjecture at this point. The early signs are not hopeful as the language of the last 30 years predominates to an ever-greater extent. For instance, we learn that, 'Our economic future depends upon our productivity as a nation. That requires a labour force with skills that match the best in the world' (DfES 2006a, foreword), and, 'We will introduce measures that put learners and employers in the driving seat in determining what is funded and how services are delivered' (DfES 2006a: 21). Whither the role of educators? With every statement, knowledge and professional practice are pushed out.

On a practical level, the body charged with developing the content of these skills explains, 'Functional skills are those core elements of English, maths and ICT that provide an individual with the essential knowledge, skills and understanding that will enable them to operate confidently, effectively and independently in life and at work' (QCA 2005b: 1). This, at least, is encouraging, in that knowledge and understanding do get a mention. Another positive indication is that, in two respects, Dearing's ideas of ten years ago are reconstituted. First, by comparison to many around him, he did not follow the skills agenda in a completely, anodyne manner and, in the same way that he desired compulsion, the award of diplomas will only occur on successful completion of functional skills at a level appropriate to that diploma. Furthermore, GCSE mathematics, English and ICT will be reformulated to include a core of functional skills which must be achieved as elements within that GCSE. The fear here is that we might be witnessing a dumbing-down as the term 'functional' certainly implies. After all, an ability to merely function represents a pretty meagre aspiration.

Optimistically, standards will be more or less adhered to and providing institutions will be forced to take these 'skills' seriously in terms of providing qualified staff with the necessary training and time to do the job properly, otherwise success rates on diplomas will plummet to a level last seen with the introduction of GNVQs. Within the next few months, we will be better placed to judge, as the first reformulated GCSEs roll out in September 2007.

Whatever the demands of your current teacher training programme in relation to literacy, numeracy, basic or key skills, you have only just begun, as this area within further education is a movable feast for the foreseeable future.

Chronology of key skills

1976	James Callaghan, PM, delivers Ruskin College Speech.
1978	Training established for unemployed young people; Youth Opportunities Programme (YOP) developed by the Manpower Services Commission (MSC).
1979	*A Basis for Choice* published by the Further Education Unit introduces the concept of core skills.
1983	YOP is transformed into the Youth Training Scheme (YTS) with college-based learning including core skills.
1985	Certificate of Pre-vocational Education as full time course with heavy emphasis on core and other 'skills'.
1986	Business Technology and Education Council (BTEC) launches 'common skills' in its full time vocational courses.
1990	National Curriculum Council responds to the Secretary of State with the suggestion that six core skills should be included in post-compulsory curriculum.
1992	NCVQ launches GNVQ courses with three mandatory and three optional core skills.
1996	School Curriculum and Assessment Authority (SCAA) releases Dearing Report with recommendations for three compulsory key skills at level 2, and the same or a free standing AS key skills at level 3.
1999	Qualifications & Curriculum Authority (QCA) releases definitive list of three skills and the 'broader' (often termed 'softer') key skills.
2000	Curriculum 2000 launched, encouraging learning providers to offer key skills.
2004	DFES releases report, *14–19 Curriculum and Qualifications Reform* (Tomlinson Report) with recommendation that three functional skills comprise major part of 'core' learning and achievement at level 2 in all three required for the award of a level 2/3 diploma.
2006	14–19 education and skills White Paper.
2007	First pilots of functional skills.
2008	National roll-out of functional skills.

Key readings

For a thorough account of employer/MSC-led unemployed youth training schemes in FE colleges, see Caroline Benn and John Fairley (1986) *Challenging the MSC on Jobs, Education and Training*. London: Pluto.

For historical accounts of the discussion and developments of core/key skills, see Ann Hodgson and Ken Spours (2002) Key skills for all? The key skills qualification and Curriculum 2000, *Journal of Education Policy*, 17(2): 29–47.

For a philosophical argument for general education, see Marshall Gregory (1997) Skills versus scholarship or liberal education knows a hawk from a handsaw. Paper presented at the Humanities and Arts Higher Education Network Conference; 17 January.

For a critique of 'skills' and transferability, see Terry Hyland and Steve Johnson (1998) Of cabbages and key skills: exploding the mythology of core transferable skills in post-school education, *Journal of Further and Higher Education*, 29(2): 163–72.

For an account of the conceptual confusion around the term 'skill' see Joanna Williams (2005) Skill as metaphor: an analysis of terminology used in *Success For All* and *21st Century Skills, Journal of Further and Higher Education*, 29(2): 181–90.

6   The rise and rise of credentialism

Neil Davenport

From parenting classes to pre-retirement courses, every aspect of life must now be supervised and assessed. Students are over-assessed. Lecturers are over-assessed and over-inspected. The rise of what is called 'credentialism' – seeking more and more qualification in more and more areas of life – seems unstoppable. There is a well-known and growing academic literature examining and criticizing the obsession with qualifications (Dore 1976, 1997; Collins 1979; Bills 1988). To no avail, in the real world credentialism continues to be a major theme with government ministers and directors of businesses and employer-bodies demanding more and better qualifications to close supposed 'skill gaps'. This chapter will examine the range of qualifications and the forces behind 'credentialism' in further education (FE). 'How to assess' is a common theme dominating text books in FE but over-assessment and the rise of credentialism is rarely explained. Credentialism may not be much discussed in the FE staff room but it is increasingly important as the proposed 14–19 'diploma' which, despite some fears, is now expected to replace A levels within ten years, embodies developments that radically extends previous forms of credentialism.

The progress of students or pupils has always been recorded in some form. Whether it was school reports or end of year exams and their associated certificates, a measurement of student strengths and weaknesses was always deemed an important part of the education system. As we shall see in this chapter, what has driven the form that assessment takes has often been motivated by factors external to the educational system. In particular, in order to understand why there is such an emphasis on credentialism today, we need to take a step back from narrow pedagogic debates and locate it in broader discussions on the role of FE today.

From a broader perspective, this chapter aims to trace the development of assessment within FE. We will examine the impact of educational reforms in the 1960s, whereby FE begins to change its 'stop-gap' nature – responding to immediate and local needs – and to develop more systematically under government direction into an important sector within the UK education system. That shift becomes embodied in a gradual shift from talking about 'technical colleges' to 'further education colleges' which was completed shortly after incorporation in 1993. It is not a mere change of name – the narrow vocational function of the 'tech' had ended.

However, we are not writing a history of qualifications offered in FE, except to set the background for New Labour's ongoing educational reforms which, since 1997, have ensured that FE has come into its own. Far from being the 'Cinderella' of the education system, FE is now seen as a vital social institution that will transform young people and adults into model citizens. The key to enabling this development is the rise of official supervision, endless assessments and further credentials.

The post-war period

The form of assessment we understand today, and one that continues to impact on FE, emerged in the post-war years. There was a demand from wider society that some type of universal examination system was required that could provide equality of opportunity. Essentially, the working classes wanted an examination system whereby they could be assessed on an equal footing to the upper echelons of society (until this time, education was the preserve of the elites). This universalism was reflected in the name of this academic qualification, the General Certificate in Education or GCE.

The GCE was originally introduced in England, Wales and Northern Ireland in 1951 replacing the older School Certificate (SC) and the Higher School Certificate (HSC). It was intended to cater for the increased range of subjects available to pupils since the school leaving age was raised from 14 to 15, in 1947. The examinations were graded into ordinary level for 16-year-olds (O levels), and advanced level for 18-year-olds (A levels). There was also an intermediate level, advanced/ordinary level (AO level) and a higher special paper (S level). By the early 1960s, O and A levels were offered in FE colleges for 16–19-year-olds, and also to mature students.

At first A levels only distinguished between a pass and a fail, although fails were divided into two types: one meaning that the student had failed a subject at A level but passed at the O level equivalent of that subject, and the other meaning that the student had not passed at either A level or O level. In 1953, another grade was introduced: the distinction, for high passes. Due to complaints from universities that the grading system was not specific enough to identify the students they wanted, a grading scale close to the current one was created in 1963, which retained an O level pass between the grades E and F (fail).

Before the revised A levels were introduced under Curriculum 2000 (see later in the chapter), candidates were expected to show a full understanding of a subject's syllabus over a two-year period. Compared to later forms of examinations, candidates were not continuously assessed but took two three hour papers at the end of their second year. The A levels were once considered the 'gold standard' of academic education because of the intensity of the syllabus content covered. They were also seen as a reliable indicator of a candidate's academic ability. Compared to later forms of assessments, O and A levels were broad but also rigorous. What has been forgotten since, however, is that A levels were an academic journey for the journey's sake, and not every aspect of the syllabus would be 'assessed' in the way A levels are today. This was because there was a widespread belief, particularly from the elites, that 'education for education's sake' should be the hallmark of the liberal education system. In recent years, though, A levels are considered too narrowly academic for the world of work. Ironically, as the assessment criteria for the new A level have increased, the actual academic content has rapidly diminished.

The New Right – education as skills training

The 1979 election victory of the Conservative Party is often seen as a watershed in changing the English education system, especially for the rise of credentialism. Many of the reforms that Conservative governments put in place, during the 1980s and 1990s, have continued to influence New Labour's approach to FE today. Nevertheless, the change in thinking from 'education for education's sake' to an increasingly instrumentalist approach to the FE sector, was first pioneered under the last Labour government of 1974/9. In 1976 the Labour Prime Minister, James Callaghan argued that education should 'contribute as much as possible to improving industrial performance and thereby increasing the national wealth' (Finn 1987: 48).

Callahan's 'Great Debate' on education simply chimed with nascent New Right thinking, which was that education should concentrate more on improving the skills of school leavers and the workforce to increase economic productivity. At the time, many critics correctly pointed out how skills-based education cannot compensate for an economy that doesn't provide skilled jobs (Finn 1987: 59). Nevertheless, both the Labour Party and then the Conservative Party pressed ahead in extending training schemes via the FE sector. Among the earlier measures included were the Job Creation Programme (1975) and the Work Experience Programme (1976). These measures, however, didn't stimulate the economy or provide job opportunities.

As unemployment continued to grow in the late 1970s and early 1980s, further training schemes were introduced, such as the Youth Opportunities Programme (YOP) which later became the Youth Training Scheme (YTS): a one-year training scheme that combined work experience with FE training courses for school leavers – representing the 'New Vocationalism'. John Clarke and Paul Willis argue that such schemes kept young people in 'suspended animation' until work became available again (Clarke and Willis 1984: 32). As such, FE became a mechanism through which potentially disgruntled individuals were given hands-on supervision by the government. The need to mask youth unemployment led inexorably to the expansion of vocational education. In turn this led to an expansion of assessment and credentials that were more workplace oriented.

As we saw previously, student assessment was largely based on displaying theoretical knowledge and understanding of a subject. In the early 1980s, though, the emphasis on assessment had moved into articulation and measurement of competencies – that is, 'of actual operations required of the employee in the workplace' (Kerry and Tollitt-Evans 1986: 82). As long ago as 1980, the CBI stated that profiles were needed 'which were meaningful to employers as a whole' (Kerry and Tollitt-Evans 1986: 83).

The introduction of the National Council for Vocational Qualifications

Vocational-based assessments previously came in the form of City and Guilds and BTEC diplomas. However, these were not as standardized as the academic-based qualifications. Thus in 1986 the National Council for Vocational Qualifications (NCVQ) was set up, with the aim of standardizing vocational qualifications related to working in specific occupations. The aim of NVQs is to reward practical achievement, with qualifications and grades being gained by demonstrating 'competencies' that are divided into different units. Each unit relates to competence in a different area of activity within a job. And each of these consists of elements of skill, knowledge and understanding that specify the performance required to demonstrate such competence.

From this, NVQs demand a far greater range of assessment than for previous examinations. In particular, NVQ assessors look in terms of *outcomes*, i.e., what must be achieved rather than the process of learning. With NVQs, assessors must take into consideration a long list of criteria that a candidate must show evidence of having. As NVQs have expanded in FE, so too has the extent of assessment and credentials. In 1993, for example, the General National Vocational Qualification (GNVQ) was introduced nationally. The purpose of GNVQs was more towards employability than gaining specific work skills, and they were seen as a vocationally-oriented alternative to traditional academic exams, such as GCSEs and A levels.

The shift towards the new vocationalism has led to a plethora of new credential qualifications. Yet the emphasis on testing and assessment has not been isolated to this area, but flowed from the New Right's approach to education during the 1980s and 1990s. The buzzword here was 'the marketization of education', meaning that rationalization of resources and increased competition between colleges would both make the services more efficient and also raise educational standards in the process. It also meant recasting FE colleges as 'producers' and students as 'consumers' which in turn led to a greater instrumentalization of the educational system at this level. Attempts to measure the 'performance' of schools and colleges, and publish the results, led automatically to intensifying the measurement of both students and lecturers alike. This was further ratified in a series of educational reforms that accelerated the rise of credentialism.

The 1988 Educational Reform Act

This piece of legislation was perhaps the most far-reaching set of educational reforms since the 1944 Butler Education Act. For the first time, a national curriculum was introduced and schools could opt out from the control of local educational authorities (LEA). Testing and attainment targets were introduced for children between the ages of 7 and 16 in the hope that standards would rise.

The 1988 Educational Reform Act also had a dramatic impact on the FE sector. Under a new system of formula funding, the financing of FE colleges was largely based upon the number of enrolments. The thinking behind this strategy was to reward successful colleges while giving less successful colleges the incentive to improve. Although such a formula is in operation in schools, in the post-compulsory sector there is far greater pressure on colleges and lecturers. Students are not legally bound to attend classes and courses and therefore the rate of retention is under constant scrutiny. As a consequence, lecturers' professional performance is now assessed on whether or not they can keep students on their courses. It also means that lecturers are open to greater managerial interference than ever before.

GCSE's replace O levels

In 1986 the General Certificate of Secondary Education (GCSEs) replaced the two-tier system of O levels for more academic pupils, and CSEs for less academically able students. Initially, it led to all students being entered for the same examination though increasingly subjects began to be seen as belonging to either a 'higher' or 'lower' tier. The new qualification also introduced a large amount of coursework in the assessment methods. This has important consequences for FE lecturers.

Traditionally, FE colleges were often a place for students of all ages seeking a 'second chance', including those who hadn't done well in what is now Year 11. Retaking GCSEs in one academic year is still a popular choice for some post-16 students. The use of coursework in the assessment method for GCSE puts lecturers under greater pressure in a number of ways. In some subjects, such as history, there are two lengthy pieces of coursework that have to be produced. Lecturers not only have to monitor these, they also have to mark entire pieces of coursework, rather than this being done by external examiners.

Accessibility to higher education through further education

In 1993 the Conservative government published a set of proposals describing the aims of the government's education reform. One such proposal was 'to make further and higher education more widely accessible and more responsive to the needs of the economy' (1993 Education Act). What this really meant was using FE to try and get people to stop claiming unemployment benefit and into higher education. Rather than expecting mature students to sit through two years of studying A levels, the Conservative government introduced access courses.

Compared to A levels or GNVQs, access to HE certificates are not graded. According to the UCAS website, 'Students acquire a mixture of knowledge and skills on Access programmes and the use of credits is a way of formally recognizing the achievement of particular learning outcomes or identifiable new skills or knowledge acquired by the learner.' Regardless of whether access courses are science- or humanities-based, they are assessed by the same 'outcome' objectives.

In order to gain the access to HE certificate, students must achieve a minimum of 12 credits at level 3 standard. Compared to traditional subject measurements, access to education eschews exams for continual assessment of essays and presentations. FE lecturers are recast as 'access providers' who, according to UCAS, make 'use of records or profiles of achievement as a way of providing more information about individual performance'. As with GCSE coursework, it is the lecturer who is expected to do the assessing, rather than external examination boards. Thus, the expansion of mature students into FE also meant the expansion of assessment tasks for lecturers.

New Labour and the rise and rise of credentialism

Even before the election of New Labour in May 1997, party leader Tony Blair said that his priorities were 'Education, Education and Education'. As we shall outline, aspects of New Right policies, especially the new vocationalism, were not only retained but expanded upon. There remains a strong belief that constant skills training – leading to 'credentials' – is needed in a highly competitive globalized economy (Mullan 2004: 3). In 2005, the then Education Secretary, Charles Clarke, justified further vocationalism and credentialism in terms that it would benefit the economy and the country. It is debatable as to whether there is a correlation between education and economic growth (Mullan 2004: 3), but the government's firm belief in this theory has led to new forms of assessment and credentials in FE.

The expansion of vocational subjects

In 2001, New Labour attempted to create a 'parity of esteem' between vocational and traditional academic subjects. (Though, as has already been pointed out, the 'aims and outcomes' framework traditionally associated with vocational assessment had already crept into the vocabulary of academic-based education.) To this end, vocational A levels and GCSEs were introduced with the aim of bridging this educational divide. In particular, the aim was to encourage more middle class students to consider vocational qualifications.

New Labour's emphasis on vocational education differs considerably to the Conservative Party line. Whereas vocational education was aimed particularly at working class youth, in order to hide the level of unemployment, New Labour wants vocational-based education to be the norm for all. Thus the assessment of a subject's content is based on whether it has any workplace 'relevance'. Previously, it was accepted that grounding in compulsory academic education was required before students achieved training at work. Now all subjects must have a form of assessment that makes then more focused on employability.

Yet the rise in accreditation for 'vocational' GCSE and A levels isn't quite what it seems either. Proper training in engineering and mechanics has been supplanted by numerous FE courses involving 'soft' skills – relating to attitudes, feelings and manners – infamously so with subjects, such as alternative therapies, counselling and care (areas that were never considered to be 'skilled work'). Instead, the vocational courses favoured by New Labour are geared towards generic skills, such as communication or group work. The separating out of rudimentary skills as being skills demanding separate accreditation is another reason why there has been a continued rise in credentialism. Nowhere is this more evident than with recasting English, maths and ICT 'skills' deserving of separate accreditation too.

Key and basic skills

The thinking behind providing key skills, sits at the heart of contemporary thinking on educational provision and assessment. Learning Shakespeare or complicated mathematical formulae, goes the argument, do not equip the learner for what is required at work. Therefore, FE students studying academic-based A levels are assessed on key skills in their work, while lecturers are also assessed on whether they are assessing students on these key skills too. Even when the Conservatives expanded vocational training in the 1980s, educationalists were keen to keep the distinction between academic and vocational education. Now *all* students are assessed on work-based aptitude.

In the *Review of Qualifications for 16–19-Year-Olds*, Ron Dearing points out that all schools, colleges and training bodies providing publicly funded education and training for 16–19-year-olds 'should provide opportunities for all young people to develop their key skills and to have them assessed and recognized' (Standish 2001: 2). The committee chaired by Dearing drew up a list of key skills, based on comments both from people in higher education and employers. Using these recommendations, the Qualifications and Curriculum Authority (QCA) developed a specification for key skills qualifications that was fully introduced in September 2000.

The QCA specifications for key skills include six defined areas where qualifications can be obtained. These are communication, application of number, information technology, working with others, improving your own learning and problem-solving. The first three are considered the core areas and the latter three wider skills. The content of key skills courses involves lessons that provide opportunities for students to work on specific objectives. They produce work towards a portfolio, which exists as evidence to be internally assessed and externally moderated. Exams are taken at the end of the year.

The Qualifications and Curriculum Authority (QCA) also notes that some of the traditional academic qualifications, such as GSCE English literature and maths, are equivalent to the new key skills qualifications. The difference with key skills specifications is that they are part of a competence-based approach to learning, which was previously the form of assessment used in explicitly vocational education.

Although surveys from employers suggest that they still prefer candidates with A level qualifications than key skills certificates, the education system is still pressing on with the vocational and 'skills-based' revolution. Not surprisingly, the traditional gold standard of academic education, A levels, has not emerged unscathed.

The modularization of advanced levels

Key Skills were to play a significant role in the newly revised A levels, that were introduced in 2000. Instead of following a syllabus over a two-year period, candidates now study three units in the first year, leading to an AS examination. If candidates are successful they can progress and take on A2 course and study a further 3 units. The combined marks from all six units make up the final A level grade. Leaving aside whether the new A levels are easier for students to pass, they are also another form of assessment for both students and lecturers to contend with.

The changes to the A level are less to do with any major problems in the old system. Universities and employers were satisfied that an A level qualification gave a reliable indicator of a candidate's abilities and potentials. The newly revised A levels are informed by the government's drive for continual tests and assessment. This is founded on the belief that regular assessments are the best mechanism to improve standards within the education system. In particular, the new A level enables FE college management to supervise and assess the performance of lecturers to a greater degree than before.

As A level exams are now sat annually – and in some institutions biannually – there is more intense and ongoing pressure for lecturers to deliver good results. This is especially the case with the introduction of coursework for many humanities-based subjects. In some humanities subjects, coursework now accounts for around 30 per cent of the total A level mark. For FE managers, the coursework option enables more students to pass A levels with good grades and thus keep OfSTED inspectors happy. FE lecturers are thus under pressure to ensure students are 'assisted' with their coursework as much as possible. Many lecturers spend extra time on examination board standardization courses to ensure that students get as much help that they need. While it is the case that students are tested and assessed more than ever, more is expected from FE lecturers than from FE students. As they are almost solely responsible for the performance of students, the over-assessment of lecturers will continue to be a key feature of FE.

PGCE/Cert. Ed in post-compulsory education training (PCET)

Increasingly, FE institutions now demand a credential for teaching at this level. As with higher education previously FE college lecturers did not have to complete a formal qualification in order to teach in the post-compulsory sector. The apparent thinking behind making the PGCE/Cert. Ed mandatory was to provide a standardization to ensure better quality teaching. It could be argued, however, that this credential undermines rather than enhances professionalism because it implies that post-compulsory lecturers can't be trusted to act on their own. Their situation is entirely different to that of doctors who must be trusted to act on their own – although even this is increasingly brought into question as medical qualifications are expected to include an emphasis on 'soft skills'.

There is no doubt that, as it is currently structured (see Chapter 8) this approach trains teachers to accept the orthodoxies of differentiation, diversity and further assessment. A key component of PCET is making sure FE teachers provide continuous assessment of students, ensure there is classroom 'inclusion' and that attention is given to cultural diversity in the classroom. This formal training has a less developmental parallel in the annual round of management observations of teaching, as a consequence of which FE lecturers will have their teaching techniques and 'learning resources' checked and graded.

None of this guarantees improvement in academic education, rather both lecturers and students are assessed on how far they match the etiquette demanded on inter-personal conduct. Thus lecturers would be marked down if they allow bright students to dominate classroom discussion, as it is recommended that students 'learn' how to co-operate in group activities. When it comes to assessing the FE lecturer's ability, a demonstration of subject knowledge is actually lower down on the list of prioritizes. Instead, encouraging 'appropriate' interaction and behaviour between students in the classroom takes greater precedence. It's no surprise, then, that there are even assessments designed to prove you can act and behave to meet 'official' standards.

Parenting classes and pre-retirement courses

As we examine in the next section, the role of FE colleges has gone beyond providing academic and vocational courses. In many cases, they are seen as crucial vehicles in providing guidelines on action and behaviour, and not with 16–19-year-old learners, but also right across the age spectrum. Couples with children can now enrol on parenting classes, designed to guide them through child psychology and 'advanced' child rearing. In the past, couples simply got on with the task of bringing up children without third parties providing check-lists and assessments. Likewise something as basic as enjoying retirement time becomes institutionalized and interfered with via pre-retirement courses. Vocational education credentials are supposed to equip learners with *work-based* skills, so why the need for a post-work course and certificate? Why are routine aspects of non-working life now recast within a credentialist framework?

Explaining the drive behind credentialism

From what we've discussed so far, the growth in credentialism has coincided with what's referred to as the 'marketization of education' – the implementation of competition and supply-and-demand guidelines within a public sector framework. This means that the education system has to deliver concrete objectives – i.e., qualifications – in order to prove itself as 'cost effective'. As students are recast as consumers, the thinking here is also that they must have a 'product' to take home after a year of studying. Hence vocational courses that didn't have a certificate to their name were given credentials by the late 1980s. Although GNVQ's didn't exactly overcome the problem of mass unemployment during this period, they did give the impression that the then Conservative government was 'proactive' in seeking solutions (however illusory that might be).

In this context, the rise of credentialism can be first explained as a compensator for a lack of genuine social policies to combat social problems. The more government and other state institutions have lacked the vision and effectiveness to steer society for the better, the more education has stepped in to fill that vacuum. Indeed, the expansion of higher education in the early 1990s, and with it the rise in qualifications, was entirely born out of exhaustion from tackling unemployment, rather than as a quest to bring higher learning to more people. Nevertheless, many of the Conservative government's changes to the education system in this period were accepted at face value. Many on the left welcomed the expansion of higher education, access courses and the enhanced status of vocational courses as a blow against educational elitism.

At a time when the Conservatives lacked the authority to forge a consensus on anything, from the nuclear family to British nationalism, expanding education was one of the few areas to guarantee a remarkable degree of cross-political support. By doing so, it also helped to redefine how society's problems should be tackled. Thus high unemployment isn't a result of the weakness of the market economy, but a problem of not enough people not having enough qualifications. Such thinking leads to the reorganization of how the state and society relates to the individual. Previously, the state was seen as a mechanism to fill the gaps left by the market system. And above all, there was a consensus in the post-war years that social problems demanded social solutions. The ending of consensus politics in the 1980s, and particularly the dismantling of labourist welfarism, undoubtedly pushed individualistic solutions to the top of the political agenda; but these were not enthusiastically supported as being a set of values to define British society (even by those who voted Conservative).

The support for the Conservatives' expanding, credentialist education succeeded in doing two things. First, it popularized the idea that individuals are to blame for social problems. Second, it suggested that the education system is ideally equipped to change individuals in order to improve society. The far reaching consequences of these ideas were to flourish considerably under New Labour. In fact, it became the defining policy drive of Tony Blair. Key to Blair's thinking on education is that it can become a vehicle through which to tackle what New Labour refers to as 'social exclusion'. In non-jargon talk, this alludes to material deprivation, but poverty isn't the prime concern for the government. The 'exclusion' part actually refers to sections of society which are outside points of contact with a variety of community and state institutions, national and local government. Whereas trades unions and grass roots party organization enabled an organic relationship between the political class and mass society, the dismantling of these ties by Thatcher, coupled with the decline of political participation, severed such mediating links for the political elites. This unease with their isolation from the rest of society constantly forces New Labour to seek new points of connection. This is where the FE sector – long considered the 'Cinderella' of the British education system – came into its own.

Compared to so many other institutions in Britain, such as the police, the monarchy or public schools, FE wasn't tainted with being a bulwark of Old Britain's class system. In fact, as FE developed out of workers' educational councils, it seemed to denote egalitarianism over elitism – something which New Labour is obsessively concerned to promote. Whereas FE was once marginal to educational policies, it increasingly becomes the model for both secondary education *and* higher education to follow. This model was about transforming education into a vehicle to combat 'social exclusion' of the working classes and ethnic minorities. Therefore finding new ways of encouraging more people, particularly young people, to enrol in FE courses became a top priority.

As we have already outlined, developing key skills credentials (see Chapter 5) and expanding on vocational courses became the major thrust of New Labour's entry into FE. The thinking here is that more students are likely to enrol if such courses appear 'relevant' and 'accessible'. In many ways, reducing the actual content of education – often by replacing it with skills training – is considered necessary if more people are to be encouraged into FE classrooms. In New Labour's world of learning, the phrase 'education for education's sake' takes on a whole new meaning. What used to be a defence against notions that academic learning must be justified in terms of economic benefit, now seems to mean that getting young people into education is justifiable even when they learn little, because at least they are included in a relationship with an institution.

Ironically enough this is why there's a symbiotic relationship between eroding educational content and increasing the available credentials. The tick box mentality of credentials becomes a phoney display of charting students' 'progression' in a technical but, ultimately, meaningless way. Dishing out certificates is seen to be as practical 'proof' that more people are becoming qualified under New Labour's 'education revolution'. The obsession with credentials becoming an educational 'receipt', however, goes beyond a PR gloss on educational reforms. This process gets to the nub of New Labour's approach to FE.

We've already outlined how New Labour continued the 'marketization' initiated by the New Right; but it would be wrong to consider recent reforms as being simply 'more of the same'. In March 2006, the government's White Paper, *Further Education: Raising Skills, Improving Life Chances*, perhaps gave unwitting insight into the credentialization process. Here, FE courses that prioritize the wider interests of 'community' and 'business' – i.e., vocational courses – will receive more funding than those that don't. In particular, FE courses that *don't* offer a qualification at the end are recast as being a 'bad provision' and liable to have their funding cut. Thus, government ministers believe that 'night courses should not be the preserve of the middle classes keen on self-improvement' (Davenport 2006: 2). As a result, the cost of non-vocational courses that don't lead to a qualification will be doubled 'to help fund job training for low-skilled workers' (Davenport 2006: 2). There is more going on here than crude bean counting – the UK's economy can easily afford to provide evening classes for art and Spanish and beyond.

What New Labour finds uncomfortable is autonomous individuals learning for learning's sake, rather than as a means to an end. It's precisely the idea that individuals might do something outside of the tick box mentality that so irks current education reformers. Credentials are considered important because they define the willingness to participate in an institutional course and thus endow them with 'legitimacy'. The flipside of this, however, is that adults become assessed, not as free-thinking citizens, but according to their portfolio of credentials. This is why educationalists now prefer 19–25-year-old learners to study in sixth form A level classes. The removal of adult learning classes suggests you're not considered a mature adult until you've gained at least one level 3 qualification. Elsewhere, as 'inadequate' individuals are now blamed for social problems, particularly in terms of child rearing and health, FE courses can somehow improve people's behaviour and improve society in the process. The idea of attending parenting classes shows how citizenship is increasingly wrapped up with proving you have the necessary credentials.

Essentially, *Raising Skills* emphasizes that both FE and its students can only be evaluated on identifiable 'outcomes'. It thus begs the question, why can't New Labour imagine the education system playing any other role? At any given historical period, a nation's education system will reflect the prevailing ideas and values of its dominant political class. New Labour's problem is that it doesn't have any galvanizing ideas and beliefs to pass down. In the 1980s, the New Right might have marketized the education system and laid the basis for creeping vocationalism, but even they had ideas they believed should be imparted through the education system, such as notions of British 'identity'. Today as political life is drearily characterized by soulless managerial-speak, so is the education system. Yet the consequences of this are altogether more pervasive and educationally destructive.

A lack of values and beliefs means education can only be assessed *technically* rather than *socially*. An identification with values leads to a voluntary and committed relationship betweens citizens and the state. When society is bereft of values, such a relationship has to be engineered in an artificial and mechanistic way. Thus when individuals appear autonomous from social institutions, New Labour's instinct is to seek regulation in order to bring individuals back within the official fold. It's this desire to create binding connections that dominates every facet of FE too. Whether it is colleges and courses or teachers and learners, at every step of the way, there has to be a clear 'aim' and an identifiable 'outcome'. As it is easier to quantify the pass rate of a course than it is the content, credentials play a key role in the process of instrumentalist evaluation.

So what is to be done?

In some important respects, providing credentials or qualifications can be a useful process within the education system. In particular, they can represent universalistic standards in society and thus, in theory, help to assist the development of a meritocratic culture. After all, the demand for GCE certificates came from the working classes who wanted to prove they could meet the demands of academic education. Then, rather than now, however, an academic education was worthy of its name. In some ways, the pursuit of knowledge and learning for its own sake meant there was little room for time consuming assessments.

In today's education system, there needs to be an expansion of the *content* of education, rather than the *outcome*. The old A levels were undoubtedly in need of reform, but the syllabus didn't need to be eroded to the extent that an AS level is now the equivalent of the old GCE O level. A return to rigorous academic standards within A levels would be a good place to start. If credentials are to exist, then they must represent something of real educational worth.

In order to assist this process, there also needs to be clear distinctions between vocational education and academic education. It needs to be acknowledged that rather than having a 'parity of esteem', they are in fact different and require different levels of aptitude and ability. A lot of the mechanistic devices in current assessments stem from this wrongheaded idea that academia can 'learn' from the processes within vocational education. Far from helping students reach their potential, vocational tick box assessments are a barrier to developing abstract thought and cogent arguments. Likewise, it's doubtful whether so many of the vocational courses on offer really need such extensive credentials. Again, providing real skills training, rather than pieces of paper saying that you have, would be of greater benefit to students.

Finally, in defiant opposition to *Further Education: Raising Skills, Improving Life Chances*, funding of FE colleges should not be decided on whether courses offer credentials or not. The liberal idea of an education for education's sake needs to be at the centre of policy within FE and beyond. This means that evening classes on critical theory and cookery should be given public funding regardless of their 'practical' outcome for individuals or the economy. Through this, we can begin to re-address the purpose of education through its content and value, and not its 'aims' and 'outcomes'.

A chronology of credentialism in FE

1951	*The introduction of the General Certificate in Education (GCE).* This replaced the School Certificate and the Higher School Certificate. Students studied academic and science subjects at ordinary level and advanced level. There was also an intermediate O/A level certificate and a higher special (S level) paper.
1953	*A levels receive new gradation.* In 1953, another grade was introduced: the distinction for high passes.
1963	*A levels receive a finer grading scale.* Due to complaints from universities that the grading system was not specific enough to identify the students they wanted, a grading scale, close to the current one, was created, which retained an O level pass between the grades E and F (fail).

cont.

1975	*Job Creation Programme introduced.* The then Labour government introduced this vocational programme into FE with the aim of providing skills in order to combat unemployment.
1976	*Work Experience Programme.* Jim Callahan believed that more vocational education was needed in order to combat rising unemployment. How more skills could compensate for less jobs wasn't made entirely clear.
1980	*Youth Opportunities Programme introduced.* Although skills training failed to combat rising unemployment, the 1979 Conservative government introduced more credential-based schemes.
1981	*Youth Training Scheme introduced.* This one-year training scheme combined work experience with FE training courses for school leavers. In place of proper jobs, young people were offered credentials as an alternative.
1986	*The National Council for Vocational Qualifications introduced.* This body standardized vocational qualifications related to working in specific occupations. The aim of NVQs is to reward practical achievement, with qualifications, and grades being gained by demonstrating 'competencies' that are divided into different units.
1988	*GCSEs replace O level examinations.* The 1988 Education Act introduced a new qualification for 16-year-olds. The General Certificates of Secondary Education (GCSE) replaced the two-tier system of O levels for more academic pupils, and CSEs for less academically able students.
1993	*The General National Vocational Qualifications (GNVQ) introduced nationally.* The purpose here was to provide a vocationally-oriented alternative to traditional academic exams, such as GCSEs and A levels. This established the basis for the 'parity of esteem' between vocational and academic education.
1993	*Access to higher education.* As part of the 1993 Education Act, the Conservative government aimed to make further and higher education 'more accessible' through the introduction of access courses.
2000	*Curriculum 2000,* the introduction of key skills as a compulsory component of all courses and records of achievement for all students. The dividing of A levels into AS and A2 qualifications further increased the range of credentials available to post-16-year-olds. *cont.*

2001	*Mandatory teaching qualifications* for the post-compulsory sector introduced. Mandatory PGCE and Cert. Ed qualifications were an attempt to standardize all aspects of teaching in the FE sector.
2004	*Parenting classes* introduced. The growth of credentialism goes beyond work-oriented areas to incorporate training on day-to-day activities, such as child rearing or enjoying retirement time. Increasingly, credentials become a way of establishing citizenship.
2006	FE funding related directly to the provision of skills-based courses. The White Paper *Further Education: Raising Skills, Improving Life Chances* aims to end night classes on the basis that they don't provide credentials and are therefore irrelevant to the needs of the economy. Such measures signal the end of education for education sake and the triumph of credential instrumentalism.

Key readings

The classic work on the explosion of qualifications is Ronald Dore's (1976) *The Diploma Disease*. Berkeley, CA: University of California Press. His subsequent reflections on the qualification explosion can be found in (1997) Reflections on the diploma disease twenty years later, *Assessment in Education: Principles, Policy, and Practice*, 4(1): 189–218.

Randall Collins popularized the term 'credentialism' in his classic work of (1979), *The Credential Society*. New York, NY: Academic Press, and is sometimes said to have coined the term.

Thinking about all aspects of credentialism has been developed by David B. Bills in (1988) Credentials and capacities: employer's perceptions of the acquisition of skills, *The Sociological Quarterly*, 29(3): 439–49. Credentialism is put in a broad sociological context in his (2004) *The Sociology of Education and Work*. Oxford: Blackwell.

A short account of the actual facts and figures from the last century in relation to the growth of provision and qualifications, which were not always collected in a systematic way available for FE, is to be found in A. H. Halsey's chapter, (2000) Further and higher education, in A. H. Halsey with J. Webb (eds) *Twentieth-Century British Social Trends*. Basingstoke: MacMillan; pp. 221–53.

Credentialism is addressed in a polemical way in Dennis Hayes's (2006) Womb for Improvement, *TES FE Focus*, 6 January. Available at: www.tes.co.uk/search/story/?story_id=2177580

7 The transition to work and adulthood

Patrick Turner

> *Modern morality consists in accepting the standard of one's age.*
> *I consider that for any man of culture to accept the standard of*
> *his age is a form of the grossest immorality.*
>
> (Wilde 1959: 191)

The New Labour government is exercised, to say the least, over the transition from youth to adulthood (DfEE 1998, 1999, 2000a, b; SEU 1999; DfES 2005c, 2006a). Policy-makers are convinced that without aggressive professional intervention into the lives of teenagers many will be destined to end up on the scrap-heap: unemployed long term, sexually incontinent, drug addicted, anti-social and depressed (DfES 2005c; Feinstein *et al.* 2005). Recent years have seen a raft of new initiatives on just about every policy front, from education, through social care, criminal justice and health promotion to employment policy and youth work (Home Office 1998a, b, 2003; DfEE 1998, 2000a, b; SEU 1999; DoH 2004; DfES 2004a, 2006a). Government has become convinced not only of the wisdom, but also of the morality of determined state intervention to prevent later negative outcomes for its young citizens (DfES 2004a). But are new forms of professional intervention genuinely required to ease the transition from youth to 'responsible adulthood'; and what of the relations between self and society thereby established (Furedi 2003, 2005)?

This chapter sets out to explain how the concept of transitions is currently being interpreted and deployed by policy-makers and in which contexts. The chapter will also aim to put the subject of youth transitions and government responses to it into some sort of broader context, and to demonstrate the degree to which the debate around transitions crystallizes a number of prevailing social, cultural and political concerns (Ecclestone *et al.* 2005a). Because so many discussions on youth transitions and risk take liberties with the real complexities of people's lives, I have decided to include a section in which I reflect upon my own teenage experience of growing up in a 'risky' environment. In doing so, I do not wish to suggest that my own experience is somehow exemplary. What is more, I am fully aware of the historical gap between the time of my own youth and the present moment. However, one of the fallacies that I seek to rebut in offering this personal testimony is precisely the oft repeated claim that the actions of the current government are fully justified because 'the ills of the world have multiplied' (Giddens 1998b, 2004). While accepting that the world today in certain particulars is radically different from that of my own youth, I believe many of the risks and dilemmas over choices, allegedly so unique, to this generation were also relevant to my own.

A few words on how the chapter is structured: divided into five parts, part one will provide a short thumbnail sketch of the broader cultural climate within which youth transitions have come to prominence among policy-makers; part two will set out some of the concerns around contemporary youth and recent government responses; part three will provide a basic introduction to the policy underpinnings of the Connexions Service and will describe the work of the Connexions Personal Adviser (PA); part four will explain the significance of direct experience in my own emergence into adulthood and briefly ponder how this sits with the current determination to ensure young people are assisted through the transition phase; and part five, the conclusion, assesses the validity of youth transitions, as currently interpreted, and some of the consequences for young people and society.

Therapy, management control

Astute critics (from at least the 1960s onwards) have been concerned with the relationship of western governments and the state to citizens, discerning the emergence of ever more intrusive forms of lifestyle regulation and both insidious and formalized modes of management, social control and surveillance (Cohen 1985; Habermas 1985; Rieff 1987; Foucault 1991; Lasch 1995; Baudrillard 1996; Donzelot 1997; Nolan 1998; Rose 1999, Rose 2000; Marcuse 2002; Palmer 2003; Ecclestone 2004; Furedi 2004a; Weatherall 2004). Interestingly, the picture is murky from a political point of view; this phenomenon does not easily map onto a left/right divide or totalitarian versus liberal (Habermas 1985; Lasch 1995; Nolan 1998; Rose 1999; Furedi 2004a; Weatherall 2004).

The rise of 'therapy culture' was given wings by the expressive individualism of the sixties 'New Left' with its concern for authenticity, subjectivity and politicizing the personal (Sennett 1986; Lasch 1991; Jacoby 1997; Weatherall 2004). And many of its staunchest critics were, and are to be found on the left/liberal end of the political spectrum (Jacoby 1997). By contrast, managerialism first emerged in the monetarist 1980s of Thatcher and Reagan, and has found its apogee in the Third Way market state of messrs. Blair and Brown (Finlayson 2003). Management consultants and credulous politicians display an almost religious faith in the power of centralized, rational control of people and processes by systems of audit, target setting and measurement. 'New Public Management' has gone way beyond bean counting and cost efficiency to become a tyrannical credo regulating the conduct of all levels of public services and their users (Fevre 2003; Marquand 2004).

The post-Fordist shift from production to consumption, the rise of a 'risk society', and the talked-up threats of capital taking flight from places with high labour costs, etc., have convinced policy-makers that both efficiency and the sovereign will of consumers in all matters must dictate policy (Bauman 2003; Finlayson 2003; Jordan 2005). As aspects of a wider cultural mood, subjectivism and a therapeutic concern with personal authenticity have merely obeyed their own utilitarian logic by demonstrating their usefulness to policy-makers in search of 'humane', frictionless methods for enhancing personal performance and increasing self-regulation (Nolan 1998; Colley 2003; Ecclestone 2004; Furedi 2004a; Weatherall 2004; McGee 2005). But what must also be added to this is the way that New Labour has attempted to address the problems of socio-economic decline and order within deprived neighbourhoods by a communitarian emphasis on personal responsibility and mutual obligation (Levitas 1998; Goldson 2000; Finlayson 2003; Jordan and Jordan 2003; Clarke 2005). In the minds of current policy-makers the pre-economic 'social capital' believed to be so critical to regeneration and social harmony is tied to old-fashioned moral ideas of normality, respect and decent conduct (Clarke 2005; Davies 2006). However, efforts to secure these things have involved a jettisoning of natural justice and civil liberties, as summary powers have been handed over to the police and local authorities (Home Office 2003). In New Labour's Britain the McKinseyite state, the police state and the therapeutic state are one.

British youth in 'late modernity'

By the time New Labour came into government in the late 1990s, making the 'transition' from childhood to adulthood had, it would appear, for many become a hazardous undertaking fraught with a host of new challenges and problems (Bentley and Gurumurchy 1999; SEU 1999; Giddens 2004). Able still to buy cigarettes, have sex and marry at 16, drive a car at 17, vote in an election and purchase alcohol at 18, contemporary youth had, nonetheless, little access to many of the tangible resources once considered pre-requisites of adult independence. With the decline of the youth labour market and work-based apprenticeships, the removal of state benefits to most 16–18-year-olds, the exorbitant cost of private housing and the dwindling of public housing, many of the means of achieving a modicum of autonomy had withered for all but the most privileged of young people (Ecclestone *et al.* 2005a; Goodwin and O'Connor 2005). With mainly casual, service industry jobs available at the lower end of the pay spectrum, government has sought to massively expand further and higher education in an attempt, arguably, to warehouse large numbers of otherwise unoccupied young people (HEFCE 2002; Wolf 2002; DfES 2003a, 2004b;). Tertiary education, it is hoped, will deliver the training in technical and dispositional skills for future work in a 'knowledge'-based economy (DfES 2006a). At the same time as receiving an education in relevant skills for the labour market, young people may also be diverted from the twin perils of unprotected sex and illegal drug use. It is the aim of policy to ensure that no young person makes the independent choice to *prematurely* confront the multiple risks of adulthood alone with regards to work, relationships and leisure (SEU 1999; DfEE 2000a, b). The Educational Maintenance Allowance (EMA), offered to disadvantaged 16–18-year-olds as an incentive to stay on at school or college, attests to this imperative. Despite physical maturity and the notional right to operate legally as independent adults, this transitional phase is being heavily extended via initiatives seeking to ensure young people's constructive use of time and space within an educational context.

In scores of once working class areas, informal networks of support that might formerly have eased young people's passage to independence have also dwindled owing to the combined effects of de-industrialization, gentrification and the absorption of migrant newcomers (Abercrombie and Warde 2000). Additionally, some argue that welfare and housing allocation policies have impacted on community cohesion and older forms of solidarity to the detriment of young people (Dench *et al.* 2006). Moreover, the periodic moral panics of the past over unruly teenagers have, in recent years, assumed a wholly different character. 'Youth', once a useful 'folk devil' for wheeling out from time to time in support of repressive law and order policies, is now regarded as a permanent enemy within (Home Office 1998a, 2003; Goldson 2000; James *et al.* 2002). Sowing fear and disorder by its mere malevolent presence, youth requires aggressive control by the state (Home Office 1998a, 2003; Goldson 2000; O'Malley and Waiton 2005). Teenage parents have become exemplars of the moral turpitude and welfare dependency of this new youth underclass: feckless and sexually incontinent (James *et al.* 2002; Gillies 2005). Any notion that starting a family while still young might possibly be the means of – if not necessarily the original motive for – acquiring maturity and a sense of responsibility is roundly dismissed as recklessly permissive nonsense. Furthermore, the widespread availability and exponential use of illegal drugs, during the 1990s, has arguably led to what some commentators persuasively term the 'normalization of adolescent drug use' (Home Office 1998b; Parker *et al.* 1998; Blackman 2004).

The social theorist, Anthony Giddens is of the opinion that the social and cultural conditions of 'late modernity' pile up disadvantage for individuals born into less well-off families (Giddens 1998b, 2004). It has robbed them of the occupational security, dependable welfare and informal solidarities of yesteryear, leaving them cruelly exposed to the caprices of the market and the remorseless seductions of consumerism. And in so doing, it has transformed the cultural 'ecologies' in which disadvantaged children are socialized. Growing up in demoralized, atomized communities, where fear and distrust reign supreme and older people are no longer able, if even available, to exercise 'horizontal' forms of social control, the young are afforded little opportunity outside the family home to develop their own 'internal locus of control' (Giddens 1998b; Feinstein *et al.* 2005). The increased availability of legal and illegal consumer commodities has made the exercise of choice fraught with previously absent ethical and personal considerations (Parker *et al.* 1998; Giddens 2004), while among the poorly-socialized, the ability to regulate impulses, sublimate wants and defer gratification has lamentably declined. In a society in which success or failure is almost entirely contingent upon the exercise of individual effort and will, and a skill in complex decision-making, the absence of such 'life skills' spells certain failure (Bauman 2003). In sum, according to Giddens, the quality of nurture and parenting provided by the 'demoralized' underclass of 'late modernity' fails to sufficiently inoculate its offspring psychologically, morally and intellectually against the proliferating challenges of society (Giddens 2004). As a consequence, social exclusion, high levels of personal danger and economic disadvantage, with all this means for mental and physical health and criminality, are passed on from generation to generation, and maintained in perpetuity.

In response to this situation, government has sought, on every front, to deal with the so called youth 'problem' by throwing a *cordon-sanitaire* around the young (Home Office 2003; DfES 2005c). At a local authority level, multi-agency partnerships now employ formal systems of surveillance for the purposes of targeting services at identified individuals (DfES 2004a, 2005c). This involves the routine exchange between agencies of the names of individuals and families. One of the key competencies for the future children and young people's workforce, as set out in the *Every Child Matters* (DfES 2004a), is a practitioner's ability to share information about children, young people and their families with other professionals. To this end information, referral and tracking (IRT) computer database systems, that store and make available personal information about children and young people to 'networks' of relevant local professionals, have recently been piloted up and down the country (DfES 2004a). Employing the communitarian language of a moral crusade seeking to reclaim neighbourhoods from alien and anti-social elements, local authorities and police implement joint strategies for the regulation of public space (Goldson 2000; Home Office 2003). CCTV cameras are placed at strategic points, professional outreach workers are detailed to groups of young people, while dispersal zones and curfews curtail movement and the scope for public assembly (Home Office 2003). Michael Keith terms this phenomenon the mapping and monitoring of 'cartographies of risk' (Keith 2005).

But the management of youth transitions is also a matter of therapeutically moulding the appropriate dispositional qualities for entering 'employment, education and training' in the new 'knowledge economy' (Colley 2003; Ecclestone 2004). Citizenship, life skills, health promotion, behaviour modification and emotional literacy training, have become incorporated into many aspects of the formal and informal educational curriculum (Turner 2006). At the same time, considerable resources and energy have been channelled into efforts to instil into parents a proper sense of their duties both to their offspring and to wider society, i.e., their rights and responsibilities. Parenting, so it seems, has come to be regarded by policy-makers as a branch of 'primary prevention'. The reconfiguration, and in many places virtual merging, of the youth service and youth justice services, as well as the introduction of ASBOs, are patent instances of a determination to profoundly alter the terms on which public professionals, based in local neighbourhoods, enter into a relationship and work with young people (Goldson 2000; O'Malley and Waiton 2005). Pre-school initiatives such as Sure Start, dedicated to parenting, health promotion and promoting employability, evidence the growth in targeted, arguably intrusive forms of 'early intervention' (DfES 2004a). In secondary and further education institutions, 'para' support and behaviour professionals and programmes now abound (DfES 2000b, 2006a). These include learning mentors, behaviour improvement programmes (BIP) and, crucially, the Connexions Service (Colley 2003). This has inevitably been a bit of a whistle stop tour through some of the issues bound up with youth transitions and the current range of initiatives that have been framed in response. The next section will look at the most high profile of these responses: the Connexions Service.

Connexions

For Giddens, the loss of previous social supports and stabilizing influences requires a whole new form of professionalized welfare. His term for this is 'life politics' or 'positive welfare' (Giddens 1998b). It being no longer a viable option to return to the bureaucratic, homogenous welfare of social democracies prior to the rise of neo-liberal economics in the 1980s, progressive governments must now frame imaginative, targeted responses that work in the cause of promoting autonomy rather than dependency on the state. This means shifting the focus of welfare to 'primary prevention' and deploying professional expertise directly on the 'damaged' and 'fragmented' psyches of individuals (Giddens 1998b). If disadvantage is as much cultural, psychological and affective as it is material, government, according to Giddens, can be of most use in developing community-based schemes and initiatives that intervene to repair the damage done by the failures of primary nurture and the immediate environment. Such 'rehabilitation' seeks, ultimately, to enable the newly recombinant individual to compete on a level playing field of risk and opportunity against those already sufficiently endowed with psychological and cultural capital by family privilege (Giddens 1998b, 2004; Giddens and Diamond 2005). Tony Blair writes:

> Getting this right offers the prospect of a double dividend. A better life for young people themselves, saving them from the prospects of a lifetime of dead-end jobs, unemployment, poverty, ill-health and other kinds of exclusion. A better deal for society as a whole that has to pay a very high price in terms of welfare bills and crime for failing to help people make the transition to becoming independent adults.
>
> (SEU 1999: 6)

In 1999 the UK government published two key reports, *Bridging the Gap*, a report by the Social Exclusion Unit on youth disadvantage and, *Learning to Succeed: A New Framework for Post-16 Learning*, by the then Department for Education and Employment (DfEE£). The former highlighted the manifold difficult 'transitions' experienced by young people in a post-industrial era of extended adolescence, minimal youth labour opportunities, community and familial fragmentation, and the extensive gaps in support for those most vulnerable and 'at-risk'. *Bridging the Gap* recommended that considerable government money and resources be channelled into providing a 'holistic', single access point youth support service interlocking with, and providing 'brokerage' for, other provision. The latter, building on an earlier 1998 green paper, *The Learning Age*, set out measures for the configuring of post-16 education around skills for the new global 'knowledge economy', employability, vocational training and life-long learning, and, crucially, the perceived obstacles to achieving these things. A critical element, moreover, in *Bridging the Gap* was its implicit critique of traditional youth services for failing to adapt their provision, focus and methods to the new socio-cultural climate (Jeffs and Smith 2002).

These complimentary perspectives on the multiple challenges, now faced by British youth, culminated in 2000 with the establishment of a new youth support service: Connexions (DfEE 2000a, b). Connexions merges the vocational and training focus of careers advice with the welfare case management of social work, and the informal support and access to recreation of traditional youth work. The core of the Connexions service is the work of the Personal Adviser (PA). The Connexions PA is, arguably, the foot soldier of Giddens' 'positive welfare'. Based within youth work projects, multi-agency youth offending teams, secondary schools and further education colleges (FECs). PAs offer the brokerage and advice service called for in *Bridging the Gap*, one that is particularly *targeted* at those 'not in education, employment or training' (NEET). The emphasis of the role, however, alters according to a number of variables. These include an individual PA's previous professional experience and identity, the institutional context they are working in, such as a school/youth offending team, etc., and the nature of the client group and their needs. With respect to the latter, this concerns whether a young person comes under the category of universal/mainstream and thus requires predominantly low level careers/training advice. If they are at the other end of the spectrum, they are deemed to require 'intensive' support with their multiple/complex needs. Hence a Connexions PA tends to be – but in actuality is not always – *either* a 'universal' *or* an 'intensive' practitioner. The work itself broadly consists of combinations of the following, again dependent on the individual PA, client and institutional context:

- one-to-one formal assessments of young people;
- managing a client caseload;
- operating advice and drop-in 'surgeries';
- doing outreach and detached work;
- accompanying clients to appointments;
- running group drug and sexual health education sessions;
- liaising with prospective employers and other services and professionals;
- making referrals;
- contributing to multi-agency panels, networks and forums; and
- writing client profiles, and recording and storing client information on computer databases.

The Connexions service makes a number of claims regarding the nature, principles and validity of its operation, foremost among them being the following:

- Connexions, a *young person-centred* service, is led by the concerns and needs of its clientbase;
- Connexions is *holistic*, seeing the young person as complex, and thereby promoting multi-agency working;

- Connexions is *evidence-based,* using the information it garners to provide a better picture, both locally and nationally, of 'what works';
- Connexions encourages a self-critical *reflective practice* among its workforce.

Of central importance is an aspiration to promote the use of a range of therapeutic techniques and interventions by Connexions PAs, such as cognitive behavioural therapy, motivational interviewing, brief solution focused therapy and neuro-linguistic programming (DfES 2003d). Such interventions are intended as complimentary to the service's chief method of fostering behavioural change: the assessment planning implementation and review (APIR) tool (DfES 2003d). The APIR is a graphical model in the form of a wheel with the client at the hub and each spoke representing a different feature of their life world, such as friends, family, education, work, etc. By subdividing these things further, via a series of concentric circles radiating out from the centre, the PA encourages the young person to literally map for themselves where they are positioned regarding the major aspects of their lives. The process is intended to work through a series of stages that follow the order of assessment, planning, implementation and review. The aim is to facilitate reflection on where changes might be made and what 'resources' these changes might necessitate. 'Resources' are literally the 'human capital' offered by the PA, the young person and others. In fact the APIR and its conduct trades on the notion that it is an embodiment of the Connexions service core principles:

- It is an assessment instrument guided solely by the client's own identified concerns: *person-centred.*
- It is broad-based and encourages due weight to be given to a range of concerns: *holistic.*
- It enables the identifying of opportunities for getting support from other services: *multi-agency working.*
- It proceeds inductively and uses past experience as a guide: *evidence-based.*
- It encourages a thoughtful, creative approach by the PA: *reflective practice.*

The use, by Connexions, of therapeutic techniques to 'work for client change' owes much to the *problem as opportunity* orientation of solution-focused therapy. This is the glass as 'half full' school of individual 'empowerment'. The therapist facilitates the discovery of hitherto unknown internal resources by framing questions in such a way as to only elicit responses that provide tangible evidence of client self-efficacy (DfES 2003d; O'Hanlon and Beadle 1997).

Experience and character

To be good, according to the vulgar standard of goodness, is
obviously quite easy. It merely requires a certain amount of sordid
terror, a certain lack of imaginative thought, and a certain low
passion for middle-class respectability

(Wilde 1959: 191)

As a young man growing up in the London of the 1970s and 1980s I enjoyed a great deal of personal freedom. On a shabby London square, as an 'experiment' in social housing, a number of lone parent families had been housed together in four Victorian buildings knocked into each other with a large communal garden at the back. This provided ample opportunity to roam free and to get to know lots of people of different social and ethnic backgrounds. But it also meant I was surrounded by what some might regard as poor role models and bad influences. Without wanting to romanticize my youth as some sort of 'picaresque' rites of passage, looked at through the puritanical, safety obsessed lens of today, it seems hard to believe that I actually made it to adulthood at all. The mere fact of growing up in social housing, the child of a female lone parent with very little money and no extended family, would doubtless these days instantly qualify me for a place on a local authority top 500 list of 'at-risk' children. Added to this list was an absent father; very little maternal supervision; exposure to second-hand smoke and the regular spectacle of adult drunkenness; inconsistent discipline; early, reckless drug taking; a general climate of permissiveness towards drugs; long periods spent hanging out on the neighbourhood streets after dark; under aged, unprotected sex; an enjoyment of wanton vandalism, theft and random acts of violence; early brushes with the law; truancy; drug dealing; a period spent in a pupil referral unit; and leaving school without any qualifications. In other words, I was exposed to many of the things that, according to current wisdom, almost certainly guarantee a one-way ticket to a life of deprivation, ill-health and mental misery (Feinstein *et al.* 2005).

And yet my experience was fairly typical of many of the people I grew up with in North London (apart, perhaps, from the time spent in a pupil referral unit) not all of whom lived in such difficult circumstances as I. Some of the people from my past are dead, incarcerated or mentally shot, but these are a very small minority. Most have gone on to have comparatively full lives of fulfilling work, travel and family. The transition to adulthood might well have been rocky at times; it certainly was not 'managed' in any calculated way. Indeed, in my own case, those years between youth and adulthood, and beyond, were largely ones of experimentation: trial and error. Usually ignoring the wise counsel of others, this meant following impulses, taking a series of whimsical routes and stop-start turns and making a great number of mistakes. None of this conferred instant wisdom, mistakes were – are – repeated. Even if, in hindsight, it is possible to discern the consequences of earlier choices and imagine what might have been, had you done otherwise, this provides no warrant for future conduct.

For many people the transition years are indeed filled with a great deal of confusion and anxiety, and a pained search for identity (Sennett 1996). And friends, family and partners are as likely to be the cause of this pain as a source of solace. Substance use, sex, creativity and individual and collective endeavour are just some of the ways of sublimating existential despair. Periods of depression and introspection, miserable at the time, can also work to burnish and refine raw experience. The question of the role of professional helpers in this, therefore, is moot. It took me a long time to settle on a career path of sorts, but I count the experiences I have had over the course of my life as invaluable. Not as a 'teacher' in any easy, settled way, but for the experiences themselves, many of them enjoyable. All of this is not to discount the fact that each person is differentially positioned by external, structural constraints that will have an enormous bearing on the range of choices he or she is capable of making at any one time (Duneier 2001; Bourdieu 2005). My failure at school and early use of substances was doubtless partly down to my social background and the absence of parental control and support (Duneier 2001; Bourgois 2003) – as also perhaps was the subsequent time it took me to settle on a more or less stable career path. And this, precisely, is one of the chief justifications for intensive professional support being targeted at particular social groups.

The essential point, however, is whether or not I and others like me would have appreciated, let alone benefited from, the sorts of assistance now offered to young people by the authorities. I am not altogether certain I would have accepted the idea that, owing to my social profile, the state had the right to decide on my behalf that I required carefully shepherding through this potentially exciting period of uncertainty. How would the pleasure of taking risks, trying new things out for the first time, and the wonderful sense of life going on forever have comported with the cold demand to carefully weigh up each and every choice, to market myself for employers and to arm myself in advance of all possible eventualities with a battery of techniques for reducing the potential harm from sex and drugs? Were I to have applied these so-called 'life skills' I may well have indemnified myself against not only pleasure, but teenage life itself. Why should official anxieties over the alleged synergistic effects of poverty and teenage risk-taking debar an individual from the right to immerse him- or herself fully in the messy business of human relations? The anthropologist, Philippe Bourgois, writing about impoverished inner city residents of East Harlem, sees in this construction of 'moral citizens' by the capitalist state as a form of structural violence working in the maintenance of existing patterns of inequality.

> Inner city residents must be constructed as moral citizens (who practice safe sex, avoid drugs, refrain from violence, and toil diligently at subordinate jobs) in order to deserve shelter, food, medical care, employment, and a modicum of public respect. Should they fail to abide by these behavioural dictates, they are blamed for producing their own material distress.
>
> (Bourgois 2002a)

The irony of this is that at the very point at which authentic opportunities for young people's independent action and responsibility are contracting, when fundamental, adult-led changes to the social order are disavowed, the demand to be autonomous and self-regulating in advance of experience has become almost deafening (Furedi 2004a). For New Labour, efficiency and the maintenance of social order dictate that particular classes of young people are armed against experience.

Conclusion: transitions

Christopher Lasch once used the term 'culture of narcissism' to describe the emergence of a new cultural situation at the end of the twentieth century (Lasch 1991). Earlier western notions of individuality, based on a broadly stable self encountering external situations of uncertainty, had been progressively replaced by a form of selfhood dedicated to the satisfaction of inner uncertainty through doomed appeals to external sources of affirmation (Lasch 1984, 1991). In a cultural climate of gnawing insecurity and shallow commitments, the concept of transitions has expanded way beyond the navigating of a risky external reality to now encapsulate each and every human relationship and point of change; every potential threat to self, imagined or real (Ecclestone et al. 2005a). The belief among policymakers that every young person would benefit from the close attentions of a personal life coach the better to cope with the infinite transitions of contemporary life, arguably speaks, therefore, to something real and worrying in our culture (Colley 2003).

The vision of society offered by *Bridging the Gap*, leading to the introduction of the Connexions service, is one that is irredeemably individualistic, fragmented and competitive (Colley 2003). The late modern self is regarded as essentially vulnerable, selfish and at risk both psychically and practically (Bauman 2003; Giddens 2004). The consequences for young people are policies and practical initiatives involving an unprecedented formalization of relations between different generations within a community (Furedi 2004a). At the level of public space, a heightened awareness of risk has legitimized increased state surveillance and the intrusive regulation of individuals and groups (Goldson 2000; O'Malley and Waiton 2005). Therapeutic interventions dedicated to the construction of 'moral citizens', such as the Connexions APIR tool, now abound (Bourgois 2002b online; Colley 2003; Ecclestone 2004). As astute observers of recent government policy have noted, structure and agency have been reversed in an effort to adapt individuals to the given social conditions (Colley and Hodgkinson 2001).

What such an analysis of the current situation highlights is the specific way in which the concept of youth 'transitions' has been greatly inflated to emphasize the risky nature of cultural individualization and economic globalization (Ecclestone *et al.* 2004a). Formerly, youth 'transitions' specifically applied to the process of leaving school and entering the labour market, and addressed the largely material and structural mechanisms that facilitated or obstructed this period of change and adaptation (Goodwin and O'Connor 2005). However, late modernity having swept away older structures, codes and certainties, allegedly makes excessive demands on an individual's ability to survive, let alone thrive in conditions of radical uncertainty (Bauman 2003; Giddens 2004). Thus each and every change, risk, challenge, temptation and, indeed, conflicting piece of knowledge, poses a potential threat to young people that is difficult both to compute and to predict the long-term outcome of. And because many of these things occur during relationships with others, such as friends and family, in relation to institutions, such as school and college, and within particular geographical, virtual and media environments, then all of these areas potentially require monitoring and regulating by the state. But what is more, in conditions of globalization there is now an absolute demand from the current political class that citizens achieve economic independence and autonomy (Finlayson 2003; Jordan and Jordan 2003; Clarke 2005; Gillies 2005). Modern welfare has become the 'investment state', dedicated to this project (Fawcett *et al.* 2004). Thus for particular classes of people, i.e. the disadvantaged, the successful management of the complex 'transitions' of late modernity cannot be left to chance. As Tony Blair says, society will have to 'pay a very high price in terms of welfare bills and crime for failing to help people make the transition to becoming independent adults' (SEU 1999: 6).

The provision, therefore, of professional intensive support, incorporating high levels of surveillance and potentially probing into areas previously considered private and off-limits is considered a fair and humane response to the nature of modern 'transitions'. But the normative concept of 'transitions', once in its conceptually limited phase of the domain of careers advice, has now been expanded to include all threats to an individual's security (Ecclestone *et al.* 2005a; Goodwin and O'Connor 2005). And this of course calls for *holistic* forms of youth support capable of responding to the multiplicity of transitional issues. The notion of youth as *rites of passage* in which agency is exercised on an individual's own behalf, mistakes are made and a character is forged out of direct experience, has been superseded by a model in which the conscious *long-term* goal is to achieve economic autonomy through modes of 'life planning' and target setting aided by a battery of professional advisors and coaches (e.g. the APIR) (Finlayson 2003; Weatherall 2004). By learning techniques for impulse control, self-regulation and how to distinguish harmful, pointless risks from those that present opportunity, the individual can be set on a productive, healthy path (Nolan 1998; Weatherall 2004). This is an order of enforced liberty – or to use an oxymoron well-suited to the temper of the times, 'libertarian paternalism' (Sunstein and Thaler 2003; DoH 2004; Halpern *et al.* 2004; *Economist* 2006). Its defining features are a commitment to the formation of an idealized self capable of endless adaptation and the constant acquisition of new skills for an unstable labour market (Weatherall 2004). Alan Finlayson neatly sums up the paradoxical nature of this regulatory enterprise: 'In order to be the kinds of people we are supposed to be, responsible for ourselves and not mediated by the state, that very same state has to act to make it so' (Finlayson 2003).

Is the prevailing pessimism about the formative role of direct life experience for young people justified? Has society become so pervaded by uncertainty, and yet so convinced of the effectiveness of therapeutic intervention, that it has lost all faith in the capacity of young people to independently undergo the sometimes painful, risky process of character formation? Pausing to consider the ways in which current notions of autonomy and its fostering are framed, there appears to be a rather circular reasoning at work in policy circles. A particular set of socio-economic conditions (globalization and economic individualism) have produced a cultural situation of maladapted individuals and groups (the so-called underclass). It is thus the state's duty to reconstruct these same individuals and groups so that the very socio-economic conditions that disadvantaged them in the first place can be successfully reproduced. But aside from the depressing political implications of this, and constraining, complex forces notwithstanding, do such interventions potentially not do a grave injustice to personal agency and dignity? And should it not alarm political progressives who understand the dialectical truth that enduring social solidarities can only ever emerge out of the collective actions of self-determining individuals?

Chronology of key policies and initiative relating to the transition to adulthood

1992   *The Health of the Nation.* Introduced by the Conservative government, this was the health policy that heralded the full emergence of an individualized, preventative approach to dealing with public health using techniques of behaviour modification.

1997   *Social Exclusion Unit (SEU).* Established by New Labour shortly after coming to power. Working cross-departmentally, the unit was set to work on a number of initiatives addressing to youth disaffection and problematic transitions. Published a series of influential Policy Action Team (PAT) reports on youth disadvantage.

1998   *Crime and Disorder Act.* Based on New Labour's zero-tolerance approach to youth crime and efforts to target irresponsible parents. Multi-agency youth offending teams put an emphasis on holistic, preventative work with young offenders and those at risk of offending. Brought in a range of new disposals for the courts including anti-social behaviour orders and curfews.

1999   *Learning to Succeed: A New Framework for Post-16 Learning.* Building on an earlier document *The Learning Age* (1998), the framework sets out New Labour's vision for an employer-led, youth training and education agenda shaped to the realities of economic globalization.

1999   *Bridging the Gap: New Opportunities for Sixteen to Eighteen-Year-Olds.* The key report calling for a single access point youth support service embedded in, and supporting the government youth employability agenda. It identifies the complex nature of late modern youth transitions and focuses on the importance of support able to mould the appropriate dispositions for employment and economic independence.

2000   *Connexions: The Best Start in Life for Every Young Person.* Following the recommendations of *Bridging the Gap,* introduces the Connexions Strategy for the UK.

2004   *Every Child Matters* (ECM). Announces the integrating of education and social care for children and young people through the formation of multi-agency children's trusts to replace local authority social services and education

cont.

	departments. Following the Victoria Climbie case, sets out plans for new information sharing protocols between professionals and the piloting of computer Information, Referral and Tracking (IRT) databases. Introduces five key outcomes for children and young people, to be guaranteed by the workforce: being healthy, staying safe, enjoying and achieving, making a positive contribution and achieving economic well-being.
2005	*Youth Matters.* Proposes an overhaul of youth services on the basis of *Every Child Matters.* Implies the days of informal, club-based work with young people are numbered. Sets out plans for a more formalized youth support service targeted at the most disadvantaged, and using a range of incentives to keep young people engaged in services. Places a question mark over the Connexions service by suggesting that individual children's trusts will be free to commission youth support services of their own choosing.
2006	*Further Education: Raising Skills, Improving Life Chances.* A White Paper proposing reforms in the skills and qualification levels for post-16 education. Stresses customized, individualized provision for learners and diversification of education providers. Again building on the employability agenda, and seeking novel ways to ensure young people stay on in some form of education.

Key readings

Other than the reports, policy papers and acts mentioned above, there are listed below, several seminal texts that look at the changed nature of contemporary culture, New Labour policies and the problematical nature of self-identity in 'late modernity'.

Finlayson, A. (2003) *Making Sense of New Labour*, London: Lawrence and Wishart.

Furedi, F. (2003) *Culture of Fear: Risk Taking and the Morality of Low Expectations*, 2nd edn. London: Continuum.

Furedi, F. (2004a) *Therapy Culture: Cultivating Vulnerability in an Uncertain Age*. London: Routledge.

Giddens, A. (2004) *Modernity and Self-Identity: Self and Society in the Late Modern Age*. Cambridge: Polity Press.
Levitas, R. (1998) *The Inclusive Society? Social Exclusion and New Labour*. Basingstoke: Macmillan.

8   Teacher training for all?
Dennis Hayes

Is it teacher 'education' or teacher 'training'? In further education (FE) and in higher education (HE) the answer was previously 'look and see'. The programmes on offer for lecturers and students were varied. They were often eccentric, following the intellectual inclinations of the tutors who devised them, and occasionally very functional, but always different. This situation no longer exists. Preparation for FE and HE teaching is now, because of government prescription, just simple *training*. This situation mirrors that of initial teacher training for compulsory education. In his inaugural lecture at the Institute of Education, University of London, Professor Len Barton gives an account of his research into the impact that the Teacher Training Agency (TTA), now the Training and Development Agency (TDA), since its creation in 1994, has had on preparation for teaching in schools. His most important finding, for our purposes, is that the TTA privileged 'a discourse of training instead of education as best characterizing these programmes' (Barton 2003: 19). This is precisely the result of the more recent work of the Further Education National Training Organization (FENTO), now absorbed into Lifelong Learning UK (LLUK) and the Institute for Learning and Teaching in HE (ILTHE), now the Higher Education Academy (HEA), all of which foster a skills-based approach. The mental alphabet soup produced by the constantly changing names of quangos is an irritant but is irrelevant except that keeping up with the restructuring and redefinitions – the bureaucratisation of Further education (FE) by the quangocracy – distracts attention from the very real loss of the essential element of education, that differentiates it from training, which is *criticism*. 'Education' is just an empty term if it is not about criticism and the device of insisting against the 'discourse' of the quangocracy that goes on in colleges and universities is 'initial teacher *education*' (ITE) rather than 'initial teacher *training*' (ITT) is, for the most part, a sham. It is a dangerous sham, as anyone with a critical inclination will incline towards cynicism as a result of such semantic manoeuvring.

   The new approaches to preparation for teaching continue to ensure that both critical thinking and, in the case of skill acquisition, the core element of *judgement* are minimized if not removed. Look through lists of 'standards' that teachers should achieve and see if the 'critical' appears. It will rarely be found, even as rhetoric. When it is found there or elsewhere, in course documents and programmes, there are dangerous changes in the meaning of the term, as we will see. With the rejection of any idea of criticism, theory also becomes irrelevant, replaced by the idea of 'reflective practice'. In fact all that is left in training courses is a concern with practice and teaching methods. This general shift can be characterized by a movement away from knowledge and understanding to practice. This is an anti-educational process and the arguments of this chapter are an attempt to reverse that movement.

The shift from ITE to ITT has been facilitated by a completely ill-founded philosophical change, the introduction of 'competence-based' approaches throughout FE programmes, and in FE teacher training, followed by a sleight of hand in the latter case involving another name change. Competencies became 'standards'. Both these approaches break any professional knowledge and skills up into small 'bite sized' chunks (see Chapter 2; Hyland 1994). Much time and effort is spent by the quangocracy on consultations with teachers and lecturers about the range, content and wording of 'standards'. The process of consultation is a displacement activity that inhibits thinking about the unacceptable behavioural basis of the 'standards' and what is being excluded. The main point that has to be made here is that critical thinking and good judgement not only *cannot* be set out in terms of 'standards' – and there is no attempt to even try to do this – because education and training in judgement are open-ended. Quite straightforwardly, what makes them so valued is that their consequences are unpredictable. The unpredictability is part of the transformative aspect of education that lures intelligent and skilled people into FE teaching and not just some prosaic interest in seeing people learn.

The introduction of government imposed 'standards' took away the professional autonomy of the teacher (see the Introduction) and undermined the teacher as an authority, as someone who is an expert in a subject. There is, as we shall see in much of the teacher training literature, a conscious attempt to weaken the authority of the teacher by undermining the idea of knowledge that is transformative (Hayes 2006e) and promoting scepticism, even cynicism, about imparting knowledge and skills. This scepticism merges with educational radicalism and contemporary relativism to produce what can only be described as a celebration of ignorance. Two examples will make this clear. One of the earliest and most popular FE teaching textbooks declares at the outset that, 'The modern teacher is a facilitator' (Reece and Walker [1992] 2003: 4). The reasons given are that adults have experience to offer and that they learn in different ways at their own pace. This orientation around students and the importance of prior knowledge and experience is radically revised in later texts that suggest that 'knowledge' itself is brought into question. We are told to 'treat understanding and knowledge as provisional and never final' and we are encouraged in a sloppy relativism that must accept that 'the interpretations [we] choose to place on any given event is only one of a list of possibilities' (Harkin *et al.* 2001: 36). There is now no using previous knowledge to enable students to learn, but an undermining of their ability to know anything other than what is based on their own experience and personal interpretation. How such views can even survive a cursory understanding, say, of medical science which is characterized not by accepting different interpretations of medical knowledge but by 'the progressive rejections of personal opinion as the basis for authority' (Tallis 2005: 110). In medicine, and much else, your personal 'interpretation' of the facts from your personal experience are worthless. In teacher training, however, talking worthless nonsense now seems to be a goal!

Much of the literature on FE teaching during the last decade and a half, constitutes a dual attack both on the authority of the teacher and on the authority of knowledge. If both are in doubt, why not just 'facilitate' classes? The latest form of 'facilitation' is open communication through 'communicative language use' (Harkin *et al.* 2001: 14). But once knowledge and authority have been done away with, what is left? Increasingly, as will be argued in this chapter, there is nothing left but a focus on either keeping students happy by letting them do what they want or to concentrate on their own and their tutors' emotions and emotional intelligence (Mortiboys 2005; Hayes 2006a; Ecclestone and Hayes 2007).

The following three sections of the chapter deal respectively with how this general undermining of education, through attacking knowledge and understanding actually happens by revising notions of criticism, theory and practice.

Six forms of 'criticism'

Although 'criticism' is the essence of education, the use of the term cannot be taken at face value anymore. There are at least five uses of the term that need to be understood and put on one side if we are to understand what 'criticism' means. As we have lost the true meaning of the term, a discussion of how it is now used is necessary if any clarity is to be regained.

1   *'Criticism' as the politicization of education.* The trouble is that most people do not see what has been lost. The absence of a concern with critical thinking might not even seem to be true. It could be pointed out that there have been commentaries about the lack of

critical thinking in education since the 1960s. The contributors to the influential Penguin special, *Education for Democracy* (Rubinstein and Stoneman 1972), make the point over and over again that 'although the idea of education as a critical activity is not dead, it is not the dominant force shaping British education today' (Arblaster 1972: 39-40) and one of the editors puts their position well:

> So if it is accepted that the pursuit of learning for its own sake is a valid purpose for a university, the conclusion is inescapable that its scholars must be allowed to investigate society, and criticise its contradictions, injustices and inconsistencies. It becomes impossible to make any divorce between the roles of critical scholar and critical citizen.
>
> (Stoneman 1972: 200).

Written in the aftermath of the student revolts of 1968, this book is premised on the contemporary reality of student militancy and the possibility of immediate and revolutionary social change. It is also premised on the post-war consensus that liberal or comprehensive education was the norm for students. It was taken for granted that there would be 'criticism' in the sense of challenging received wisdom in the subjects, in science, English, history and so on. The demand for 'critical thinking' from the 1960s was, therefore, about the politicization of education.

2   *'Criticism' as the adoption of 'critical theory'*. This 'politicization' continues today in the advocacy of another approach by those who draw upon 'critical theory'. 'Critical theory', of which more below, draws on the writings of thinkers reacting to the defeat of political revolution in the 1920s in Germany. The political context of that time was the rise of the Stalinist distortion of communism in the Soviet Union and its domination of political movements throughout the world. Shifting in isolation from involvement in any social movements, the thinkers of the 'Frankfurt School' drifted into philosophy. A popular idea that writers take from the work of Jurgen Habermas, who is associated with the Frankfurt School, is the idea that in a communicative situation there exists the basis for free conversation. The simplified adoption of his work can lead to the tempting and idealistic belief that open, equal and critical communication is possible in the FE classroom, if we approach teaching in a certain way. Being 'critical' in the sense that you, however distantly, associated yourself with the ideas of 'critical theory', although popular with some teacher trainers, is an esoteric and unusual use of the term 'critical'.

3   *'Criticism' as a 'skill'*. The real shift in the meaning of 'critical' away from the sort of criticism that is at the cutting edge of subjects is no longer towards social or political criticism but towards thinking of 'criticism' as a skill. Books and qualifications abound aimed at developing 'critical thinking' (see: lsneducation.co.uk and www.criticalthinking.org and www.lsda.org.uk/files/PDF/unpthinkingskills_taxonomies_bibliography.pdf). Even worse, the 'thinking skills' that these books and resources offer are generalized from any particular subject and therefore have no real application. What is on offer is not a study logic. It does not involve the simple spotting of informal fallacies or the identification of formal logical arguments. There could be no objection to this. There is some value in knowing when an argument is false, for example, because it is *ad hominem*. *Ad hominem* statements attack the person who is arguing by using attitudes, feelings or prejudices about them instead of addressing what they say. Often when unhappy with an argument some academics of either sex, unable to answer a point, will make the gibe – 'Typical of a male middleclass perspective!' No need to respond by feeling guilty, which is the speaker's aim: the gibe embodies a fallacy. Spotting invalid arguments in formal logical is also useful, but harder. Consider this example from syllogistic logic:

> All terrorists are dangerous.
> All terrorists criticize the New Labour government.
> Therefore, all critics of the New Labour government are
>   dangerous.

This is a well-known fallacy where the minor term is said to be 'illicit' because no statement is made about all critics in the premises, although the conclusion makes a statement about *all* critics. There are good books on logic covering such topics (a standard work, for anyone interested is Copi and Cohen ([1953] 2004) *Introduction to Logic*). Books on critical thinking do now introduce you to the rigours of logic, but propose strategies for thinking differently without making what they do relevant to subject content. Being 'critical' in this sense is a mysterious, metaphysical thing.

Application of thinking or critical thinking skills is often thought of as something purely mechanical. Critical thinking, we are often told, is a skill and can easily be part of higher or any level 'key skills' (see Chapter 5). This is a familiar comment from employers' representatives, such as the CBI, but government and hardly anyone is exempt from this fundamental error. Critical thinking involves judgement and new thinking, it cannot by definition be applied mechanically.

4   *'Criticism' as political correctness.* Worse still, 'criticism' as often used by teacher trainers means something like removing your previous assumptions and views and getting you to think correctly. When a young colleague of mine talked about teachers in her experience needing to be much more critical, I was surprised until I realized it meant critical of their assumptions and views. They simply did not have the right perspectives and had to become more critical of themselves so that they could accept politically and educationally correct views.

5   *'Criticism' as cynicism.* Criticism can often mean cynicism. In today's political climate there exists a cynical attitude towards politicians, with mistrust, even fear, of almost any devotion to an ideal. The danger of this climate of cynicism is that traditional philosophical scepticism, which questions the normal understanding of concepts, common sense attitudes to truth and conventional ethical position, no longer acts to challenge everyday views by awakening the mind to the need for criticism of the assumptions on which its ideas are founded but simply reinforces that cynicism. As well as doubting politicians, people are encouraged to doubt knowledge, truth, aesthetic values and ethics. To do its job today, philosophy needs to shore up beliefs not question them. It is all too easy because it will meet with a positive response from many FE lecturers to simply perpetuate and deepen this culture of cynicism as if it were criticism.

6   *Criticism as advancing human understanding.* 'Criticism' in its proper meaning in education applies only to thinking that a base of substantial knowledge and understanding is required as the basis for advancing human knowledge. In Matthew Arnold's famous discussion of the 'Functions of criticism at the present time', he defines criticism as: 'a disinterested endeavour to learn and propagate the best that is has been known and thought in the world' (Arnold [1864] 2003: 50). It is impossible to be critical unless you are a master of a subject. You may *opine* but that is not criticism.

Criticism is out of fashion, but only in part, because of the attack on knowledge and the knowing subject. This attack from teacher trainers is complemented by a removal of all criticism from teacher education by government and its quangos to ensure compliance: not out of fear of the power of critical thinking, which is real, but much more of a 'we know better than you' nannying. This modern nannying is not in the old mode, where there was a conflict between opposing views and they knew best for people, but a more intrusive form in which all forms of independence are frowned upon because they might lead to harm for lecturers or students (see the Introduction; Hayes 2006e; Ecclestone and Hayes 2007).

Criticism does not sell, as publishers will tell you. Functional approaches are what people want. On ITE courses, teachers read only as much as they need to read to get through a course, often no more than a core text (Lawes 2004: 215–18). Volumes written by teacher trainers in FE now flood the market but they are notoriously uncritical works, in the proper sense of 'uncritical'. They are uncritical in that they, for the most part, reject the knowledge – the theory – that might constitute education as a subject.

A discussion of types of criticism in this way is an important step towards understanding what is missing from ITT for FE and a first step to rebuilding ITE. A second step is to understand that the acceptance of training implies a commitment to a philosophy of education or to a theory of education. In teacher training this is often approached through a discussion of 'ideologies' of education, which are presented in such a way that students often think they can pick and choose between them in an arbitrary manner.

The ideologies of teacher trainers

In a companion volume to this, there is a discussion and activities aimed at drawing the attention of practitioners to the educational ideologies that lie behind or are expressed in various FE programmes and courses (Armitage *et al.* 2007: Section 7.4). The five ideologies and their aims presented there are: classical humanism (cultural transmission), liberal humanism (knowledge for a fairer society), progressivism (personal growth for a democratic society), instrumentalism (skill delivery) and reconstructionism (social change). This use of 'ideology' is loose and refers to a 'set of ideas', that does not approach any level of complexity. The idea of 'ideology' as a 'false consciousness' of the world is not addressed, although it has ready application to some of the policy suggestions of recent governments and various quangos. Exercise 7.13 in the companion volume, invites readers to 'spot the ideology' in a range of courses. Occasionally, a sharp Certificate in Education student has been known to apply this exercise to the course they are undertaking. The results are not always welcomed by teacher trainers, who prefer a posture of ideological neutrality. The neutral teacher trainer is as much a straw person as the neutral teacher and not only do Certificate in Education programmes and teacher trainers have explicit or implicit ideologies but so do the major textbooks. The important point is that 'ideologies' or theories of education are not 'tools' for use in the game of education, but are serious intellectual attempts to understand education and are passionately defended as true or equally passionately attacked as false. They matter, not least, in determining what education is given to students. For the most part they are contradictory, if not incommensurate, and cannot be adopted in a 'pick and mix' or eclectic way. To treat them in this way is to encourage cynicism about education.

Taking 'spot the ideology' a step further, here is a brief guide to the standard texts FE lecturers may come across, set out under sub-headings indicating their broad ideological sweep and their attitude to 'criticism'.

Theorists

L. B. Curzon's book, *Teaching in Further Education* is in, what is now considered to be, the old school of theory before practice. Despite revisions, it has embodied for three decades the idea that FE lecturers' thinking needs grounding in basic theories in order to understand what they are doing. The latest edition of his book starts with a quotation that argues that unless the teacher has 'some definite idea of what constitutes an education' they make work to very little purpose ([1976] 2005: 3). Curzon's work is largely focused on educational psychology with some philosophy, and this is typical of such works produced in the 1960s and 1970s.

Teachers newly on a training programme might well seek out J. W. Tibble's *The Study of Education*, published in 1966, to see that once teachers were expected to have some understanding of what the relevant forms of knowledge, philosophy, psychology, sociology and history had to tell us about education. It is still a useful work if, as Brian Simon says, talking of the study of the history of education, you want to go beyond concern with day-to-day practical issues and gain 'a wider perspective and a deeper understanding' (Simon 1966: 126).

Curzon's work has been thoroughly revised but is still relatively hard going and unfashionable in these untheoretical times. It might be considered an exception to the anti-theoretical and critical drift. Nevertheless, as it gets revised, the views of theories start to be accommodated to fashion. For example, his note on teaching and training ('instruction' is added in the most recent edition) puts forward a sophistry that all three are fundamentally similar 'and their rationale is an intensification of the rate of human development – an important aspect of educational activity' (Curzon [1976] 2005: 29) and are therefore conducive to human growth. This is supposed to undermine Richard Peters' argument in *Ethics and Education*, published in 1966, that 'training' is not part of education because it is always for specific ends, whereas education is worthwhile in itself. Curzon merely glosses over important distinctions. An 'intensification of human development' uses speed as a criterion to connect education and training. But learning how to use a gun faster and learning to read Shakespeare carefully and well but faster (if such a thing is possible) remain different, the first being a means to an end the latter an end in itself. This is the sort of thinking that you get in education policy when literature is seen as building self-awareness and values. Happily, Shakespeare is no good for citizenship and reading him may turn out more Iagos than Henry Vs.

Anti-theorists: reflective practice

The rhetoric of promoting 'reflective practice' is so ubiquitous it seems unexceptional. Everyone accepts that a good lecturer 'strives for continuous improvement through reflective practice' (LLUK 2006: 2). However, I don't accept that 'reflective practice' is a good thing. It is a meaningless term that promotes a dangerous anxiety-making, navel gazing that undermines a lecturer's ability to be a good teacher. Of course if you are a nominalist like Humpty Dumpty in Lewis Carroll's *Through the Looking Glass* you might declare, 'When *I* use the term reflective practice it means just what I choose it to mean –neither more nor less.'

Yvonne Hillier's book, *Reflective Practice in Further and Adult Education*, is the opposite of Curzon's. Its general drift is anti-theoretical. This may seem surprising as she claims that if we (critically) reflect:

> we not only challenge our assumptions about why we do what we do, we can also help ourselves identify where we feel lacking and why we may be setting ourselves unnecessarily unachievable standards. How can we reflect on our approaches to our practice? What can we do? What can we uncover in the process?
>
> (Hillier 2002: 7)

Already the reader feels insecure. Worried. And we should be, as human knowledge is about to be undermined. The method Hillier uses in her opening chapter is a model of how to cast doubt on knowledge and teacher authority by simply referring to others who also undermine it. What she uses is what can be called the 'charm bracelet' approach to theory. In her introductory chapter she tells us, following post-modern thinkers, that practice is all, and that by looking at knowledge as problem solving 'the gap between theory and practice' is bridged (Hillier 2002: 12). Then we are told we might think there are too many formal and 'informal theories', and that 'universal theory' is no use (2002: 14), then Karl Popper's work is invoked to cast doubt on scientific truth (Hillier 2002: 14) and finally 'critical theory' is introduced to further question the 'scientific or positivist paradigm' (2002: 16). Not many readers will have a clue about whether what she says about these thinkers' philosophies is true. No one will have read serious and difficult works on the theory of knowledge, such as Susan Haack's work on reconstructing, rather than deconstructing and undermining, truth (1993). The message is clear. Practice not theory is what you need because there are no truths, and science is questionable.

All that is left is a vague and literally confusing (Hillier 2002: 17) notion of reflective practice. It is opposed to reasoning, objective truth and science. Adding 'critical' before it is spurious. We are pushed towards self-questioning and therapy, and told to 'think of [ourselves] as learners and to ask, 'What does it feel like?' (2002: 27). This approach takes away the lecturers' knowledge, authority and ability, and promotes anxiety and insecurity. Reflecting all the time on personal experiences is the opposite of theorizing. Of course, for reflective practitioners theory is practice (for a critique, see Lawes 2004).

Hillier is the most well-known advocate of 'reflective practice' in FE, and her work is one of the reasons why the term is so widely accepted. Yet it remains an ill-defined term. It has no meaning other than 'be worried about what you do, and talk about it or write it down'.

There are even more extreme manifestations of the anti-theoretical impulse behind 'reflective practice'. For example, Jean McNiff has even taken solipsistic individualized anti-theory as far as it can go with the development of what she calls 'I theory', or what ordinary folk would call floundering about in ignorance (McNiff with Whitehead 2002; McNiff 2003)

Descriptive practice

Whatever the textbooks say, much of what is presented by trainee teachers as 'reflective practice' in terms of diaries, logs and evaluations seems to have no purpose other than to express and worsen lecturers' fears about all aspects of teaching. Most of the writing is also crude, no more than postcards from the classroom or tutorial. Much of it is so brief, unclear or merely summative, it is incomprehensible to an external reader. A better approach would be for the trainee teacher to abandon the 'reflective' part and to engage in straightforward *descriptive practice*. Descriptive practice requires the careful observation and recording of the classroom, the students' and the teacher's actions and utterances. This is not an easy task. The best examples of how to do it come from literature. A model might be Ursula Brangwen's struggle with her pupils in D. H. Lawrence's *The Rainbow* ([1915] 1995: 288–361) or Gradgrind's teaching of facts in the opening chapter of Charles Dickens' *Hard Times* ([1854] 2003). More recently, the model for any work on education must be Alan Bennett's *The History Boys* (2004).

Functionalists

Functionalist approaches are popular. This is how to do the job, put simply with no fuss, no ambiguity or challenges. The model functionalist texts are Minton's *Teaching Skills in Further and Adult Education* (2005) and Reece and Walker's *A Practical Guide to Teaching and Learning*, first published in 1992. Reece and Walkers' work is a good example of this sort of text. The first edition is in the tradition of 'tips and ideas', while the second edition, of 1994, introduced competencies and led the trend towards the entirely functional 'meeting the standards' approach of Fawbert and Donaldson (2006). The tradition is continued in Coles (2004). Now every university offering a training course is producing its own functional textbook. A worrying recent shift away from 'functioning' to just surviving is Jim Crawley's 'survival guide', *In at the Deep End* (2005).

Mixed in with this functional approach, which is entirely uncritical, are snippets of what could be called the ideology of social engineering. Fawbert and Donaldson (2006), Coles (2004) and Crawley (2005) all have broad social justice or even socialist aims, which come out more in the 'food for thought' exercises they add or in the sections on education policy. For a more thorough work on social engineering through education in the New Labour tradition, Tom Bentley's *Learning Beyond the Classroom* (1998) is required reading. Whether social justice issues are raised or not, functionalist textbooks fit in well with the New Labour technicist approach to problems. We know what we want from FE: achieving it is a technical matter.

Neutralists

Armitage *et al.*'s *Teaching and Training in Post-Compulsory Education* (2007) really takes no stance on any ideological issue. This is true of the companion volume, Lea *et al.*'s *Working in Post-Compulsory Education* (2003). Both books take a position which is that there are normally two clear sides on any issue and they ask the reader to think for themselves about a topic. This is, in part, a device that covers clear differences of opinion between the authors and in part it is a useful methodological tool. Neutralists like Armitage *et al.* clearly value critical thinking but in a rather abstract way. Critical thinking is valued for its own sake rather than as manifested in any clear battle of ideas. This is less true of Lea *et al.* but, even there, there is difference but no engagement.

Therapists

Textbooks for FE teaching as therapy are sure to be on the increase and we can expect *Circle Time in FE* to be a best seller soon – publishers should note the title is under copyright! We already have Alan Mortiboys' *Teaching with Emotional Intelligence. A Step-by-Step Guide for Further and Higher Education Professionals* (2005) and his training programmes offering the same. One sixth form college is already offering all students emotional quotient (EQ) testing and training in emotional literacy (see Chapter 3). But the new therapeutic ethos runs through many other textbooks.

Harkin, Dawn and Turner are typical of many teacher educators with a radical orientation who slip into therapeutic education. They argue that 'Much of what passes for education is dull and of little relevance to learners' (Harkin *et al.* 2001: 140). They add:

> It is time to build a high-trust, democratic education system that respects learners and their experiences, listens closely to their expressions of interest and need, builds partnerships between teachers, learners, parents, the community and employers so that young adults learn what they wish to learn, and how they wish to learn.
>
> (2001: 40)

The language they use: 'trust', 'partnership', and 'respect' for 'learners and their experiences', is that of the therapist rather than the educationalist. They also provide a focus on communication and the notion of striving for an 'ideal speech community' in which the 'learner voice' will no longer be silent (2001: 142). The therapeutic implications of this should be obvious. Indeed the shift towards the therapeutic culture in FE is becoming focused on the 'learner's voice' rather than on the student, quietly engaged in studying.

Norman Lucas, in his otherwise excellent book, *Teaching in Further Education,* argues that FE teaching needs a new concept to frame our thinking, which is that of 'the learning professional'. The key to achieving learning professionalism is that teachers and students should move from a 'curriculum to a "learner-led" perspective' (Lucas 2004: 176). There you have it: no more curricula just learning. Lucas, despite his intentions, is creating a professional framework with no content, a vacuum to be filled by therapeutic education. If you give up on knowledge all you have left is therapy, helping young people to deal with their personal issues and inner selves.

Humanists

Hayes, Marshall and Turner's book *A Lecturer's Guide to Further Education* (2007). contains contributions from FE lecturers and others who are broadly working within what might be described as in the 'humanist' tradition.

From varying backgrounds, they all believe in progress and that humanity is capable of controlling its destiny through the development of knowledge and understanding. They are pro-science and pro-technology. To some extent, each contributor supports a distinction between 'knowledge' and 'skills' and hence, 'education' and 'training'. In an age where writers like John Gray popularize the idea that 'progress is a superstition' and that we should not try to 'remake the world' or try to live in a 'world of our own making' (Gray 2002: xi–xv) they are an antidote to misanthropy and the idea that, in particular, young people cannot change what they are or the world they live in. People are not animals. Above all else, Hayes *et al.* would defend criticism in the proper sense.

Teaching without purpose

If criticism and theory are abandoned then all teaching is bad teaching. This is true no matter how much effort is put into improving teaching. The consequence of all the effort being put into developing teachers will be that teaching will get worse. The publication of the LLUK, revised professional 'standards' for teachers in the 'learning and skills sector', shows how serious a business improving teaching is becoming. Every FE and adult education lecturer will soon have to prove they meet revised and demanding professional 'standards'. As has been noted – like the equally demanding and recently revised TDA 'standards' for the wider workforce and school teachers and the HEA Standards for university teachers – the standards for teacher trainers in FE can be searched in vain for any mention of the development of students' critical thinking that is the essence of education. Unless lecturers have some understanding and commitment to a theory of education and, in every lesson, critical thought is developed, then the 'standards' are about socialization. Teaching becomes just a form of group-based social work backed by an over-complicated and ruthlessly monitored exercise in ensuring compliance of lecturers in meeting the 'standards'.

But if the government and its quangos have given up on education in favour of 'inclusive' social training of a therapeutic nature, just what will lecturers do when they are supervising those unthreatening and safe learning spaces for 860 hours a year?

If you're not being asked to work at giving hard lectures, challenging seminars or at imparting difficult skills, what are you supposed to do? Why worry? Why not relax with this 'survivor's guide' to teaching that lists the main techniques for skiving that are familiar to every experienced lecturer (Hayes 2006b).

The FOFO technique

This is the classic skiving technique. The initials stand for 'F*** off and find out!' The original technique was simply to send your students to the library to research a topic or find the answer to a question. In its modern form it involves getting students to surf the Web in order to research a topic or answer a question. Whatever form is appropriate the result is the same, no students and some peace! The ICT form of FOFO has the added benefit of not disturbing the repose of librarians. Paul Mackney, the General Secretary of NATFHE for many years, claims that he has the copyright on this technique along with its more generic form, the yo-yo technique.

The yo-yo technique

This is a technique that was universally applied by employers in the Thatcherite 1980s and early 1990s, but has now gained institutional recognition by those lecturers who simply do not want to teach. It stands for 'You're on your own'. The students can complete packs in student study or support centres, or work through pre-packaged materials in book or electronic form.

The wilt technique

Make your teaching relevant by adopting this cynical technique inspired by Tom Sharpe's novels about the liberal studies lecturer, Wilt. This is more demanding than FOFO, as the lecturer has to listen to what the students are talking about and pursue that line of discussion before just letting them continue to talk. Only now it's a lesson and not just chatting. 'Wasn't that interesting!' they'll say as they leave. If you hit on the right topic for most of the session you can daydream, only waking up and interjecting a point here and there if the level of chatting diminishes.

The circle time technique

This will now be familiar to students since primary school, so it's easy to use and almost expected. Sit your students in a single group or, preferably, in independent small groups and encourage them to express their feelings about whatever topic is on the syllabus. Get one person in each of the circles to write the group's feelings down on a flip chart and discuss them with the whole class. Apart from odd moments of sitting near each group and pretending to listen and then, at the end of the session, saying, 'Tell me what your group thought', this is a really undemanding way of spending a few hours.

The amanuensis technique

An amanuensis is a person who copies things down. The amanuensis technique involves the lecturer getting students to copy work from the board or a slide. You get students to copy down lots of notes from the whiteboard or an OHT, or better still from the Web, which is the ICT form of the technique. This is something they find rewarding, as files and notebooks fill up. It usually keeps them quiet for most of a lesson. Many students use the amanuensis technique instinctively in essays, where it is called 'plagiarism'.

The sociological technique

This approach involves keeping students occupied by getting them mentally confused. Its origins are in sociology and it works well with access and in-service groups. A warning is necessary as some effort is involved at first in producing a worksheet and a set of questions, or giving out a textbook. Once started you can relax and leave the students to discuss seven or more definitions, or complex views, on any topic, such as 'class'. By the end of the session a student will say with awe and respect, 'I haven't a clue what that was about. It just shows you how difficult everything is!'

The 'Socratic' technique

The 'Socratic' technique is often said to be about questioning. Lecturers sometimes say, 'I use the "Socratic" method. I ask my students questions and encourage them to ask questions.' This often results in a sort of therapy of endless questioning and ultimately to uncertainty about everything. There is no understanding of the Socratic combat or 'eristic', in which endless questioning leads to self-contradictions – the 'elenchi' – that stuns the student and spurs them onwards towards truth (Ryle 1966: 193–215). Questioning of this sort is more akin to the public philosophical 'prize fighting' of the intellectually uncommitted and morally relativistic Sophists than to Socrates.

The subversive technique

Despite the findings of some surveys, the trendy, subversive and, preferably, young or young at heart lecturer, is very popular and need hardly teach at all: take up some issue that's close to the social or personal life of students or give them their 'voice' and conspire against the programme, other staff, the college or the examination system. As long as no action ever emerges from this form of free communication, the radical lecturer will gain respect and the students' self-esteem will grow. They will even work in their spare time so as not to get the subversive lecturer in trouble with management.

The workshop technique

This is another way of letting students teach themselves; unfortunately the lecturer has to stay in the room. This technique is adapted from motor vehicle and craft workshops. All students have individual programmes they have negotiated and they learn at their own pace, while the tutor, although technically available, can sit at a desk and read. 'Personalized learning' will extend to all courses and programmes: the whole learning and skills sector is about to go on a big skive!

The portfolio technique

Spend several sessions allowing students to build their portfolios. Lots of lever arch files and plastic wallets are needed but there is nothing demanded of the tutor but some knowledge of alphabetical order and presentation. Once, as an external examiner, I weighed a set of portfolios and the average weight was 1.5 kilos! When they were first introduced and ridiculed as a trivialized form of assessment, one lecturer commented that portfolio building was so demanding her students never had time to watch *Coronation Street*!

By now any attentive reader attuned to irony will have noted that these are not normally considered to be techniques for skiving, but techniques at the cutting edge of teaching. They use a variety of methods to engage students. Throughout FE, and in HE as well as in compulsory education, these 'techniques' are really about keeping students happy or at least about keeping them occupied in some therapeutic activity (Ecclestone and Hayes 2007). Happiness is, of course, a 'new science' (Layard 2006) which is spreading as a new 'subject' in education.

'Chill out' about pedagogy

'What would good teaching in FE look like, then?' The answer is: 'Chill Oout! Don't worry about it'. Get away from thinking about process and teaching methods and ask a different question. The key question for every lecturer to ask is, 'Why should any student listen to a lecturer?'

Students may be given extrinsic rewards for listening (see Chapter 3) but this means nothing if, when they get into the classroom, there is nothing there for them. A lecturer has authority because a lecturer *knows* something. It is the knowledge and skills that a lecturer is offering as part of 'the best that has been known and thought in the world' that makes students listen. A lecturer has authority over students because a lecturer is an authority. The single criterion or standard that is necessary for good teaching is 'Does this person know their stuff?' If a lecturer knows a subject, whether academic or practical, it can be passed on in many ways.

Personal characteristics have nothing to do with this. A good lecturer who knows something might be a bad person. In FE many teachers are, to say the least, eccentric. Looking back at the 'tech' where I first started teaching, I recall that among the staff were a couple of 'one hit wonder' pop stars, a playwright, a Mills and Boon writer, an alternative comedian, a cartoonist, several academics 'manqués', a few experts in obscure skills and sports, political activists from several extreme socialist parties, some members of strange religious groups and more than a few freemasons! All of them brought their eccentric ideas and hobbies into the classroom. They made the lecturers in Tom Sharpe's *Wilt* seem ordinary. Bit they were great teachers, however eccentric their approaches (Hayes 2006d).

The eccentric FE teacher is now an endangered species. For 20 years, since the establishment of the National Council for Vocational Qualifications in 1986, they have been qualified into conformity. Staff development, Certificate in Education programmes and the various mandatory 'assessor' qualifications have imposed conformity and dullness on the sector. The result of checklists on behavioural competencies is exactly what was intended. Dull compliant teachers were created who would turn lively students into compliant dullards conforming to the demands of whatever faddish and patronizingly simple courses or poor jobs they were offered.

One thing we can be sure of is that what makes a good teacher in FE has nothing to do with being able to tick off all those Lifelong Learning UK 'standards'. It's something else. As an aside, I will add that the person who makes a good teacher trainer in FE will never be the lecturer who meets the new 'standards' that are being prepared to try to define this even more eccentric beast! And no one, except those who score highly, believes that good teaching has anything to do with inspection grades. The best teacher I know always does badly in such things. He or she is a genius but more than a little dull. The difference is in what he or she has to say. The inspectors have their 'edutainment' check lists and are just 'job's worths' when it come to looking for what is different. The 'different' or 'eccentric' part of a person is something that can't be put on a check list, so they can't spot it.

Eccentricity itself is not enough, although it is the best rough guide, because eccentrics can be just that and not necessarily good teachers. I put the question, 'What is it that makes someone a good FE teacher?' to some eccentric FE teachers in a 'focus group'. They were very certain that, 'A good FE teacher relates well to students'. Pressed further on this, they said that 'relate' meant that the teacher not only would have knowledge, but they would also possess a love of their subject. Bad lecturers could have knowledge but unless they were inspired to pass it on to their students they wouldn't be able to 'relate' to them. Another sort of bad lecturer they identified was the one who had no knowledge, or little knowledge, and thought that trying to 'relate' to students was what was most important.

The know-alls and the know-nothings were roundly condemned. As to the good teachers, my focus group said that it was not just their eccentric passions and past lives that were of interest, but the fact that their eccentricities were a peculiar expression of the deep love they had for their subject and that this caught the imagination of their students.

The fact is that the best teachers are bound to be the eccentric ones: the ones that can't be assessed using check lists. It's time those obsessed by setting out formulae for quality teaching learned to 'chill out' and accept good teachers even if they don't meet half or any of the criteria on their check lists.

Managers, inspectors and teacher trainers may well ask, 'How do we assess teachers then?' The answer is simply, 'Don't'. Don't *measure* them. They have knowledge. *Get to know* them and you will improve your understanding of what teaching in FE or any sector or education is about.

A Chronology of Teacher Training for FE

1944	The McNair Report projected the post-war need for over 500 new FE lecturers every year. Training was to be given on an in-service basis, with some pre-service courses.
1950	In the 1950s the C&GLI's 730 series was established, with the first Technical Teacher's Certificate being awarded.
1957	The Supply and Training of Teachers in Technical Colleges (Willis Jackson Report).
1959	Crowther Report: 75 per cent of FE teachers were found to have no teaching qualification.
1964	Industrial Training Boards established.
1966	*The Supply of Trained Teachers in Further Education* (Russell Report): seven years after the Crowther Report only a third of FE lecturers were teacher trained.
1973	Haycocks I *Report of the Advisory Committee on the Supply and Training of Teachers* (ACSETT) recommended induction courses and in-service training for experienced staff.
1977	Haycocks II, looked at provision for the training of part-time lecturers.

cont.

1977	Circular 11/77, 'The training of teachers for further education', asked regional advisory councils to draw up plans and report back by September 1978. The intention was to make induction training mandatory by 1981.
1978	Haycocks III, *Training Teachers for Management in Further and Adult Education*, looked at how management and management training in FE could be improved.
1979	CNAA sets up a Further Education Board and, by 1981/2 16 centres were running a two-year part time Cert. Ed.
1981	SCETT formed by the school and FE teacher unions to promote the training and development of teachers and lecturers.
1990	TDLB established, leading to the introduction of TDLB Assessor Awards for those teaching NVQs such as the C&GLI units D32, D33, for assessors D34, D35, for internal verifiers and D36 for APL advisors.
1996	Further Education Staff Development Forum established.
1999	FENTO launched as the NTO for FE.
2001	Statutory Instrument No 1209 makes initial teacher training mandatory for all newly appointed lecturers from 1 September.
2002	Common Inspection Framework established leading to the first inspections of FE colleges by OfSTED and ALI.
2002	IfL(FE), later the IfL (PCET), then the IfL, held it's first AGM in June 2003 as a nascent professional body for FE.
2003	OfSTED's report, issued on 11 November, *The Initial Teacher Training of Further Education Teachers* declared FE teacher training to be unsatisfactory: 'The current system of FE teacher training does not provide a satisfactory foundation of professional development for FE teachers at the start of their careers' (2003 Summary). The DfES response that came out on the same day, *The future of initial teacher education for the learning and skills sector* set out an agenda for reform.
2004	QTLS. The award of 'Qualified Teacher Learning and Skills' was announced on 2 November by Kim Howells, Minister of State, and is described in *Equipping our Teachers for the Future: Reforming Initial Teacher Training for the Learning and Skills Sector*, which names the IfL as the professional body for the sector.

cont.

2005	Foster Review, *Realizing the Potential: A Review of the Future Role of Further Education Colleges* (November), calls for a new 'workforce development' strategy.
2006	LLUK revises the teacher training standards for FE.
2006	LLUK Consultation on Standards for Teacher Trainers in FE.
2007	ITALS and QTLS. From September all new entrants to teaching are required to complete the Initial Teaching Award Learning and Skills (ITALS) to lead to a threshold status to teach. QTLS to be awarded by the IfL, which will register all teachers and seek to provide coherence in ITT awards with other sectors of education. All serving lecturers to complete 30 hours CPD every year and maintain a portfolio overseen by the IfL. All trained teachers will have to keep their portfolio updated to retain their 'Licence to Practise', which is to be awarded on the completion of initial training.

Key readings

Armitage, A., Bryant, R., Dunnill, R., Hayes, D., Hudson, A., Kent, J., Lawes, S. and Renwick, M. (2007) *Teaching and Training in Post-Compulsory Education*. 3rd edn. Maidenhead: Open University Press.

Crawley, J. (2005) *In at the Deep End: A Survival Guide for Teachers in Post-Compulsory Education*. London: David Fulton.

Curzon, L. B. ([1976] 2005) *Teaching in Further Education: An Outline of Principles and Practice*, 6th edn. London: Cassell.

Harkin, J., Turner, G. and Dawn, T. (2001) *Teaching Young Adults. A Handbook for Teachers in Post-Compulsory Education*. London: RoutledgeFalmer.

Hillier, Y. (2002) *Reflective Teaching in Further and Adult Education*. London and New York: Continuum.

IfL papers. Available at: http://www.ifl.ac.uk/members_area/code_prof.html and http://www.ifl.ac.uk/members_area/code_ethics.html

Lea, J., Hayes D., Armitage, A., Lomas, L. and Markless, S. (2003) *Working in Post-Compulsory Education*. Maidenhead: Open University Press.

Lucas, N. (2004) *Teaching in Further Education: New Perspectives for a Changing Context*. London: Institute of Education, University of London.

Minton, D. ([1976] 2005) *Teaching Skills in Further and Adult Education*, 3rd edn. Basingstoke and London: City & Guilds and Macmillan.

Reece, I. and Walker, S. ([1992] 2003) *A Practical Guide to Teaching, Training and Learning*, 5th edn. Bath: Business Education Publishers.

Walklin, L. ([1990] 2000) *Teaching and Learning in Further and Adult Education*. London: Nelson Thornes.

9 Symposium: the future of further education

Ian Nash, Kathryn Ecclestone and Claire Fox

Ian Nash: Colleges must get the Government off their backs. College leaders need to challenge publicly many of the policy reforms and funding changes imposed on their institutions. Too often, new demands from political paymasters have more to do with getting their governments out of a spending hole than with wider public benefits.

Following incorporation of colleges in 1993, when they were 'freed' from local authority control, it was suggested that the new age of the entrepreneur had arrived. Instead, it created the age of the accountant. Money rules; utilitarianism dictates. The world of further education became more pragmatic than visionary.

There are three key reasons for this. First, college principals and governors were seduced by the idea of local independence. They did not think hard enough about the centralized control, incorporation would bring. Second, they responded too uncritically to the idea of an education 'marketplace'. Third, they were too willing to oblige other people in order to chase the money. As a result, many colleges lost sight of their own vision and objectives and of what colleges can do best.

The purpose of a college can be defined in very straightforward terms. The core strength of the college is in giving people of all abilities an enhanced curriculum, beyond the utilitarian, that gets them into work, enriches their lives and keeps them on the ladder of success.

It is simple, clear and is the core idea behind the American community college, which does what it says on the tin: it serves the local community in all its aspects. It also reflects to a lesser extent – though still substantially – the Australian further education and training college.

To achieve a truly independent status, colleges in England must do three things: first, challenge the current hegemony that dictates terms regardless of which political party is in power; second, be more confident of the fact that college managers and staff know their communities better than do the politicians; and, third, learn to say 'No'.

College directors, managers and staff need to coalesce around a single mission. They should adopt the maxim (or one like it) created in 2002 by the Universities Council for the Education of Teachers in its report *Beyond Compliance*, that stated:

The intention was to move the focus . . . beyond a culture of control and compliance and a preoccupation with accountability to consider how universities, colleges and schools can once again become a driving force in educational thinking and the improvement of quality.

(UCET 2002: 1)

Leaders of colleges and their representative organizations, nationally and locally, need to take the risk of telling ministers, 'Yes, we will do it', but, 'Not with the paltry cash you are offering'. Market forces can drive down costs for governments. Fear drives necessity: fear of missing whatever cash is up for grabs. Unfortunately, the same forces are not guaranteed to drive up quality. Witness Britain's railways under the current franchizing system: government spending may be contained, but fares rise, while the quality of service plummets. For 'rail fares', read 'college fees'.

Ministers quote national statistics suggesting a desire by the public to see higher fees for non-vocational courses (and a willingness to pay them), but such data are insensitive to local issues. National edicts follow, constraining much of the flexibility local planning agents (local learning partnerships) may wish to have.

Ministerial priorities change with the political wind and with short-term economic contingencies. Flavours of the month, since 1993, have included an all-out push for 16–19 education expansion. Then it was adult recruitment at all costs. There was a new swing back to 16–19 education and a widening of that remit to cover 14–19-year-olds. Now skills for life and work-related courses take spending priority.

Government-created or -supported cash raising initiatives to boost spending have ranged from franchizing courses out to industry to expansion, on the cheap, through an accountants' creation known as 'demand-led' element of funding. Then there was the disastrous foray into individual learning accounts (ILAs), which was stopped by the government amid claims of wide-scale fraud. In fact, the Treasury had already called a halt because of a massive overspend of around £60 million. Ministers refused to take the blame, instead, private training providers were accused and court action followed. Colleges, meanwhile, deprived of that cash, plunged deeper into debt.

What happened to all the fine initiatives espoused by New Labour in their early years in power? Remember *The Learning Age* green paper in which David Blunkett, then Education Secretary, said opportunities for all had to be far wider than just employment:

As well as securing our economic future [lifelong] learning has a wider contribution. It helps make ours a civilized society . . . promotes active citizenship . . . helps us fulfil our potential and opens doors to a love of music, art and literature. That is why we value learning for its own sake.

(DfEE 1998: 7)

Blunkett wanted colleges to be part of the big story of community involvement and active citizenship. He knew he could not do this by merely marshalling the troops under a single skills-for-work banner. His successors, notably Charles Clarke and learning and skills minister Bill Rammell, had other ideas. Many colleges are persuaded that the skills agenda is paramount. But on whose terms is it to be pursued? Whose agenda is it? At what cost to other 'local' priorities?

Other flavours of the month have emerged, including proposals in the Foster and Leitch reviews for the future of colleges and the wider UK skills needs. On what terms do colleges accept, challenge or reject them?

At the moment, the college sector is the repository of everyone else's brands. Colleges rarely say, 'No'. While they continue to do everyone's bidding but their own, they will not be taken seriously.

Kathryn Ecclestone: At the LSDA's research conference on 28 February 2006, an optimistic Andrew Thomson, head of the new Quality Improvement Agency (QIA), challenged colleges to develop 'self-improving', 'risk-taking' and 'engaged' staff, and to reject the instrumental compliance with inspection and instrumental quality and funding systems that has grown up over the past 13 years.

His enthusiastic call for a re-energized sector is welcome. Yet, the QIA and new inspection agency, and the growing emphasis on 'skills' for work, announced in the White Paper in March 2006, are the latest in a long series of reforms and restructurings. Each time ministers promise 'a new dawn' for the sector, and Bill Rammell, speaking at the same conference, was no exception.

It is not easy to see how to rally staff in FE colleges, who have been on the receiving end of endless chaos, confused missions, spending crises, initiatives, restructuring and 'reforms'. It is perhaps time, as Ian says, to call on colleges to come out from under the political cosh and to assert a clear, broad and optimistic educational mission in the face of Foster's call for a utilitarian focus on skills.

But we need to ask why it has become so difficult for those who lead and teach in FE colleges to assert a challenging, constructively critical opposition to this litany of mayhem and waste of tax-payers' money over the past 13 years. Or to create and agree on a clear educational mission, let alone to be a driving force in education as Ian hopes.

One reason is that a growing number of college managers and teachers seem to be loosing their belief that they can educate anyone. Instead of education or even the development of utilitarian skills for work, it's commonplace to hear practitioners and policy-makers presenting a diminished, down-trodden view of learners and the sector itself. FE is now seen as the place to repair fragile identities and to deal with vulnerable young people and adults. Although well-meant as a response to the exporting of failure from the school sector, this pitying and negative image of students is increasingly taking hold.

It is a far cry from the optimistic, radical view of students and educational aspirations that many lecturers and managers held about the purposes of FE in the 1980s. Despite mass unemployment, poverty and high levels of failure and drop-out from the school system at that time, goals for all learners were broad, educational, upbeat and aspirational. Now the language of fragility and vulnerability stalks the sector. Utilitarian skills and heavy handed inspection and quality systems must be resisted but these are only part of the barrier to a real educational vision: diminished images of students are a problem too.

And if lecturers are to play a part in asserting an educational vision, we need to challenge the impoverished forms of education that they get in their initial teacher training and in the limited professional development on offer through their careers. Under the culture of compliance that Ian describes, initial teacher education is in dire straits. Reduced to the dreary narrowness of the FENTO/LLUK standards and the pronouncements of inspectors about good practice, universities and colleges have colluded in the erosion of initial teacher education into a mixture of compliance and disempowered criticism of government policy.

If teacher education has no educational mission, no upbeat view of teaching and learning and no positive view of students' potential, it is difficult to see how it can equip teachers with resilience and optimism. Many universities either take no interest in FE teacher training or have let their involvement decline into tinkering with the FENTO standards. There is minimal engagement with research. And continuing professional development, always precarious in FE, has fallen away to comprise little more than a training day on the latest initiative or an expensive event to promote the latest fad, be it learning styles, emotional intelligence or 'learning to learn'.

Finally, confidence to challenge the government has to be rooted in a recognition that the 'skills agenda' is a chimera. There is a serious debate to be had about what skills the economy really needs, what role employers should have in developing the skills they say they want and whether educational institutions are the place to develop them.

Exposing and challenging the constant U-turns, confusion and the narrowing vision for the sector is the first step. But a belief in education, an upbeat view of students' potential and some decent professional training and development are needed if the sector is to find its own voice after years of compliance with the repeated false promises of new dawns.

Claire Fox: You have both highlighted some of the key issues in FE today but I fear you are both in danger of putting the cart before the horse. Surely what is missing is a clear sense of what the purpose of education – let alone further education – should be.

Ian correctly points out that there is a lack of autonomy in the sector. the new quality watchdog, with its national network of expert advisors, promises yet more micromanagement on the horizon. But a critique of the QIA will only echo Sir Andrew Foster's complaint about the 17 existing monitoring, inspection and improvement agencies interfering in college affairs without ever getting to grip with what college principals, and other key players, would do if they were offered such autonomy. I welcome Kathryn's positive suggestion that we move beyond the narrow functionality of meeting the FENTO/LLUK targets in teacher training and go beyond running with fads like 'learning styles'. However, something that would really drive resistance to compliance with banal sets of standards and inspire resilience and optimism in FE staff would be a surer sense of what further education might mean educationally for students.

In some ways, everyone agrees that FE needs to find its niche and identity. Ian suggests that college directors, managers and staff 'need to coalesce around a single mission'. But what should that mission consist of? Surely this should be the focus of debate and, indeed, this exchange. Foster's report also urged the sector to have a much clearer sense of purpose. But do we agree with his focus, that colleges' prime role should be to provide skills for the economy, now warmly embraced by Ruth Kelly? Bill Rammell says the two key aims of education should be 'building a strong, highly skilled workforce to fuel the economy; and increasing social mobility'. Do we agree? Surely this should be pivotal to the debate.

I do not embrace the skills agenda – more of that below – but for now my point is that if we don't make the purpose of education a key debating point, we will lose on all other points. Once we acquiesce to the prioritization of skills and employability, it is not surprising that the government concludes that employers have every right to identify courses that should be axed in favour of those more suitable to the workforce. The clarion cry of autonomy makes no sense unless we can explain that FE should be primarily about educating students rather than about training, and that education as a concept is not in thrall to the economy, but rather it is about knowledge and developing the mind. These tasks are not within the expertise – even the skills-base – of the average employer; they should be left to those trained both in the art of teaching and the subject specialism they have developed over years.

Deciding on the core educational role of FE will dictate a range of outcomes. If enhancing skills is the name of the game, who can argue, as I would, that FE's contribution to lifelong learning should be ample provision of adult education classes? Those classes so brutally axed by New Labour's instrumentalists! Sad to note that it has been left to the Women's Institute to fight the government on this issue. Where are FE professionals leading the charge in defending the right to study for no reason other than a thirst to know more? Who would accept my premise that the students on NVQ catering and hairdressing courses should be entitled to a curriculum that embraces literature (note not literacy), science, modern foreign languages and history just to allow them to think beyond the immediate demands of earning a living.

For all of Gordon Brown's platitudes about second chances, we cannot argue these chances might include utterly useless knowledge, not even attached to qualifications, but available as a right not a target, if we have succumbed to the idea that FE is merely an outpost for employer training schemes. Indeed, students who dare to choose 'non-priority courses' will have to pay.

More pertinent for educators, the obsession with boosting students' employability is often at the expense of intellectual development. Education is a transformative process, about developing thought processes and opening up minds – and as such, a solid, academic education is as crucial for plumbers as for poets. Even in a narrow sense, education is distinct from training. Training in skills can be acquired on the job, but the underpinning knowledge is the job of educators. Plumbers need geometry and trigonometry or how will they figure out the angles to lay pipes? Electricians need algebra and physics or they will be a danger to themselves and others. To quote one vocational tutor, 'Electricity is an unforgiving tutor'.

For what it's worth, the intellectual battle on skills should be easy. This is not just about whether any aspect of educational provision should, in principle, become the servant of the economy, but whether there is any validity in the claim that the extension of education is positively associated with increased productivity or national economic growth. Despite the conventional thinking, there is no empirical evidence to show this link and a rather obvious point is that correlation does not itself establish causation. The likes of Professor Alison Wolf and economist Phil Mullan have exhaustively made this case before, but a few points are worth repeating:

- Hong Kong's rapid growth wasn't accompanied by substantial investment in education; that came later as prosperous parents used their new found wealth to give their children a better education than they had had.

- The OECD country with the lowest university attendance is Switzerland, one of the richest.
- The 97 per cent secondary school enrolment rate in the US is only slightly higher than the Ukraine's 92 per cent, but the US has nine times the per capita income of the Ukraine.

Of course, workers and their skill levels are part of the mix, but we should be wary of FE taking the brunt of responsibility for the UK's economic performance. What about capital investment in research and development (R & D) and the effective use of technology? The problems for Britain's biotechnology industry are not the lack of trained plant scientists or technicians, but rather the regulatory and political barriers to its growth.

We all know these arguments, but they are too rarely at the forefront of debates about FE. Too frequently we plead FE's case as useful for a range of non-educational reasons. For those who find the economic justifications unpalatable, other arguments are brought to the fore. FE can bolster communities, aid social inclusion and provide a source of self-esteem for the hard to reach. I agree with Kathryn's suggestion that college managers and teachers no longer believe that they can educate anyone, and instead view students more as recipients of welfare and therapy. But again, this emerges from a lack of debate in the sector about the possibilities for education to transcend social background, and fixed views of intelligence.

I would welcome your views of whether such a debate is indeed a precondition of any real change in the sector and if so, how leading figures, such as yourselves, can initiate or engage in it?

Ian Nash: Claire is right to point out that the debate must start with the question, 'What is FE for?' What is the curriculum? What is the broad purpose? Is it merely a utilitarian instrument or does it have a deeper cultural purpose? We all agree there is a need to define and to coalesce around a single mission.

A big problem, however, is the polarization of so-called vocational and leisure strands, as though there was a clear distinction between an individual's aspirations and society's needs. The separation has become rooted in recent tradition and reinforced by this government, which has done FE and the people who use it an injustice by creating the notions of 'learning and skills'. They form a clumsy and inept business-led definition of adult education that precludes any serious androgogic analysis. Claire's reference to adult education classes for enrichment as being 'utterly useless in contributing to economic prosperity' – whether meant literally or ironically – exposes the folly of such distinctions.

Kathryn falls into a similar trap when distinguishing between today's and yesterday's students as 'then' optimistic and 'now' downtrodden. Where is her empirical evidence? If anything, today's further education students are ready as never before to be galvanized into action. The radicalism of the 1980s was a 'grown-up' version of the same passions that fed the 1960s. It came from a wider but still narrow group of new HE elite. Today's students are a more robust and far broader church, typified by the NUS Vice President, Ellie Russell – an FE student who will speak her mind to ministers on the need for a broader liberal education entitlement.

Nor should the debate on what FE is for be left to the 'professionals'. The mission around which they should coalesce is one on which everyone should have a say. It is a priority for all. Why is it not top of the agenda in the Institute of Ideas? Why isn't the Institute, in Claire's words, 'leading the charge in defending the right to study for nothing more than a thirst to know more?' If the professionals had the backing of politically astute lobbies similar to those fighting HE's corner, FE would not be in the frustrating under-funded mess it is in today.

A mission needs a movement that cuts across the profession and laity, which gives all interest groups a purpose and platform, and adds weight to the profession's arguments about the essential curriculum. The lack of this has allowed politicians to hijack the agenda and create what FE is today: a supply chain model, not about the real purpose of education but an extension of human capital theory that sees people as a commodity, as cogs in a machine. Is it coincidence that FE has lately become central to the 'skills' debate within 11 Downing Street, appearing on the front page of Chancellor Gordon Brown's Treasury report?

Since so many people have gone along with the polarized arguments around FE and skills, we handed the agenda to ministers. Their justification of the current dominance of skills reduces to two points: (1) If we don't have profit, we can't pay for leisure education; and (2) No one would thank you for free leisure education when what they need is skilled work and a day's pay.

This is, however, sophistry. Giving primacy to the skills agenda is damaging in two ways. First, it assumes that education is for the super-intelligent and everything else is about skills. It is steeped in the old fashioned hierarchical concepts of the different values of learning. Second, it obviates the need to discuss the issues of wealth and investment. Again, it is an old fashioned approach (which ministers laughably call modernization). For more than 150 years, since the 1850s, official reports have expressed concern that British industry was more obsessed with dividends for shareholders than with investment in training and the plant. What is happening today in the City, with the haemorrhaging of the manufacturing base, disappears from public debate. It is easier for governments to regulate things they can control than those they cannot – and to apportion blame accordingly. Of course, dividends are important: they pay our pensions. But to let industry off the investment hook and make skills for work the raison d'être of colleges through a highly regulated market is just madness. Witness – ministers almost boasting over the loss in one year of 500,000 'non-vocational' adult learners, arguing that this is evidence of an effective shift of resources to the more valuable skills agenda.

Two recent reports, among so many, illustrate just how nonsensical is the switch of government priorities. First, the National Institute for Adult Continuing Education (NIACE) report, *One in Ten*, highlighted the overwhelming need for so-called 'leisure' classes to entice reluctant second-chance adults back to college – from where they would regain the confidence to acquire work skills. Second, a Frontier Economics report for the Learning and Skills Development Agency (LSDA) showed that the Government's obsession with skills-driven targets led colleges and other providers to concentrate on those groups that would most easily gain the skills – 'Hitting the targets but missing the point'. And the point is that colleges should be free to identify where need is greatest and foster that wider desire to learn – the twin goals of every good educator.

So a huge part of the public economy is spent compensating for inadequate investment from industry, giving people narrow rigid skills in place of broad flexible minds. What we need is a clearer definition of adult educational entitlement. But an entitlement to what? Is it a 16–19 or lifelong learning entitlement? Claire touches on the notion of a core or national curriculum in asserting a right to 'literature, science, modern foreign languages and history', whether for plumbers or poets. The danger here is that you end up patronizing students by telling them what is good for them. That said, at least this could be the starting point for a debate that is long overdue. It would also provide a baseline for the broader initial and in-service teacher training for which Kathryn rightly argues.

What happens when those who acquire skills 'essential' today face redundancy tomorrow? Evidence suggests those with a love of learning will go on to learn new things, those without it finish up on the scrapheap. We saw this with the collapse of heavy industry, the disappearance of apprenticeships and the rise in urban wasteland under Thatcherism. Undoubtedly, skills should be a focus of FE, but as part of a wider remit to create and sustain cultural value and quality of life. Ten national learning and skills organizations in the Concord Group – with widespread representation ranging from students to principals and training bosses – have debated this point. This, however, is the profession largely without the laity.

We can and should argue about what the wider remit constitutes. But, most of all, we need to reinterpret liberal education in terms of democratic experience. This raises further questions. To what extent do professors, such as Bernard Crick and Richard Layard, offer answers through education for citizenship, social cohesion and happiness? Professional educators know best about what, where and when to teach. But if the curriculum becomes a secret garden hidden from the laity – as it was in schools in the 1960s and 1970s – politicians will usurp the ground. The question of who takes part in the debate is as crucial as what the debate is about.

Kathryn Ecclestone: It is of course true that a serious debate needs to be had about the respective roles of FE in promoting leisure, skills, education for its own sake, the place of growing interest in citizenship and happiness and employer-led interests. And we cannot support Foster's narrow focus on work-based skills as the main reason for FE colleges to exist. So we all agree about that!

It is probably a cul-de-sac to keep discussing which comes first, the need for a debate about purposes for FE or a focus on the many problems preventing that debate. Perhaps the key, as Ian argues, is to extend the debate to a more democratic set of constituencies and to start asking how colleges can offer inspiring, horizon-widening and life-changing education. I guess we agree that it cannot be left to the profession which is too fragmented, too lacking in time and space for decent initial teacher education and professional development and just too diverse to agree on key purposes for FE. Nor, as the sorry tale of policy shows, can it be left to government.

So perhaps the next step could be for someone to start off a similar debate to this one at a national level. The difficulty is to imagine who would initiate it. The TES? The Institute of Ideas? DEMOS? Once some influential institution or body took the lead, it might spur groups like the Universities Council for the Education of Teachers (UCET), the Institute for Learning (IfL), and the teaching unions to lift their heads from the technicalities of conditions, bursaries and competencies and get involved too. It is shocking how arid and technical professional development and initial teacher education have become, as far removed from big questions of purpose and equipping teachers to debate them as you can imagine.

Perhaps this is at the root of the problems besetting the sector? There is little discourse of resistance in FE. None of the groups you would expect to be resisting Foster are doing so. The few well-known academics who are researching around FE currently show no sign of leading a debate either. So it's a long way to get to the public, democratic vision Ian calls for.

Finally, the students. Yes, there are lots who are galvanized ready for action and adept in talking to ministers and so I agree that it is wrong to present a romantic then-as-opposed-to-now picture of them. Yet, you only have to listen to teachers and talk to students to know that there is also a rapidly growing new language of vulnerability and fragility and a growing preoccupation with education being for self-esteem and feeling good about oneself. This distorts the purpose of FE in another direction: towards a focus on individuals and their feelings. People encouraged to dwell on questions of identity and how they feel about their learning are not likely to be very interested in bigger questions of the purposes of FE in a democracy, etc. We therefore have to consider this trend, for which there is much evidence, as we try to get a debate off the ground.

Anyway, we can go round in circles between ourselves over the place of new-style liberal education, skills, knowledge – a good place to start is to resist the word 'learning' and reinstate 'education' and branch bravely out from there!

Claire Fox: Ian worries that there is a danger of patronizing students by telling them what is good for them. But what is patronizing about championing education above the immediate demands that students might perceive as good for themselves? Surely this is leadership. Understandably, many post-school students see FE as a place merely to acquire job-related qualifications, rather than as offering an opportunity to gain additional education. It is surely up to educators to challenge this narrow view of FE and present them with opportunities to gain knowledge that may enrich their minds, not just their job prospects. It is allowable and understandable that the young exhibit an instrumentalist philistinism about 'useless' knowledge. However, when asked, 'What's the point in studying that?' one would want FE lecturers to say, 'I know better than you, and studying "this" is indeed worthwhile.'

Because of reluctance to assert that we know better than the young, we now say that even school age children should be accommodated when they ask to give up on academic subjects because they see them as irrelevant. The new specialist diplomas, soon to be available to every young person aged between 14 and 19, and delivered in FE colleges, are a case in point. I don't care how popular these diplomas might be with 14-years-olds who, surveys reveal, welcome doing more relevant job-related courses. What these diplomas effectively mean is that educators have accepted that we should abandon giving some 14-year-olds even the semblance of an academic curriculum, and instead ascribe them with only the relevant and useful knowledge required by the labour market. Any debate on the future of FE should resist the siren call of expansion and refuse to become a Trojan horse for selling a narrow brand of vocationalism to ever-younger teenagers.

That said, for all my idealism about promoting the educational part of FE against the skills pundits, I am aware there is a flaw in my argument. It is true that some students post-school may well need to acquire vocational training. While I want to ensure that trainee chefs can access the liberal arts as part of their education, they also do need to be taught how to make a soufflé rise and produce the perfect omelette. If you want to be a car mechanic, someone has to explain the workings of an engine. FE colleges' relationship with training has to be negotiated and debated. Colleges are certainly no substitute for employer-funded on-the-job training, and I regret the passing of proper apprenticeships with FE acting as a place for day-release teaching of underpinning knowledge.

One loss suffered from disguising vocational training as education is that many people now want to feel their training is really of educational worth. GNVQs singularly failed this test. However, too few argue that FE can deliver high-level educational input for 16 plus students, in addition to training. Instead some vocations now dress up training in the dubious and flimsy clothes of pseudo-academic vocational degrees and diplomas. Hence, everything from nursing to sports coaching is packaged as a degree and spurious academic modules are added into the course. More experienced nurses complain that this means new nurses can spout psychology but are less adept at the practical tasks, such as administering injections. Other unskilled jobs, such as care work, are now presented as being more valued, not through the wage packet, but through awarding educational certificates for the assessment of the most mundane tasks. It seems nothing short of a con to wrap up the banal routine tasks of McJobs in the language of educational achievement. The new idea of 'licence to practice' promises ever more paper qualifications to cover every possible job a young person might end up in. But this will not necessarily mean there's more education – or even training – on offer to the 16–24 cohort.

One irony is that for all the government's talk of 'raising skills and improving life chances', high standard training is woefully rare. Design and engineering guru, James Dyson, is so appalled at the state of technical training in this country, he is setting up his own school, with the first intake of 900 16–18-year-olds planned for September 2008. Official attempts at improving training seem in a muddle with an unsavoury standoff between industry and government. My fear is that, because FE is so unclear about its own mission, it can haplessly wander into dishing out the latest political initiatives without critiquing their real worth to students.

The new specialist diplomas are a case in point, neither satisfactory for training nor educating students. The Qualifications and Curriculum Authority (QCA) stresses they are not vocational qualifications, again insisting on their educational worth: 'They are a mixture of general and applied learning'. While linked to employment sectors, such as retail, engineering, health and social care, they are designed to make youngsters 'work-ready' not 'job-ready' to quote the official literature. This means they focus on generic skills, such as functional literacy, numeracy and ICT as well as thinking skills and team-working. This diet of general life skills is hardly going to lead to high-level practical and theoretical training or indeed any expertise. This approach mirrors the process over content orthodoxy now afflicting education in general. Specific subject content is being sidelined by a series of behaviourist outcomes unlikely to enhance either the nation's skill base or students' knowledge base. However, by dressing these qualifications up with the title of a diploma, students can feel they are being offered something worthwhile.

That takes me back to the debate I feel we need to be having: what is the worthwhile education that FE should be offering? Ian concludes by asking us to reinterpret liberal education in terms of the democratic experience and cites Crick's and Layard's work on citizenship, social cohesion and happiness. Oh please no! I would rather FE students were offered courses dictated by the disciplines of any subject – whether of chemistry or plumbing – rather than these new 'subjects', which explicitly aim to socially engineer happy citizens. I would argue that the right of a citizen is to be offered high-quality educational input from which he or she might know more after completing the course, rather than a therapeutic model aimed at improving young citizens' psyche and well-being. I think Kathryn is right to warn of the dangers in allowing FE to move in the direction of promoting 'self-esteem and feeling good about oneself', whatever form it takes. Ian might want to create courses which aim to make people feel better about themselves while others endorse giving out diplomas and qualifications of little objective worth but which seem to reward everyone's subjective desire to succeed.

So Ian, Kathryn and I don't always agree on what direction FE should go in, but we do agree on the need for debate, and my colleagues' cogent remarks should be given a wide hearing. Ian and Kathryn encourage think-tanks, political lobbyists, newspapers and the likes of the Institute of Ideas to enter into this debate, and indeed this would be good. However, this is no excuse for the lack of leadership from within the sector. There are still many professionals within FE who care passionately about its future and are educators first and foremost. In fact, it has often been outside 'policy pundits' who have done so much harm in distorting the aims of FE.

In many ways, FE is being asked to do too much. The White Paper charges FE with 'improving life chances' while Geoffrey Holland, Chair of the QIA, says: 'Further education is pivotal to the government's aim of bringing social justice and economic prosperity to everyone'. How ridiculous. Politicians may see FE as a convenient instrument to assuage their consciences on the lack of social and economic opportunities they can offer young people outside of colleges. But I would encourage FE educators to have the confidence to restate and fight for a more modest set of aims based on what they do best – that is to offer people post-school another chance at gaining an education. FE colleges are merely one other educational structure, which can allow education to be gained by anyone post-16. That is enough of a mission when one considers what it comprises: there are school leavers who want to repeat their GCSEs, some who want to pursue A levels in a setting other than school, adults who want help with their basic skills, pensioners who want to return to study for the sake of it, work trainees who need to gain underpinning knowledge for their chosen careers, etc., etc. – all that is important enough in itself. But the key word is education, and it is that which the sector must grapple with.

Bibliography

Abercrombie, N. and Warde, A. (2000) *Contemporary British Society*. Oxford: Blackwell.

Alfino, M., Caputo, J. and Wynyard, R. (eds) (1998) *McDonaldization Revisited: Critical Essays in Consumer Culture*. Westport, CN/London: Praeger.

Allen, M. (2006) Core skills, key skills . . . now we're getting functional skills, *Post-16 Educator*, 32: 16–17.

Arblaster, A. (1972) Education and Ideology, in D. Rubinstein and C. Stoneman (eds) (1972) *Education For Democracy*. Harmondsworth: Penguin Books, 34–40.

Armitage, A., Bryant, R., Dunnill, R., Flanagan, K., Hayes, D., Hudson, A., Kent, J., Lawes, S. and Renwick, M. (2007) *Teaching and Training in Post-Compulsory Education*, 3rd edn. Maidenhead: Open University Press.

Arnold, M. ([1864] 2003) The function of criticism at the present time, in S. Colllins (ed.) *Culture and Anarchy and Other Writings*. Cambridge: Cambridge University Press, 26–51.

Avis, J., Bathmaker, A-M. and Parsons, T. (2002) Communities of practice and the construction of learners in post-compulsory education and training, *Journal of Vocational Education and Training*, 54(1): 27–50.

Baker, K. (1993) *The Turbulent Years: My Life in Politics*. London: Faber and Faber.

Barber, M. (1996) *The Learning Game: Arguments for an Education Revolution*. London: Victor Gollancz.

Barton, G. (2004) Guides for young and old hands, *TES Friday Magazine*, 23 January.

Barton, L. (2003) *Inclusive Education and Teacher Education*. London: Institute of Education, University of London.

Baudrillard, J. (1996) *Selected Writings*. Cambridge: Polity Press.

Bauman, Z. (2003) *The Individualized Society*. Cambridge: Polity Press.

Beaumont, G. (1995) *Review of 100 NVQs and SVQs*. A Report Submitted to the Department of Education and Employment. London: DfEE.

Beckett, F. (2006) Goodbye to all that, *Education Guardian*, 30 May.

BECTA (British Educational Communications and Technology Agency) (2002) *Impact2*. London: BECTA.

BECTA (British Educational Communications and Technology Agency) (2003) *ICT and Attainment*. London: BECTA.

BECTA (British Educational Communications and Technology Agency) (2005a) *Post-16 E-Learning Strategy*. Available at http://becta.org.uk /post16elearningstrategy/overview.cfm

BECTA (British Educational Communications and Technology Agency) (2005b) *ICT and E-Learning in Further Education*. London: BECTA.

Benn, C. and Fairley, J. (eds) (1986) *Challenging the MSC on Jobs, Education and Training*. London: Pluto Press.

Bennett, A. (2004) *The History Boys*. London: Faber and Faber.

Bentley, T. (1998) *Learning Beyond the Classroom: Education for a Changing World*. London/New York, NY: Routledge/Demos.

Bentley, T. and Gurumurchy, R. (1999) *Destination Unknown Engaging with the Problems of Marginalized Youth*. London: Demos.

Bills, D. B. (1988) Credentials and capacities: employer's perceptions of the acquisition of skills, *The Sociological Quarterly*, 29(3): 439–49.

Bills, D. B. (2004) *The Sociology of Education and Work*. Oxford: Blackwell.

Blackman, S. (2004) *Chilling Out: The Cultural Politics of Substance Consumption, Youth and Drug Policy*. Maidenhead: Open University Press.

Blair, T. (1998) *The Third Way: New Politics for the New Century*. London: Fabian Society.

Bloomer, M. (1996) Education for Studentship, in J. Avis, M. Bloomer, G. Esland, D. Gleeson and P. Hodgkinson (eds) *Knowledge and Nationhood: Education, Politics and Work*. London: Cassell, pp. 140–63.

Bloomer, M. (1997) *Curriculum Making in Post-16 Education – The Social Conditions of Studentship*. London: Routledge.

Blunket, D. (1999) *Tackling Social Exclusion: Empowering People and Communities for a Better Future*. London: DfES.

Bolton, T. and Hyland, T. (2003) Implementing key skills in further education: perceptions and issues, *Journal of Further and Higher Education*, 27(1): 15–26.

Bourdieu, P. (2005) *The Logic of Practice*. Cambridge: Polity Press.

Bourgois, P. (2002) *The Power of Violence in War and Peace: Post-Cold War Lessons from El Salvador*. Available at: www.denison.edu/collaborations /istmo/n08/articulos/power

Bourgois, P. (2003) *In Search of Respect: Selling Crack in El-Barrio*. Cambridge: Polity Press.

Brennan, J. (2005) *TES*, 8 July/

Bright, M. (1999) State schools, private profits, *Red Pepper*, October. Available at: www.redpepper.org.uk/cularch/xstate.html

Brine, J. (1999) Economic growth, social exclusion and the European discourse of equality: pathologizing the unemployed, *Research Papers in Education*, 14(1): 93–105.

Brooks, R. (1991) *Contemporary Debates in Education: An Historical Perspective*. London: Longman.

Bryan, J. (2004) Why FE cannot save the economy, in D. Hayes (ed.) *The RoutledgeFalmer Guide to Key Debates in Education*. London: RoutledgeFalmer, 143–6.

Bynner, J. and Parsons, S. (2001) Qualifications, basic skills and accelerating social exclusion, *Journal of Education and Work*, 14(3): 279–91.

Caputo, J. S. (1998) The rhetoric of McDonaldization: a social semiotic perspective, in M. Alfino, J. Caputo and R. Wynyard (eds) *McDonaldization Revisited: Critical Essays in Consumer Culture*. Westport, CN: Praeger, 37–51.

Charlton, D., Gent, W. and Scammells, B. (1971) *The Administration of Technical Colleges*. Manchester: Manchester University Press.

Clancy, J. (2005) Protest is fully rapped, *TES FE Focus*, 30 September, p. 7.

Clarke, J. (2005) New Labour's citizens, *Critical Social Policy*, 25(4): 447–63.

Clarke, J. and Willis, P. (1984) Introduction, in Bates, I., Clarke, J., Cohen, P., Finn, D., Moore, R. and Willis, P. (eds) *Schooling for the Dole?* London: Macmillan.

Coffield, F., Edward, S., Hodgson, W., Spours, K., Steer, R. and Finlay, I. (2005) Wanted: greater clarity of vision, *TES FE Focus*, 24 August.

Cohen, S. (1985) *Visions of Social Control*. Cambridge: Polity Press.

Coles, A. (2004) (ed.) *Teaching in Post-Compulsory Education: Policy, Practice and Values*. London: David Fulton.

Colley, H. (2003) *Mentoring for Social Exclusion*. London: RoutledgeFalmer.

Colley, H. and Hodgkinson, P. (2001) Problems with 'Bridging the Gap'. The reversal of structure and agency in addressing social inclusion, *Critical Social Policy*, 21(3): 335–59.

Collins, R. (1979) *The Credential Society*. New York, NY: Academic Press.

Commission on Social Justice (1994) *Social Justice: Strategies for National Renewal*, The Report of the Commission on Social Justice. London: Vintage.

Copi, I. M. and Cohen, C. ([1953] 2004) *Introduction to Logic*, 12th edn. New Jersey, NJ: Prentice-Hall.

Coughlan, S. (1998) Cleaning up further education, *BBC News Online*, 24 June. Available at: news.bbc.co.uk/hi/education/features/108992.stm

Crawley, J. (2005) *In at the Deep End: A Survival Guide for Teachers in Post-Compulsory Education*. London: David Fulton.

Curzon, L. B. ([1976] 2005) *Teaching in Further Education: An Outline of Principles and Practice* 6th edn. London: Cassell.

Davenport, N. (2006) Free thinking not allowed, *Spiked-Online*. Available at: www.spiked-online.com/index.php?/site/article/278/

Davies, P. (2005) *The Student Experience of Further Education*. Available at: www.dfes.gov.uk (accessed 12 June 2006).

Davies, W. (2006) Beyond communitarianism and consumerism, *Renewal: The Journal of Labour Politics*, 14(1): 66–72.

Davies, P. and Owen, J. (2001) *Listening to Staff*. London: LSDA.

Day, C., Kington, A., Stobart, G. and Sammons, P. (2006) The personal and professional selves of teachers: stable and unstable identities, *British Educational Research Council*, August, 2(4): 601–16.

Dearing, R. (1996) *Review of Qualifications for 16–19-Year-Olds*. London: SCAA.

Dench, G., Gavron, K. and Young, M. (2006) *The New East End*. London: Profile Books.

Denham, D. (2002) Marketization as a context for crime: the scandals in further education colleges in England and Wales. *Crime, Law and Society*, 38(4): 373–88.

DES (Department of Education and Science) (1978) *Special Educational Needs*, the Warnock Report. London: HMSO.

DfEE (Department for Education and Employment) (1998) *The Learning Age: A Renaissance for a New Britain*. London: The Stationery Office.

DfEE (Department for Education and Employment) (1999a) *Learning to Succeed: A New Framework for Post-16 Learning*. London: The Stationery Office.

DfEE (Department for Education and Employment) (1999b) *The National Curriculum: Handbook for Secondary Teachers in England*. London: DfEE.

DfEE (Department for Education and Employment) (2000a) *Connexions: The Best Start in Life for Every Young Person*. London: The Stationery Office.

DfEE (Department for Education and Employment) (2000b) *Implementing Connexions in Schools*. London: The Stationery Office.

DfEE (Department for Education and Employment) (2000c) *Skills for all: Proposals for a National Skills Agenda*. London: The Stationery Office.

DfES (Department for Education and Skills) (2002a) *Good Practice Guide: Planning and Delivering Induction*, Key Skills Support Programme. London: DfES.

DfES (Department for Education and Skills) (2002b) *Success for All: Reforming Further Education and Training*. London: DfES.

DfES (Department for Education and Skills) (2002c) *14–19 Extending Opportunities, Raising Standards*, Consultation Document. London: DfES.

DfES (Department for Education and Skills) (2003a) *21st Century Skills: Realizing our Potential*. London: DfES.

DfES (Department for Education and Skills) (2003b) *The Future of Higher Education*. London: The Stationery Office.

DfES (Department for Education and Skills) (2003c) *14–19 Opportunities and Excellence*. London: DfES.

DfES (Department for Education and Skills) (2003d) *The Behaviour of Young People*. Sheffield: Connexions.

DfES (Department for Education and Skills) (2003e) *The Future of Initial Teacher Education for the Learning and Skills Sector*. Sheffield: Standards Unit.

DfES (Department for Education and Skills) (2004a) *Every Child Matters*. London: The Stationery Office.

DfES (Department for Education and Skills) (2004b) *The Higher Education Act*. London: The Stationery Office.

DfES (Department for Education and Skills) (2004c) *Children Act 2004*. London: The Stationery Office.

DfES (Department for Education and Skills) (2004d) *Award of Key Skills Qualifications: October 2000 to September 2003* (Provisional). London: DfES.

DfES (Department for Education and Skills) (2004e) *14–19 Curriculum and Qualifications Reform. Final Report of the Working Group on 14–19 Reform. Summary for Employers*, October. London: DfES.

DfES (Department for Education and Skills) (2004f) *14–19 Curriculum and Qualifications Reform (Tomlinson Report)*. Nottingham: DfES.

DfES (Department for Education and Skills) (2005a) *14–19 Education and Skills*. London: DfES.

DfES (Department for Education and Skills) (2005b) *Harnessing Technology*. London: DfES.

DfES (Department for Education and Skills) (2005c) *Youth Matters*. London: The Stationery Office.

DfES (Department for Education and Skills) (2005d) *Realizing the Potential: A Review of the Future Role of Further Education Colleges*, the Foster Review. London: DfES.

DfES (Department for Education and Skills) (2006a) *Further Education: Raising Skills, Improving Life Chances*. London: The Stationery Office.

DfES (Department for Education and Skills) (2006b) *Further Education and Training Bill (HL)*. Norwich: The Stationery Office.

Dickens, C. ([1854] 2003) *Hard Times*. London: Penguin Books.

DoH (Department of Health) (2004) *Choosing Health: Making Healthy Chooses Easier*. London: The Stationery Office.

Donzelot, J. (1997) *The Policing of Families*. Baltimore, MD: John Hopkins.

Dore, R. (1976) *The Diploma Disease*. Berkeley, CA: University of California Press.

Dore, R. (1997) Reflections on the diploma disease twenty years later, *Assessment in Education: Principles, Policy, and Practice*, 4(1): 189–218.

Duneier, M. (2001) *Sidewalk*. New York, NY: Farrar, Straus and Giroux.

Ecclestone, K. (2004) Learning or therapy? The demoralization of education, *British Journal of Educational Studies*, 52(2): 112–37.

Ecclestone, K. and Hayes, D. (2007) *The Dangerous Rise of Therapeutic Education: How Teaching is Becoming Therapy*. London: Routledge.

Ecclestone, K., Blackmore, T., Biesta, G., Colley, H. and Hughes, M. (2005a) Transitions through the lifecourse: political, professional and academic perspectives. Paper presented at the Annual TLRP/ESRC Conference, University of Warwick.

Ecclestone, K., Hayes, D. and Furedi, F. (2005b) 'Knowing Me, Knowing You' – legitimizing diminished expectations in post-16 education, *Studies in the Education of Adults*, 37(2): 182–200.

Economist (2006) The avuncular state, *Economist*, 8 April, 75–7.

Education Select Committee (1998) *Education and Employment*, 6th Report of the House of Commons Education Select Committee. Available at: http://www.publications.parliament.uk/pa/cm199798/cmselect/cmeduemp/264/26402.htm

Eraut, M. (1999) The key skills project: sound innovation or wishful thinking? *College Research*, 2(3): 4–6.

Evans, K. (2000) Beyond the work-related curriculum: citizenship and learning after sixteen, in R. Bailey (ed.) *Teaching Values and Citizenship Across the Curriculum*. London: Kogan Page, 157–70.

Fawbert, F. (ed.) (2003) *Teaching in Post-Compulsory Education: Learning, Skills and Standards*. London: Continuum.

Fawcett, B., Featherstone, B. and Goddard, J. (2004) *Contemporary Child Care Policy and Practice*. New York, NY: Palgrave.

FEFC (Further Education Funding Council) (1996) *Inclusive Learning: Report of the Learning Difficulties and/or Disabilities Committee*, the Tomlinson Report. London: The Stationery Office.

Feinstein, L., Bynner, J. and Duckworth, K. (2005) *Leisure Contexts in Adolescence and Their Effects on Adult Outcomes*. London: Centre for the Wider Benefits of Learning.

Fevre, R. (2003) *The New Sociology of Economic Behaviour*. London: Sage.

Field, J. (2000) *Lifelong Learning and the New Educational Order*. Stoke-on-Trent: Trentham Books.

Finlayson, A. (2003) *Making Sense of New Labour*. London: Lawrence and Wishart.

Finn, D. (1987) *Training Without Jobs: New Deals and Broken Promises*. London: Macmillan.

Foucault, M. (1991) *Discipline and Punish*. London: Penguin.

Fox, S., Collinson, D.L., Collinson, M., Kerr, R. and Swan, S.E. (2005) *Local Management and Leadership*. Available at: www.dfes.gov.uk (accessed 12 June 2006).

Fuchs, T. and Woessmann, L. (2004) *Computers and Student Learning: Bivariate and Multivariate Evidence on the Availability and Use of Computers at Home and at School*. Available at: http://papers.ssrn.com/sol3/papers.cfm?abstract_id=619101

Furedi, F. (2003) *Culture of Fear: Risk Taking and the Morality of Low Expectations*, 2nd edn. London: Continuum.

Furedi, F. (2004a) *Therapy Culture: Cultivating Vulnerability in an Uncertain Age*. London: Routledge.

Furedi, F. (2004b) *Where Have All the Intellectuals Gone? Confronting 21st Century Philistinism*. London: Continuum.

Furedi, F. (2005) *Politics of Fear: Beyond Left and Right*. London: Continuum.

Giddens, A. (1998a) *The Third Way: The Renewal of Social Democracy*. Cambridge: Polity Press.

Giddens, A. (1998b) *Beyond Left and Right: The Future of Radical Politics*. Cambridge: Polity Press.

Giddens, A. (1999) *Runaway World: How Globalization is Reshaping our Lives*. London: Profile Books.

Giddens, A. (2004) *Modernity and Self-Identity: Self and Society in the Late Modern Age*. Cambridge: Polity Press.

Giddens, A. and Diamond, P. (2005) *The New Egalitarianism*. Cambridge: Polity Press.

Gillies, V. (2005) Raising the 'meritocracy': parenting and the individualization of social class, *Sociology*, 39(2): 835–53.

Gleeson, D., Davis, J. and Wheeler, E. (2004) On the making and taking of professionalism in the further education (FE) workplace. Paper presented at the BERA Annual Conference, UMIST.

Golden, S., O'Donnell, L., Benton, T. and Rudd, P. (2005) *Evaluation of Increased Flexibility for 14–16-Year-Old's Programme Outcomes for the First Cohort*, DfES Research Report 668. London: DfES.

Goldson, B. (ed.) (2000) *The New Youth Justice*. Aldershot: Russell House Press.

Goleman, D. (1996) *Emotional Intelligence: Why It Matters More Than IQ*. London: Bloomsbury.

Goodchild, S. (2006) Happiness lessons for all, *Independent*, 9 July.

Goodwin, J. and O'Connor, H. (2005) Exploring complex transitions: looking back at the 'Golden Age' of from school to work, *Sociology*, 39(2): 201–20.

Grant, D. S. (2002) *Motivation for Teens*. Chigwell, Essex: Upwards Publishing.

Gray, D. E. and Griffin, C. (eds) (2000) *Post-Compulsory Education and the New Millennium*. London: Jessica Kingsley Publishers.

Gray, J. (2002) *Straw Dogs: Thoughts on Humans and Other Animals*. London: Granta.

Gregory, M. (1997) Skills versus scholarship or liberal education knows a hawk from a handsaw. Paper presented at the Humanities and Arts Higher Education Network Conference at the Open University, 17 January.

Haack, S. (1993) *Evidence and Inquiry: Towards Reconstruction in Epistemology*. Oxford: Blackwell.

Habermas, J. (1985) *Theory of Communicative Action*, Vol. 2. Boston: Beacon.

Hall, L. and Marsh, K. (eds) (2005) *Professionalism, Policies and Values.* London: Greenwich University Press.

Halpern, D., Bates, D. and Mulgan, G. (2004) *Personal Responsibility and Changing Behaviour: The State of Knowledge and its Implications for Public Policy.* London: Prime Minister's Strategy Unit.

Halsall, R. and Cockett, M. (1996) *Education and Training 14–19: Chaos or Coherence?* London: David Fulton.

Halsey, A. H. with Webb, J. (eds) (2000) *Twentieth-Century British Social Trends.* Basingstoke: Macmillan, 221–53.

Harkin, J., Turner, G. and Dawn, T. (2001) *Teaching Young Adults. A Handbook for Teachers in Post-Compulsory Education.* London: RoutledgeFalmer.

Hartley, D. (1993) Confusion in Teacher Education: a post-modern condition? in P. Gilroy and M. Smith (eds) *International Analyses of Teacher Education, Journal of Teacher Education Papers One.* Abingdon: Carfax Publishing Company, 83–93.

Hattie, J. (1999) *Influences on Student Learning.* Available at: www.arts .auckland.ac.nz/staff/index.cfm?P=3694

Hayes, D. (1993) The myths of incorporation, *Socialist Teacher*, 51: 18.

Hayes, D. (2002) Taking the hemlock? The new sophistry of teacher training for higher education, in D. Hayes and R. Wynyard (eds) *The McDonaldization of Higher Education.* Westport, CN/London: Bergin & Garvey, 143–58.

Hayes, D. (2003) New Labour new professionalism, in J. Satterthwaite, E. Atkinson and K. Gale (eds) (2003) *Discourse, Power, Resistance: Challenging the Rhetoric of Contemporary Education.* Stoke-on-Trent: Trentham.

Hayes, D. (ed.) (2004a) *The RoutledgeFalmer Guide to Key Debates in Education.* London: RoutledgeFalmer.

Hayes, D. (2004b) The therapeutic turn in teacher education, in D. Hayes (ed.) (2004) *The RoutledgeFalmer Guide to Key Debates in Education.* London: RoutledgeFalmer, 180–5.

Hayes, D. (2005) Diploma? Is that with fries? *TES FE Focus*, 2 September .

Hayes, D. (2006a) Womb for improvement, *TES FE Focus*, 6 January. Available at: www.tes.co.uk/search/story/?story_id=2177580

Hayes, D. (2006b) Wise up and take it easy, *TES FE Focus*, 3 March.

Hayes, D. (2006c) Emotional altercations, *TES FE Focus*, 28 April.

Hayes, D. (2006d) Dare to be different, *TES* Supplement *Get Smart;* 9 June, p. 20.

Hayes, D. (2006e) Re-humanizing education, in D. Cummings (ed.) *Debating Humanism.* Exeter: Imprint-Academic/Societas, 84–92.

Hayes, D. and Hudson, A. (2002) Basildon: The Mood of the Nation. London: DEMOS.

Hayes, D. and Wynyard, R. (2002a) Whimpering into the good night: resisting McUniversity, in G. Ritzer (ed.) *The McDonaldization Reader*. Thousand Oaks, CA: Pine Forge Press, 116–25.

Hayes, D. and Wynyard, R. (eds) (2002b) Introduction, *The McDonaldization of Higher Education*. Westport CT: Bergin and Garvey, 1–18.

Hayes, D., Marshall, T. and Turner, A. (eds) (2007) *A Lecturer's Guide to Further Education*. Maidenhead: Open University Press.

Haysom, M. (2005) Make spaces fit the future, *TES FE Focus*, 1 April, p. 39.

Hayward, G. and James, S. (eds) (2004) *Balancing the Skills Equation*. Bristol: Policy Press.

Hayward, G., Hodgson, A., Johson, J., Oancea, A., Pring, R., Spours, L., Wilde, S. and Wright, S. (2005) *The Nuffield Review of 14–19 Education and Training Annual Report 2004/5*. Oxford: OUDES.

HEFCE (2002) *Diversity in Higher Education*. London: The Stationery Office.

Hillier, Y. (2002) *Reflective Teaching in Further and Adult Education*. London: Continuum.

Hiscock, D. (2003) Could text messaging be used to engage new students? *Education Guardian*, 25 February, p. 45.

Hodgson, A. and Spours, K. (eds) (1997) *New Labour's Educational Agenda: Issues and Policies for Education and Training from 14+*. London: Kogan Page.

Hodgson, A. and Spours, K. (2002) Key skills for all? The key skills qualification and Curriculum 2000, *Journal of Education Policy*, 17(2): 29–47.

Holt, M. (ed.) (1987) *Skills and Vocationalism: The Easy Answer*. Milton Keynes: Open University Press.

Home Office (1998a) *Crime and Disorder Act 1998*. London: The Stationery Office.

Home Office (1998b) *Tackling Drugs to Build a Better Britain*. London: The Stationery Office.

Home Office (2003) *Respect and Responsibility: Taking a Stand Against Anti-Social Behaviour*. London: The Stationery Office.

Hook, S. (2002) Brush up flirting skills with adult learning, *TES FE Focus*, 13 September, p. 35.

Hook, S. (2005) Colleges' plea for more cash, *TES FE Focus*, 8 July.

Huddlestone, P. and Unwin, L. ([1997] 2002) *Teaching and Learning in Further Education: Diversity and Change*, 2nd edn. London: RoutledgeFalmer.

Hyland, T. (1994) *Competence, Education and NVQs: Dissenting Perspectives*. London: Cassell.

Hyland, T. and Johnson, S. (1998) Of cabbages and key skills: exploding the mythology of core transferable skills in post-school education, *Journal of Further and Higher Education*, 22(2): 163–72.

Hyland, T. and Merrill, B. (2003) *The Changing Face of Further Education: Lifelong Learning, Inclusion and Community Values in Further Education*. London: RoutledgeFalmer.

IfL (Institute for Learning) (2006a) *Towards a Code of Good Environmental Practice*. Available at: www.ifl.ac.uk/members_area/code_environ.html

IfL (Institute for Learning) (2006b) *Towards a Code of Professional Practice*. Available at: www.ifl.ac.uk/members_area/code_prof.html

IfL (Institute for Learning) (2006c) *Towards a Code of Ethics*. Available at: www.ifl.ac.uk/members_area/code_ethics.html

IfL (Institute for Learning) (2006d) FE White Paper: response to the consultation. Available at: www.ifl.ac.uk/news/fe_white_paper_response.html

Independent ICT in Schools Commission (Stevenson Commission) (1997) *Information and Communications Technology in UK Schools: An Independent Inquiry*. Available at: http://who.ultralab.anglia.ac.uk/stevenson/ICT.pdf

Jacoby, R. (1997) *Social Amnesia: A Critique of Contemporary Psychology*. New Jersey, NJ: Transaction.

James, A., Jenks, C. and Prout, A. (2002) *Theorizing Childhood*. Cambridge: Polity Press.

Jannigan, J. (2006) MPs cannot compare, *TES FE Focus*, 10 February, p. 4.

Jeffs, T. and Smith, M. K. (2002) Individualization and youth work , *Youth and Policy*, 76: 39–65.

Jonassen, D., Carr, C. and Yueh, H-P. (1998) *Computers as Mind Tools for Engaging Learners in Critical Thinking*. Available at: www.coe.missouri.edu/~jonassen/Mindtools.pdf

Jordan, B. (2005) New Labour: choice and values, *Critical Social Policy*, 25(4): 427–44.

Jordan, B. and Jordan, C. (2003) *Social Work and the Third Way: Tough Love as Social Policy*. London: Sage.

Keith, M. (2005) *After the Cosmopolitan*. London: Routledge.

Kelly, A. (2001) The evolution of key skills: towards a tawny paradigm, *Journal of Vocational Education and Training*, 53(1): 21–35.

Kennedy, H. (1997) *Learning Works: Widening Participation in Further Education*. Coventry: FEFC.

Kerry, T. and Tollitt-Evans, J. (1986) *Teaching in Further Education*. Oxford: Blackwell.

Kingston, P. (2004) Mix and match: research shows teenagers like learning with adults, but is there enough evidence to convince MPs, *Education Guardian*, 24 February, p. 17.

Kingston, P. (2005a) Hello. How are you? *Education Guardian*, 18 January, p. 14.

Kingston, P. (2005b) Reformer opts for sparkle, not big bang, *Education Guardian*, 15 November.

Kumar, K. (1995) *From Post-Industrial to Post-Modern Society: New Theories of the Contemporary World*. Oxford: Blackwell.

Labour Party (1987) *Election Manifesto*. Available at: www.psr.keele.ac.uk/area/uk/man.htm

Labour Party (1992) *Election Manifesto*. Available at: www.psr.keele.ac.uk /area/uk/man.htm

Labour Party (1997) *Election Manifesto*. Available at: www.psr.keele.ac.uk /area/uk/man.htm

Lasch, C. (1984) *The Minimal Self: Psychic Survival in Troubled Times*. New York, NY: W. W. Norton.

Lasch, C. (1991) *Culture of Narcissism*. New York, NY: W. W. Norton.

Lasch, C. (1995) *Haven in a Heartless World*. New York, NY: W. W. Norton.

Lawes, S. (2004) The end of theory: a comparative study of the decline of educational theory and professional knowledge in modern foreign languages teacher training in England and France. PhD thesis; Institute of Education, University of London.

Lawrence, D. H. ([1915] 1995) *The Rainbow*. London: Penguin Books.

Layard, R. (2006) *Happiness: Lessons from a New Science*. London: Penguin.

Lea, J., Hayes D., Armitage, A., Lomas, L. and Markless, S. (2003) *Working in Post-Compulsory Education*. Maidenhead: Open University Press.

Learning and Skills Council (2004) *National Learner Satisfaction Survey Further Education Summary Report 2002/3*. London: Learning and Skills Council.

Leitch, Lord S. (2005) *Skills in the UK: The Long-Term Challenge*, Interim Report. Norwich: The Stationery Office.

Leitch, Lord S. (2006) *Prosperity for All in the Global Economy – World Class Skills*, Final Report. Norwich: The Stationery Office.

Levitas, R. (1998) *The Inclusive Society? Social Exclusion and New Labour*. Basingstoke: Macmillan.

LLUK (Lifelong Learning UK) (2006) *Standards for Teaching and Supporting Learning in Further Education in England and Wales*. London: Lifelong Learning UK. (LLUK Standards for QTLS Area A). Available at: www.lifelonglearninguk.org/standards/standards_index.html

LSC (2006) *Leading Change: Annual Report and Accounts 2005/6*. London: LSC.

Lucas, N. (2000) Towards professionalism: teaching in further education, in D. E. Gray and C. Griffin (eds) *Post-Compulsory Education and the New Millennium*. London: Jessica Kingsley, 231–49.

Lucas, N. (2004) *Teaching in Further Education: New Perspectives for a Changing Context*. London: Institute of Education, University of London.

Maclure, S. (1986) An industrial education lesson for the UK, *TES*, 13 June.

Marcuse, H. (2002) *One-Dimensional Man*. London: Routledge.

Marquand, D. (2004) *Decline of the Public*. Cambridge: Polity Press.

Maslow, A. H. ([1958] 1970) *Motivation and Personality*, 2nd edn. London: Harper & Row.

McGee, M. (2005) *Self-Help, Inc: Makeover Culture in American Life*. New York, NY: Oxford University Press.

McGrath, J. (2004) Management and leadership in post-compulsory education, in A. Coles (ed.) *Teaching in Post-Compulsory Education: Policy, Practice and Values. London:* David Fulton.

McNiff, J. (2003) How do we develop a twenty-first century knowledge base for the teaching profession in South Africa? How do we communicate our passion for learning? Available at: www.jeanmcniff.com/21.html

McNiff, J. with Whitehead, J. (2002) *Action Research: Principles and Practice.* London: RoutledgeFalmer.

Midgley, S. (1998) The Ward legacy, *TES FE Focus*, 27 March.

Minton, D. ([1976] 2005) *Teaching Skills in Further and Adult Education*, 3rd edn. Basingstoke and London: City & Guilds and Macmillan.

Morris, E. (2001) *Professionalism and trust.* The future of teachers and teaching. A speech by Estelle Morris, MP, Secretary of State for Education and Skills, to the Social Market Foundation, November. London: DfES.

Mortiboys, A. (2005) *Teaching with Emotional Intelligence. A Step-By-Step Guide for Further and Higher Education Professionals.* London/New York, NY: RoutledgeFalmer.

Mounts, P. and Bursnall, M. (2004) *FE Colleges.* Available at: www.dfes .gov.uk (accessed 12 June 2006).

Mullan, P. (2004) Education: 'It's not for the economy stupid'. Available at: www.spiked-online.com

Munro, N. (2002) Emotions are key to focus on learning, in *TES Scotland*, 20 December, p. 32.

NAO (2002) *Individual Learning Accounts.* London: The Stationery Office. Available at: www.nao.org.uk/publications/nao_reports/01-02 /01021235.pdf

Nash, I. (2002) Pump the punters or lose business, *TES FE Focus*, 8 March, p. 3.

NATFHE (National Association of Treachers in Further and Higher Education) (1984) *The Great Training Robbery: An Interim Report on the Role of Private Training Agencies within the YTS in the Birmingham and Solihull Area.* Birmingham: NATFHE.

NATFHE (National Association of Treachers in Further and Higher Education) (2004) *NATFHE 100 Years On.* London: NATFHE.

Newman, J. (2001) *Modernizing Governance: New Labour, Policy and Society.* London: Sage.

NFER (National Foundation for Educational Research) (2003) *Basic skills and key skills: A Review of international literature.* London: NFER.

NIACE (National Institute for Adult and Continuing Education) (2003) *Every Child Matters: A NIACE Response to the Department for Education and Skills' Consultation on the Green Paper Every Child Matters*, November. Available at: www.niace.org.uk/Organisation/advocacy /DfES/EveryChildMatters.htm

Nolan, J. L. (1998) *The Therapeutic State: Justifying Government at Century's End.* New York, NY: New York University Press.

Nuffield Foundation, The (1994) *GNVQs 1993/4: A National Survey Report.* London: The Nuffield Foundation.

NUS (National Union of Students) (2006) *Loud and Clear: Developing the Student Voice in FE Colleges.* Available at:http://resource.nusonline.co.uk /media/resource/loudandclearguide%20UPDATE2.pdf

OfSTED (Office for Standards in Education) (2001) *Common Inspection Framework for Inspecting Post-16 Education and Training.* London: OfSTED.

OfSTED (Office for Standards in Education) (2003) *The Initial Training of Further Education Teachers: A Survey,* HMI 1762. Available at: www.ofsted .gov.uk/publications/index.cfm?fuseaction=pubs.summary&id=3425

OfSTED (Office for Standards in Education) (2006a) *Framework for Inspecting Colleges.* London: Ofsted.

OfSTED (Office for Standards in Education) (2006b) *Handbook for Inspecting Colleges.* London: OfSTED.

O'Hanlon, B. and Beadle, S. (1997) *A Field Guide to Possibility land: Possibility Therapy Methods.* London: Brief Therapy Press.

O'Malley, C. and Waiton, S. (2005) *Who's Anti-social? New Labour and the Politics of Anti-Social Behaviour.* London: Institute of Ideas.

Osborn, M. (1997) When being top is not seen as best, *TES,* 10 January, p. 14.

Palmer, G. (2003) *Discipline and Liberty: Television and Governance.* Manchester: Manchester University Press.

Parker, H., Aldridge, J. and Measham, F. (1998) *Illegal Leisure: The Normalization of Adolescent Recreational Drug Use.* London: Routledge.

Parker, J. (1999) School policies and practices: the teacher's role, in M. Cole, (ed.) *Professional Issues for Teachers and Student Teachers.* London: David Fulton Publishers, 69–84.

Persaud, R. (2006) Friday Forum, *TES Friday,* 20 January, p. 14.

Peters, R. S. (1966) *Ethics and Education.* London: George Allen & Unwin.

Phillips, M. (1996) *All Must Have Prizes.* London: Little, Brown and Company.

Postman, N. (1987) *Amusing Ourselves to Death.* London: Methuen.

Postman, N. (1993) *Technopoly: The Surrender of Culture to Technology.* New York, NY: Vintage Books.

Prensky, M. (2001) *Digital Natives: Digital Immigrants.* Available at: www.marcprensky.com

PriceWaterhouseCoopers (2001) *Building Performance: An Empirical Assessment of the Relationship Between Schools' Capital Investment and Pupil Performance,* Research Report 242. London: DfEE.

QCA (Qualifications and Curriculum Authority) (2005a) Functional skills. Update 1, Autumn. London: QCA.

QCA (Qualifications and Curriculum Authority) (2005b) Functional skills. Update 2, Winter. London: QCA.

QCA/ACCAC/CCEA (2003) *The Review of the September 2000 Key Skills*, Interim Report. London: QCA/ACCA/CCEA.

Raggatt, P., Edwards, R. and Small, N. (eds) (1996) *The Learning Society: Challenges and Trends*. London: Routledge.

Reece, I. and Walker, S. ([1992] 2003) *A Practical Guide to Teaching, Training and Learning*, 5th edn. Bath: Business Education Publishers.

Richardson, L. (2006) iPods lure students back to college, *TES FE Focus*, 6 January, p. 1.

Rieff, P. (1987) *The Triumph of the Therapeutic*. Chicago: Chicago University Press.

Ritzer, G. ([1993] 2000) *The McDonaldization of Society*, New Century edn. Thousand Oaks, CA: Pine Forge Press.

Ritzer, G. (ed.) (2002) *The McDonaldization Reader*. Thousand Oaks, CA: Pine Forge Press.

Robson, J. (2000) A profession in crisis: status, culture and identity in the further education college, in L. Hall and K. Marsh (eds) *Professionalism, Policies and Values*. London: Greenwich University Press, 11–16.

Rose, N. (1999) *Governing the Soul*. London: Free Association.

Rose, N. (2000) *The Unwanted Gaze: The Destruction of Privacy in America*. New York, NY: Random House.

Rubinstein, D. and Stoneman, C. (eds) (1972) *Education For Democracy*. Harmondsworth: Penguin Books.

Rudd, T., Colligan, F. and Naik, R. (2006) *Learner Voice: A Handbook from Futurelab*. Available at: www.futurelab.org.uk/research/handbooks /04_01.htm

Ryle, G. (1966) *Plato's Progress*. Cambridge: Cambridge University Press.

SCAA (School Curriculum and Assessment Authority) (1996) *Review of Qualifications For 16–19-Year-Olds*, Dearing Report. London: SCAA.

Schön, D. (1983) *The Reflective Practitioner: How Professionals Think in Action*. New York, NY: Basic Books.

Seldon, A. (2001) The net Blair effect, in A. Seldon (ed.) (2001) *The Blair Effect*. London: Little Brown & Company, 593–600.

Selwyn, N., Gorard, S. and Furlong, J. (2005) *Adult Learning @ Home*. Available at: www.esrc.org

Sennett, R. (1986) *The Fall of Public Man*. London: Penguin.

Sennett, R. (1996) *The Uses of Disorder*. London: Penguin.

SEU (Social Exclusion Unit) (1999) *Bridging the Gap: New Opportunities for Sixteen to Eighteen-Year-Olds*. London: The Stationery Office.

Sharpe, T. ([1976] 2002) *Wilt*. London: Arrow Books.

Sieminski, S. (1993) The 'flexible' solution to economic decline, *Journal of Further and Higher Education*, 17(1): 92–100.

Simon, B. (1966) The history of education, in J. W. Tibble (ed.) *The Study of Education*. Londn: Routledge & Kegan Paul, 91–132.

Skinner, B. F (1958) *Teaching Machines*. Available at: www.bfskinner.org /teachingmachines1958.pdf

Slater, J. (1999) Taxpayers face £1m bill for Bilston mess, *TES FE Focus*, 27 August.

Smith, G. (2000) Schools, in A. H. Halsey with J. Webb (eds) (2000) *Twentieth-Century British Social Trends*. Basingstoke: Macmillan, 179–220.

Smithers, A. (1996) Core skills, *General Educator*, 38: 12–14.

Smithers, A. (2001) Education policy, in A. Seldon (ed.) *The Blair Effect*. London: Little Brown & Company, 405–26.

Standish, A. (2001) *The Key to Skills*. Available at: www.spiked-online.com

Stock, A. (1996) Lifelong learning: thirty years of educational change, in P. Raggatt, R. Edwards and N. Small (eds) *The Learning Society: Challenges and Trends*. London: Routledge.

Stoneman, C. (1972) The purpose of universities and colleges – and their government, in D. Rubinstein and C. Stoneman (eds) *Education For Democracy*. Harmondsworth: Penguin Books, 199–206.

Sunstein, C. R. and Thaler, R. (2003) *Libertarian Paternalism is not an Oxymoron*, Working Paper. London: The Brookings Centre.

Taaffe, P. (1995) *The Rise of Militant*. London: Militant Publications.

Tallis, R. (2005), *Hippocratic Oaths: Medicine and its Discontents*. London: Atlantic books.

Tibble, J. W (ed.) (1966) *The Study of Education*. London: Routledge & Kegan Paul.

Tomlinson Report (2004) *14–19 Curriculum and Qualifications Reform*. Londn: DfES.

Tuckett, A. (2001) You've got to laugh in lifelong learning, *TES FE Focus*, 14 December, p. 44.

Turner, P. (2006) Why does youth matter? A response to the youth matters November Consultation 2005, *Policy Watch*. London: Institute of Ideas.

UCET (Universities Council for the Education of Teachers) ([1997] 2000) *Ethical Principles for the Teaching Profession*. Occasional Paper No. 7. Available at: www.ucet.ac.uk/op7.html

UCET (Universities Council for the Education of Teachers) (2002) *Beyond Compliance*, UCET Annual Conference Report. London: UCET.

Unison (2004) *The Facts – Colleges, Choices for Young People and the Adult Skills Revolution*. London: Unison.

Usher, R. and Edwards, R. (1994) *Post-modernism and Education*. London: Routledge.

Walklin, L. ([1990] 2000) *Teaching and Learning in Further and Adult Education*. London: Nelson Thornes.

Wallace, S. (2002) *Managing Behaviour and Motivating Students in Further Education*. Exeter: Learning Matters.

Wallace, S. (2003) *Teaching and Supporting Learning in Further Education and Training*. Exeter: Learning Matters.

Weatherall, R. (2004) *Our Last Great Illusion: A Radical Psychoanalytic Critique of Therapy Culture*. Exeter: Imprint Academic.

Whittaker, M. (2003a) Learning from the listener, *TES FE Focus*, 11 April, p. 48.

Whittaker, M. (2003b) I'm on the training, *TES FE Focus*, 15 August, p. 30.

Whittaker, M. (2005) Dancing feat earned award, *TES FE Focus*, 8 April, p. 3.

Whitty, G. (1989) The New Right and the national curriculum, state control or market forces, *Journal of Education Policy*, 40(4).

Whitty, G. (2002) *Making Sense of Education Policy*. London: Sage.

Wilde, O. (1959) *The Wit and Wisdom of Oscar Wilde*. New York, NY: Dover.

Williams, J. (2005) Skill as metaphor: an analysis of terminology used in *Success for All* and *21st Century Skills*, *Journal of Further and Higher Education*, 29(2): 181–90.

Williams, S. (2004) Accounting for change in public sector industrial relations: the erosion of national bargaining in further education in England and Wales, *Industrial Relations Journal*, 35(3): 233–48. Available at: http://eprints.libr.port.ac.uk/archive/00000026/01/FEBARG4.pdf#search=%22Ward%20new%20CEF%20formed%20in%201992%22

Willis, P. (1987) Foreword, in D. Finn (ed.) *Training Without Jobs: New Deals and Broken Promises*. London: Macmillan, xiv–xxi.

Wolf, A. (2002) *Does Education Matter? Myths About Education and Economic Growth*. Harmondsworth: Penguin.

Index